HOW TO IMMIGRATE TO THE US

Adam Starchild

Books for Business
New York - Hong Kong

How to Immigrate to the US:
Live, Work and Retire-The Easy Way

by
Adam Starchild

ISBN: 0-89499-066-7

Copyright © 2001 by Books for Business

Reprinted from the 1994 edition

Books for Business
New York - Hong Kong
http://www.BusinessBooksInternational.com

All rights reserved, including the right to reproduce this book, or portions thereof, in any form.

In order to make original editions of historical works available to scholars at an economical price, this facsimile of the original edition of 1994 is reproduced from the best available copy and has been digitally enhanced to improve legibility, but the text remains unaltered to retain historical authenticity.

TABLE OF CONTENTS

WELCOME TO AMERICA 1
TERMS YOU NEED TO UNDERSTAND 8
NON-IMMIGRANTS AND TEMPORARY RESIDENTS 10
    General information on non-immigrant visas 10
    Class A visa: diplomatic status 12
    Class B visa: temporary visitor or businessman 14
    Class C visa: transit aliens 16
    Class D visa: crewmen 17
    Class E visa: treaty traders/treaty investors 18
    Class F visa: academic student 22
        Employment and Training 23
        Employment for Training or as Continuing Education 24
        Creative Uses of a Student Visa 24
        Exceptions to F-1 Visa Requirements 25
    Class G visa: representatives of international organizations 25
    Class H visa: aliens of distinguished merit and ability/temporary workers
        and trainees 27
        H-1A Professional Nurses 27
        H-1B Specialized Occupations 28
        H-2A Temporary Agricultural Workers 29
        H-2B Non-Agricultural Temporary Workers 29
        H-3 Trainees 30
    Class I visa: representative of foreign information media 31
    Class J visa: exchange visitor 32
    Class K visa: fiance or fiancee 34
    Class L visa: intra-company transferees 34
    Class M visa: vocational students 36
    Class N visa: family members of G-4 special immigrants 36
    Class O visa: extraordinary ability entertainers, athletes, and others ... 37
    Class P visa: entertainers and athletes 37
    Class Q visa: international cultural exchange aliens 38
    Class R visa: ministers and religious workers 39
VISITING WITHOUT A VISA 41
CANADIAN FREE TRADE AGREEMENT 42

- Special Work Privileges for Canadian Visitors 42
- IMMIGRANTS/PERMANENT RESIDENTS 44
  - General information for immigrant visas 44
- EMPLOYMENT-BASED IMMIGRATION 49
  - Labor Certification for Second and Third Preferences 50
  - Filing The Petition and Obtaining the Visa 52
  - The B List 53
  - Household Domestic Service Workers 55
  - Special Exceptions for College Teachers 55
  - The First Employment-Based Preference for Priority Workers 55
    - Aliens With Extraordinary Ability 56
    - Outstanding Professors and Researchers 57
    - International Executives and Managers 58
  - The Second Employment-Based Category for Exceptional Ability Aliens and Advanced-Degree Professionals 60
    - Aliens With Exceptional Ability 60
    - Advanced-Degree Professionals 61
  - The Third Employment-Based Preference For Skilled Workers, Professionals, and Other Workers 62
    - Professionals 63
    - Skilled Workers 63
    - Other Workers 63
  - Information Common To The First Three Employment-Based Preferences ... 64
  - The Fourth Employment-Based Preference for Special Immigrants 66
    - Religious Workers 67
    - Miscellaneous Fourth Preference Visas 68
  - The Fifth Employment-Based Preference for Immigrant Investors 68
- FAMILY-SPONSORED IMMIGRATION 71
  - The Accompanying Relatives Problem 72
  - Automatic Conversion in the Family Category 75
    - Legal definitions of "child" – more openings than you might think 76
    - The marriage game 79
    - Relatives of Former Illegal Immigrants – Special Category Available only until September 30, 1994 84
- DIVERSITY IMMIGRATION 86
  - The Transitional AA-1 Program 86

The Permanent Diversity Program		88
SPECIAL IMMIGRANT VISAS FOR NATIVES OF HONG KONG		89
REFUGEES AND ASYLUM		90
WHO CANNOT ENTER THE US		94
Medical Grounds for Exclusion		94
Criminal Activity Grounds for Exclusion		95
Security Grounds for Exclusion		97
Special Rules for Former Communist Party Members		98
The Immigration Fraud Ground for Exclusion		100
The "Public Charge" Ground For Exclusion		100
DEPORTATION AND APPEALS		101
RIGHTS AND OBLIGATIONS OF ALIENS		103
BECOMING A CITIZEN		104
The Requirements for Citizenship		104
The Citizenship Test		106
Denaturalization		107
Dual Nationality		107
Renouncing US Citizenship and Why You Might Want To		111
LEGITIMATE TAX TRICKS FOR IMMIGRANTS		115
Choosing Your Arrival Date		115
Tax Treaty Exemptions		115
The $70,000 Exclusion		116
The Puerto Rico Loophole		120
A Pension From the US Government (even if you are not an American)		122
UNDERSTANDING AMERICA		124
APPENDIX - SAMPLE IMMIGRATION FORMS		135
OP 156	Non-immigrant Visa Application	137
I-765	Application for Employment Authorization	141
I-129	Petition for a Non-immigrant Worker	144
I-134	Affidavit of Support	155
I-129F	Petition for Alien Fiance(e)	159
G-325A	Biographic Information	163
I-129L	Petition to Employ Intra-company Transferee	165
I-20M-N/I-201D (M-1)	Certificate of Eligibility for Non-immigrant Student Status for Vocational Studies	169
ETA 750	Application for Alien Employment Certification	173

Form	Description	Page
I-526	Immigrant Petition by Alien Entrepreneur	179
I-140	Immigrant Petition for Alien Worker	183
I-130	Petition for Alien Relative	187
I-600	Petition to Classify Orphan as an Immediate Relative	193
I-600A	Application for Advance Processing of Orphan Petition	197
I-539	Application to Extend/Change Non-immigrant Status	201
I-693	Medical Examination of Aliens Seeking Adjustment of Status	207
I-751	Petition to Remove the Conditions on Residence	211
I-589	Request for Asylum in the United States	215
I-485	Application to Register Permanent Residence or Adjust Status	223
9003	Additional questions to be Completed by All Applicants for Permanent Residence in the United States	229
N-400	Application for Naturalization	231
N-402	Application to File Petition for Naturalization in behalf of child	237
FD-258	FBI/US Department of Justice Fingerprints	241
ER-731	Color Photograph Specifications	243

The law changes constantly and is subject to different interpretations. It is up to you to check it thoroughly before relying on it. Neither the author nor the publisher guarantees the outcome of the uses to which this material is put.

WELCOME TO AMERICA

Give me your tired, your poor,
Your huddled masses yearning to breathe free,
The wretched refuse of your teeming shores,
Send these, the homeless, tempest-tossed to me:
I lift my lamp beside the golden door.

(Inscription on the Statue of Liberty, New York Harbor, USA)

The United States is a nation of immigrants. From the beginning of this country's history, people have come to its shores from other parts of the world.

Once, America's attitude toward foreigners was one of unrestrained welcome. The nation was eager to embrace any and all who could survive the long and perilous journey to its shores.

America was a vast empty continent starving for people to build and cultivate and fill up her bountiful spaces. She was a treasure chest waiting to be opened. During the first hundred years of America's history, there was room for all. The United States had a seemingly-limitless ability to absorb and accommodate the rich melange of European, Middle Eastern and Asian cultures. America was rightly called the melting pot of the world.

This is not to say that the melding of greatly different ethnic cultures was an easy task. Each group had to fight for its place in the American sun. But one of the greatest achievements of the American system is that the combining of different cultures did occur and each nationality contributed something special to the development and growth of America. The United States is a nation whose system of government and way of life is unique in all the world because it is a fine mixture of the best aspects of all nationalities.

One of the national treasures of the United States is the heritage created by the millions of immigrants from every country in the world who fused into a new community of persons dedicated to creating and preserving a society and a government which provides, first and foremost, for individual freedom and unlimited opportunity. From their multi-racial multi-national beginnings, the citizens of the United States in a little more than 200 years have evolved into Americans — "one nation, indivisible, with liberty and justice for all."

Is there a place for you in America? Yes . . . perhaps.

Since the turn of the century, the United States' policy towards the immigration of foreigners has gradually changed until today the admittance of foreign nationals has become a process of much more restricted selection. There are reasons for the change in attitude.

Primarily, the United States doesn't need people the way it once did. It is now a populous thriving country.

In addition, more and more people desire to secure the benefits of living in the United States. The world gets smaller every day. It is much easier to travel from one part of the world to another and more people have the financial means to get to America. Many took unfair advantage of the relative ease of entering America on a temporary basis. In the past, floods of "visitors" and "students" have entered the US and never left.

And there is, of course, the problem of persons entering the United States illegally without any papers at all.

The impact on the American economy of this huge flow of foreigners into the United States has resulted in a noticeable change in attitude on the part of the American people. Their mood generally has become one of "less is better".

For these and other reasons, legislation has been enacted to protect the United States from an unrestrained influx of foreign migrants. The Immigration Act of 1990 made major changes to the system.

Basically, the regulations are designed to: (1) restrict the number of foreigners entering the United States; (2) to measure the quality of foreigners entering the United States; (3) to protect the United States from those who might jeopardize the security of the nation.

The United States restricts the number of aliens entering the country each year in order to prevent what the voting public sees as an unfavorable impact on the American economy. Forgetting their own origins, they believe that unrestricted admission of vast numbers of uneducated and unskilled workers could create a serious situation in the job market wherein there would be more workers than available jobs. The public and politicians also believe that such a situation could also seriously strain the US welfare system if unskilled aliens could not find employment or were unable to earn enough to support themselves and their families. These considerations become especially critical during times of economic recession when many American citizens might also become unemployed.

To help prevent such a situation, the United States generally restricts the persons it does admit to those of good health and good character who have a certain level of education. Those requirements help ensure that aliens entering the United States are of a caliber that can reasonably be expected to make positive contributions to the American economy and cause few problems. To this end, aliens who are physically or mentally incompetent would also be denied admission.

Further, the United States has an obligation to its citizens to assure the continued well-being and security of the nation. Thus, persons whose stated political aims or ideological beliefs might endanger the security and peace of the nation would be denied admittance. Others who would be excluded are those whose professions (such as prostitutes, persons who traffic in narcotics, convicted criminals, etc.) would be considered detrimental to the general well-being of the country.

In 1990 the Congress of the United States enacted legislation which greatly changed the regulations governing numerical quotas and the admittance of refugees. However, many of the basic personal requirements and restrictions on immigrants remain.

But in spite of the restrictions on immigration, the United States still embodies the golden promise: a country of unlimited opportunity for economic and social betterment, and a country of unparalleled political and personal freedom. And so, whatever their motives, every year thousands of foreigners make the decision to move to the United States either permanently or on a temporary basis. Each classification of immigration has its own special requirements, qualifications and restrictions.

Unlike many other countries, bribery of officials doesn't work. In the US even the attempt is likely to land one in prison for a long time. But America is a very legalistic society and a detailed knowledge of the ins and outs of the immigration law can work wonders for you. The result of combining these two basic principles is that you are more likely to be successful at gaining entry to the US by careful study of the regulations and handling the application process yourself, than by paying an immigration lawyer to "take care of things" for you. All he is really doing for his fee is applying his knowledge of how to process the paperwork correctly and efficiently – but if you have read the rules and the instructions on the forms, you can accomplish 95 per cent of that for yourself anyway.

If someone you know insists he walked into a consulate and got a green card immediately just for the asking, or successfully bribed a US immigration official, you can be almost certain that person has an over-active imagination. There are always rare unusual incidents but the hard fact is that shortcutting the US immigration system is close to impossible. While bribing public officials is generally tolerated in some countries, it is not so in the United States. Unfortunately, immigrants from certain countries where bribery is a common practice believe the same tactic will work in the United States. It won't, and more unfortunately, most of those who try spend some time in a US prison, which is most definitely not a pleasant experience. Any US government employee found guilty of "selling" visas is sure to be severely punished. If one thinks that you are even hinting at a bribe, without your offer having become explicit enough for them to be certain, they will usually try to avoid involvement with your application, or it mysteriously will be denied. The bottom line is that immigration officials don't take bribes. Should one respond favorably to your suggestion, the odds are about 100 to 1 that he doesn't intend to take the bribe, but is setting you up for an arrest.

You will see several comments in this book about criminal penalties for various immigration violations. It is very easy for someone not used to US legal and cultural attitudes to do things that seem perfectly acceptable anywhere else in the world, and find a massive over-reaction from the US authorities. This is just another aspect of a highly legalistic society. Keep in mind that the US has the world's highest per capita incarceration rate. Many things that would not be seen as serious in most countries can result in long prison sentences and this is particularly true of crimes like bribing a government official, making false statements on a government form, or other violations of immigration laws. And unlike most countries, the US tends to imprison violators, rather than just deport them.

An even greater danger than having too little information is having incorrect information. Common sources of confusion are well-meaning friends and relatives as well as general rumor mongers, all of whom are only too happy to share their ignorance with you. Of all the false information in circulation, the stories from those who claim to have obtained green cards or visas by ignoring the rules or using special influence are by far the most creative. Enjoy them for their entertainment value but don't harm yourself by believing them.

Many dishonest immigration lawyers are well aware that aliens unfamiliar with American society may believe that they can "fix" things through bribery, and use that perception to charge their clients outrageously high fees to cover the imaginary bribes. Very few lawyers will make such a false claim explicitly to a client but a much larger dishonest group of these shysters know that the client believes it to be possible and does nothing to explain to the client that the large amounts of money charged aren't needed for bribes. It does not cost $5000 to fill in a visa application for you – a few hundred dollars at most is a reasonable fee.

But in reality you don't necessarily need that help and it may not be projecting the image that will most readily get your application approved. Do you want your visa in a pile of applications submitted by a lawyer who the immigration authorities know has a sleazy reputation? Do you want your first dealings with the government of the country you are moving to handled in a highly legalistic and confrontational appearing way? Do you want somebody at the immigration service wondering why you think you even need a lawyer? For the simple truth is that most immigrants to most countries of the world have a straightforward case to present and do so on their own.

Another plan popular among those determined to bypass the system is asking for help from US congressmen or senators. The offices of these officials are besieged with such requests. While a US politician will always treat you courteously and may write a letter to the immigration authorities asking for a status report on your case, one thing he will not do is fight with the immigration authorities to get you a green card or visa. No matter how strong your political influence might be, no government official can get immigration benefits for someone who is not truly qualified, nor will he try to do so. It is a point of pride among Americans that even congressmen and senators are not above the law. Another problem with this tactic is that an inquiry letter from a politician is likely to annoy the immigration officers who have to answer it. They have enough work to do without wasting time answering political inquiries on behalf of impatient applicants.

If you have an unusual situation, consider taking advice from a consultant or lawyer, without retaining a lawyer to actually process the application for you. Knowledge of the rules and the loopholes can help you immensely and that is what this book will do for you.

Because of this, you should read the entire book and not just turn to the sections whose headings appear relevant to you at first glance. Beneficial surprises may be in any section.

A good example of this comes under diplomatic visas – a section many readers might ordinarily skip over because they are not a diplomat. But don't because hidden in that section is a little gem called household staff of diplomats, which might be a way to get in the door, look around, and find something else for yourself.

It is often difficult to get detailed regulations and admissions criteria from the immigration authorities. Whenever it has been possible, the regulations have been quoted at length. This will help you in several ways. It will keep you from wasting time on a category that you cannot qualify for and perhaps hurting your chances for some other category later. It will keep you from spending money on a lawyer telling you that he'll try an application for a particular category, when you can tell for yourself that you wouldn't have a chance. And having detailed regulations may show you some loophole that you can use that would not be obvious from the category.

Some of this may make the book sound overly legalistic but remember that America is a highly legalistic society – with many times more lawyers per capita than any other country in the world. It is a country where your knowledge of the rules and laws is far more important than who you know. Your friend working in the US government can't get you into the US but your knowledge of the immigration law can help get you into the US. Show a bureaucrat in the immigration service that you qualify under some particular section, and the visa is most likely yours.

This book is designed to give information and to answer questions about immigrating to the United States. Further, it is the intention of the author to help the prospective immigrant gain an understanding of American culture and customs so that the move to America and becoming a part of the American way of life will be a pleasant rather than a distressing experience.

Not everyone can immigrate to the United States, but you can improve your chances by knowing the inside information on immigration. That's exactly what you'll find in this book. If you don't qualify to immigrate right now, we will examine the possibilities for you becoming qualified in the future. It isn't hopeless. There are things you can do. We're going to remove the mystery surrounding immigration and tell you what those things are. The key to winning at US immigration is information: the information you'll find in these pages. An early mistake can frustrate or, at the least, complicate your plan to move to the US, since it is easy to overlook the strict standards applied by the US immigration authorities on all persons entering the US.

The United States of America is still the most open country in the world, politically and personally. In spite of the present restrictions governing immigration, the United States still has one of the most generous immigration policies and consistently admits more immigrants and refugees than any other nation in the world. For decades, immigration was not a political issue in the US and the average American was unaware of immigration. Today, scarcely a week goes by without the national news media featuring stories about the subject and this makes the issue more political since politicians react to what they think concerns voters. The 1990 immigration law was a reflection of those feelings and it is quite possible that there will be additional restrictions in the future. So if you intend to immigrate to the US, and are eligible for one of the short-term special programs, such as the diversity immigration program, it might be well to act sooner rather than later.

The Statue of Liberty still extends her arms generously and says ''Welcome to America!''.

TERMS YOU NEED TO UNDERSTAND

The government of the United States lists persons seeking to enter the country by many classifications. It is important that you understand the terms which may be used in setting forth descriptions, restrictions and requirements for visa applications.

Alien: any person who is not a citizen or national of the United States of America. (Although the term may seem strange or uncomfortable to you, it is the word normally used in the immigration field and, therefore, is used throughout this book. It is the term Congress has used since 1798, when the first immigration law was enacted.)

Beneficiary: an alien who is the recipient of an application filed on their behalf by another individual or organization

Common nationality: persons owing personal allegiance to a colony, territory, or other dependency of a sovereign nation.

Exchange visitor: an alien who is a genuine qualified student, scholar, trainee, teacher, professor, research assistant, or leader in a field of specialized knowledge or skill who is entering the United States *temporarily* for the purpose of teaching, lecturing, studying, observing, conducting research, consulting, demonstrating a skill, or receiving training.

Foreign investor: an alien who (1) has invested, or is in the process of investing, substantial money in an enterprise in the United States, (2) will be the principal manager of the enterprise, and (3) will employ in the enterprise one or more US citizens or nationals or one or more aliens other than the investor or his immediate family.

Green card: a slang term for a permanent resident identification card. Many decades ago these cards were green. Today they are not green but contain the alien's photo and fingerprint. The term is in very common usage, but only applies to resident visa holders not to non-resident visa holders.

Immigrant: any alien entering the United States for the purpose of establishing permanent residence. Immigrant is another name for permanent resident alien.

Minor children: children under 18 years of age.

National: a person who is not a citizen of the country in which he has permanent residence but who owes permanent allegiance to that country.

Non-immigrant: any alien entering the United States on a *temporary* basis and who does not intend to give up residence in or allegiance to a country other than the United States.

Reciprocity: a mutual exchange. An arrangement between two countries whereby corresponding advantages and privileges are granted by each country to the other.

Sponsor: a person, business, institution, organization, etc., who makes a promise or pledge to be responsible for someone.

Visa: a temporary permit entered on the alien passport by the United States consular office issuing the visa allowing the bearer entry into or passage through the United States.

Visitor: a person having a residence in a country other than the United States which he has no intention of abandoning and who is visiting the United States *temporarily* only for business or pleasure.

NON-IMMIGRANTS AND TEMPORARY RESIDENTS

GENERAL INFORMATION ON NON-IMMIGRANT VISAS

Non-immigrants, or those persons who wish to enter the United States on a temporary basis, generally are not subject to US immigrant numerical quota restrictions. Nor are they usually restricted by some of the other requirements persons applying for entrance as permanent residents are.

For these reasons many aliens attempt to enter the United States on a visa as a "visitor", hoping either to apply for a change in status once they are securely in the United States, or to simply "get lost in the crowd" and become one of millions of unregistered aliens living illegally in the US Recent legislation has made the success of this tactic much more difficult to achieve and the penalties for getting caught much more severe. The lucky ones get deported – the unlucky ones spend several years in a federal prison and then get deported.

Despite all this, some of the greatest opportunities exist within the non-immigrant visa categories, particularly for somebody who wants to work or do business in the US but not become a citizen. Time spent in the US on an immigrant visa (green card) counts towards the five-year requirement for citizenship. Time spent in the US on a non-immigrant visa generally does not count towards the residence requirements for citizenship. So if citizenship is not your object, there are many more possibilities to get into the US, and it is much more likely that some visa category can be made to fit your purpose.

People not familiar with the immigration laws often have an obsession with getting a "green card" and often overlook less obvious categories that are both easier to obtain and more likely to suit their purpose with fewer obligations. With this book you will be able to avoid this mistake. (Although a permanent resident visa is popularly called a "green card", the alien registration card which is issued to a permanent resident visa holder hasn't been colored green in decades.)

For example, a "green card" holder is always taxable on his worldwide income – as a non-immigrant visa holder you may be able to avoid this. And should the military draft or a similar national service program be activated, as the Clinton administration has proposed, younger "green card" holders may find that they are required to participate or have their visa revoked.

Only those aliens who can positively prove that they wish to enter the United States for some temporary purpose will be issued with a visa. This is not always easy because the burden of proof of intent is *always* on the applicant. Such proof might include requiring you to post a substantial cash bond with the United States Attorney General, although that would be an unusual requirement.

An applicant for a non-immigrant visa must further convince the consular office on a number of points:

1. That while in the United States he will observe the conditions of the particular nonimmigrant visa classification under which he wishes to be admitted, or to such classification to which he might be reclassified while in the United States.
2. That he will in fact leave the United States before the expiration of his allowable stay or any authorized extension thereof.
3. That while in the United States he will not seek or accept any employment unless he is specifically granted permission to do so by the United States Immigration and Naturalization Service.
4. That his passport is valid for six months *longer* than the period of time he intends to stay in the United States.
5. That he will observe the restrictions of his visa classification.
6. That he will comply with any other conditions which the consular office may impose on him in order to ensure that he will indeed leave the United States at the end of the time allowed.

A visa probably will be denied if the applicant suffers from a contagious disease, has or has suffered from a mental illness, has a criminal record, is a drug addict or is a trafficker in drugs, has previously attempted to obtain a visa by fraudulent means or by misrepresenting himself on his application, or is a member of or affiliated with a communist organization.

A visa may not be granted unless the applicant can show evidence that he will be able to proceed to the United States within the period of a visa's validity. Such proof might include airline or ship tickets, a valid passport, and proof that the applicant has or will be able to obtain the necessary exit permits and visas from his own government.

There is no charge for filing an application for a visa (except an L-1 visa), but there may be a charge if one is issued. Fees or charges for the issuance of non-immigrant visas are set on a basis of reciprocity, taking into account any visa, entry, residence or other similar fees, taxes, or charges levied against citizens or nationals of the United States by the country of which the visa applicant is a citizen. In other words, if your country charges Americans a fee for a visa to visit your country, you will be charged the same amount to obtain a US visa.

The period for which a visa is valid may also be set by determining the period US citizens of a similar classification would be allowed to stay in the visa applicant's country. Generally, the length of stay in the United States is limited to the period necessary to accomplish the intended purpose of the alien's temporary stay. Under no conditions will the term of the visa exceed any limits fixed by law or regulation which applies to a particular nonimmigrant classification.

Once a US visa is issued there is *no guarantee* that entry into the United States will be allowed. Visas are issued by US consular offices but only the US Immigration and Naturalization Service controls actual entry. The holder of a valid visa can be refused admittance to the United States for any number of reasons. Only when an alien arrives at a United States port of entry is he examined to determine his admissibility. No decision to admit or to refuse admittance is ever made in advance of arrival at a port of entry.

VISAS ARE NOT TRANSFERABLE. You may not give it to or sell it to someone else. So if you obtain a visa in one of the quotas or lotteries, only you can use the priority status.

Non-resident visas are classified alphabetically – A through R. Each classification indicates a special status or condition of the holder.

CLASS A VISA: DIPLOMATIC STATUS

A-1 ISSUED TO:

– an ambassador, career officer, consular officer or public minister;
– members of his immediate family.

Class A-1 visas are issued only to officials of foreign governments that have been legally and officially recognized by the government of the United States. Diplomats and/or officials of a foreign government not legally and officially recognized by the United States who are proceeding to or through the US on an official mission, must apply for a Class B, C, or G visa.

Class A-1 visa holders are entitled to full diplomatic immunity. An A-1 visa is issued for the duration of the official assignment.

A-2 ISSUED TO:

– other officials and employees of the diplomatic missions of legally and officially recognized governments and members of their immediate families.

A-2 visas are issued on the basis or reciprocity; that is, only insofar as US citizens are accorded the same diplomatic advantages and privileges in the A-2 applicant's country.

Holders of A-2 visas may claim diplomatic immunity but administrative, clerical and service personnel may not be as completely protected as are officials of high rank. An A-2 visa is issued for the duration of the official assignment.

A-3 ISSUED TO:

– servants, attendants, and personal employees of persons holding A-1 or A-2 visas;
– their immediate families.

A-3 visas are issued on the same basis or reciprocity as are A-2 visas. A-3 visa holders may claim diplomatic immunity but protection is not guaranteed. An A-3 visa is issued for a term of one year but may be renewed on a yearly basis.

Talking about diplomatic visas may seem irrelevant to most of our readers, but the A-3 category can be useful if you have a friend in your country's embassy, or one of its consulates, who can hire you for a time. It can get you into the US for long enough to establish some social and business connections of your own, at which time you could then apply for a different category of visa. Unlike many countries, in the US it is normally possible to apply for a change of status from within the country – you do not need to leave the country and apply again at an embassy. One of the advantages to this is that you can deal personally with the immigration service personnel in the city in which you are living, instead of dealing at a distance through an embassy visa section.

Usually, all paperwork and legal formalities are handled by the government employing A-1, A-2, and A-3 applicants.

CLASS B VISA: TEMPORARY VISITOR OR BUSINESSMAN

B-1 ISSUED TO:

– an alien coming to the United States temporarily for business purposes such as trade shows or business conferences or meetings;
– an alien employed by foreign corporations coming to the US for special training;
– an alien who is widely recognized as an outstanding expert in his field and who is coming to the US to render expert services (teaching, lecturing, consulting, etc.) and who is not sponsored by a US-based corporation;
– their immediate families.

To obtain a B-1 visa an applicant must show a clear intention to retain his foreign residence. Usually this means that only those persons who are employed by a foreign-based company and who will be paid by that company from abroad will be considered.

Consulates are hesitant to issue B-1 visas in cases where the services rendered or the business conducted by the applicant appear to be of more benefit to a US corporation rather than the foreign company; or, if the consular office feels that the purpose of applying for a B-1 visa is to avoid the requirements of other visa classifications; or, if the consular office feels the purpose of the trip would require presence in the United States for more then one year. Holders of a B-1 visa may not take any job other than the one for which the visa was issued.

The term of a B-1 visa may be set from one week to one year; six months is the usual time permitted. Application may be made for an extension of the visa and it may be renewed in six month increments. Many people have renewed such visas many times, particularly if they can show frequent travel in and out of the US instead of a continuous stay in the US that might imply employment.

For B-1 business visitors, the list of permissible activities includes engaging in commercial transactions not involving gainful employment, such as taking sales orders or making purchases of inventory or supplies for a foreign employer; negotiating contracts;

consulting with business associates; engaging in litigation; or participating in scientific, educational, professional or business conventions or conferences.

The main requirement for permissible B-1 activities is that the alien receives no salary or fee from a US source for activities amounting to local employment. In determining whether the activity is local employment, the main issue is where the benefit of the activity lies. An independent business person marketing his own professional services who comes to the United States to solicit business is engaged in local employment and receives a fee from a US source, even if the professional services are actually rendered abroad. In that case, the INS considers that the business person is essentially setting up a US business and is paid directly from a US source for services rendered. In contrast, an employee of that same independent businessman who comes to the United States to consult on specifications for a contracted service is not directly paid from a US source, but rather is paid a salary from the employer abroad. The activity in the US principally benefits the foreign employer, and as long as the actual work on the contract is performed outside of the United States, the employee is engaged in legitimate B-1 activities.

There is another very interesting and little known purpose for the B-1 visa. It is available for serving as a personal or domestic servant (a) for another non-immigrant who is on temporary assignment in the United States; (b) for a US citizen whose principal residence is abroad and who makes only temporary visits to the United States; or (c) for a US citizen who is subject to international transfers and is on a temporary assignment of four years or less in the United States. The general rule is that the employer-employee relationship must have existed prior to the application for admission, and the servant must have some specified amount of experience. Prior to commencing employment in the United States, the servant must obtain explicit employment authorization from the INS by filing INS Form I-765 with the local INS district office. The servant will receive an employment authorization document granting renewable authorization to work.

B-2 ISSUED TO:

- an alien who wishes to travel to the United States for pleasure, vacation, or holiday travel. Pleasure travel might include persons coming to the US to visit friends or relatives.

A B-2 visa can also be used for aliens coming for medical treatment, for aliens participating in conferences or conventions, and amateur athletes or musicians who will receive no pay.

To obtain a B-2 visa an applicant must show a clear intention to retain his foreign residence. Evidence of long-term employment at the same company or proof of family obligations might be ways of proving this.

Holders of a B-2 visa are not allowed to accept any sort of employment in the US The term of a B-2 visa is usually for six months, but may be issued for up to one year. Extensions are permitted in exceptional circumstances – such as prolonged medical treatment.

For a B-1 visa, application is made on Form OF 156 – Non-immigrant Visa Application accompanied by a letter from the applicant's employer stating the purpose of the trip, the anticipated length of the trip, and the employer's intention to pay all or substantially all of the applicant's expenses,

For a B-2 visa, application is also made on Form OF 156 – Non-immigrant Visa Application, accompanied by a letter or statement outlining your planned visit and when and why you will be returning to your home after your visit to the US; and evidence of ability to finance your trip and your stay in the US.

If you lack sufficient funds to pay for the trip to and your stay in the US, you must submit Form I 134 – Affidavit of Support. This is a statement from a close relative guaranteeing financial responsibility for you.

CLASS C VISA: TRANSIT ALIENS

This category is not of much use to an intending immigrant but is mentioned here for completeness. In some cases a person may have a use for a transit visa as a way to make a short visit without meeting the visitor's visa requirements.

C-1 ISSUED TO:

– an alien intending to travel *through* the United States without stopping.

C-2 ISSUED TO:

— an alien qualified to travel to the United Nations Headquarters District from abroad, and is valid only within 25 miles of the UN headquarters.

C-3 ISSUED TO:

— foreign government officials in transit through the United States to or from official business in another country.

C-3 visas are issued solely on the basis of reciprocity. It is possible for citizens of many countries to be granted transit privileges through the US *without* a visa, under certain conditions. Such a transit privilege is limited to five days and issued only at certain US ports of entry. However, the transit-without-visa privilege is often suspended without notice. If you plan to attempt to travel through the United States without obtaining a visa first, you should check with the nearest US Consulate to determine if you are in fact eligible for this kind of travel and if such privilege is being granted for the time you plan to be in transit through the United States.

The term of all Class C visas is for 29 days maximum. It is possible under exceptional circumstances to obtain an extension, but be advised it is extremely difficult to do so.

Application for all Class C visas is made on Form OF 156 – Non-immigrant Visa Application, accompanied by proof that the applicant has permission to enter another country after traveling through the US, or, proof that the country to which they are traveling does not require a permit to enter. The request also requires possession of a ticket to or a guarantee of transportation to the intended destination, and proof that the applicant has enough money to cover travel, living, business or any other expenses which he might incur during the trip.

CLASS D VISA: CREWMEN

Issued to an alien employed as a crewman on a seagoing vessel or an aircraft who has an honest and sincere intention of serving as a crewman on that vessel or aircraft until it returns to its home port or base of operations, and who intends to land temporarily in the US solely for the purpose of fulfilling his function on the vessel or aircraft, and who will depart from the United States with the vessel or aircraft.

Class D visas will not be issued to alien crewmen serving on a fishing vessel having its home port or base of operations in the United States. The term of a Class D visa will be set at whatever period of time the admitting Immigration Officer decides is necessary to accomplish the purpose of the vessel's/ aircraft's stay in the United States.

The shipping company normally submits a crew list to the US consulate – no other application is required. Application requires proof of employment as crewman serving in good faith in any capacity required for normal operation and service on board such vessel or aircraft.

While this would not appear to be a very useful visa category for the prospective immigrant, we do know of some interesting uses of it. For example, businessmen with their own yacht or small freighter using this category as an inconspicuous way to do business in the US without establishing a taxable residence, or even being noticed. After all, if one is a crew member on a boat making allegedly weekly sailings from the Bahamas (for the East Coast) or Mexico (for the West Coast), an incredible amount of business may be routinely done in one's Miami or Los Angeles office between sailings. But such activities could result in immediate deportation for violating the condition that the visa is only for shore leave while the ship or aircraft is in port.

It also lets the wealthy yacht owner appear on the papers just as a hired captain of the tax haven company (perhaps purporting to be a charter company) owning the yacht, rather than being conspicuous as the owner.

CLASS E VISA: TREATY TRADERS/TREATY INVESTORS

E-1 ISSUED TO:

– an alien qualified to enter the United States under a treaty of commerce and navigation, solely for the purpose of carrying on substantial trade mainly between the United States and the country of which the applicant is a citizen or national;
– his spouse and minor children.

To be eligible for an E-1 visa the following conditions must be met:
1. A treaty between the United States and the foreign country in question must be in effect;
2. The applicant must be a native or national of that foreign country;

3. The applicant must meet the treaty requirements for a bona fide trader.

An E-1 Treaty Trader may be self-employed, but if not, must be either an executive, supervisor, or hold a position requiring special qualifications in the employing business. The employing business must be engaged in substantial trade principally between the United States and the treaty country, and the enterprise must be majority-owned by nationals of the treaty country.

An E-1 Treaty Trader may not change the business or activity for which the visa is issued unless specifically authorized by the District Director of the US Immigration and Naturalization Service. This means that it is useful to draft the purpose of the business in as broad a way as possible, to avoid any arguments later as to whether it is within the purposes for which the visa was granted. A particularly useful type of business to qualify for this category is to open a consultancy specializing in trade between the United States and the home country. Under such a broad business one can do nearly anything on behalf of a client. Of course, the client may be another company owned by the visa holder but he pays his personal salary only from the consulting company.

E-1 visas may be renewed almost indefinitely as long as the holder can give sufficient evidence that his continued presence in the United States is necessary for the development and operation of the enterprise for which the visa was issued. The E visa is issued for a period of validity and number of entries to the United States based on reciprocity between the United States and the alien's home country. For most treaty countries a five-year period of visa validity is typical, as is a multiple entry visa.

E-2 ISSUED TO:

- an alien entitled to enter the United States under a treaty of commerce and navigation solely to develop and direct the operation of an enterprise in which he has invested a substantial amount of money;
- his spouse and minor children.

  To be eligible for an E-2 visa the following conditions must be met:
1. A treaty between the United States and the foreign country in question must be in effect;
2. The applicant must be a native or national of that foreign country;

3. The applicant must meet the treaty requirements for a bona fide investor;

4. There must be a substantial investment of money in the enterprise by the applicant. There are no set dollar amounts for these investments;

5. The nature of the enterprise and the amount of money invested must be such as to assure the employment of other persons, either US citizens or nationals, or qualified registered aliens. The applicant's immediate family cannot be counted as those other persons.

An E-2 Treaty Investor is usually self-employed but if not must be either an executive or manager of the employing business. In this case the employing business may be headquartered either in the United States or abroad but the business must be incorporated or registered in the treaty country – otherwise he would be a transferred executive rather than a Treaty Investor.

As a Treaty Investor, some of the types of business you might be engaged in could be commercial trade, international banking, maritime insurance, transportation, communications, news-gathering activities, or tourist agencies selling tickets.

The investment must be active not just passive investment such as in stock or real estate. It must involve funds and assets for which the investor is personally at risk; loans secured by the assets of the enterprise are not acceptable. The enterprise cannot be marginal, in that it only supports you and your family, and does not generate sufficient revenues to employ US workers.

For treaty investor status (E-2), the investment enterprise must be at least 50 per cent owned by nationals of the treaty country.

The "substantial" amount of investment required is a discretionary matter, depending upon the nature of the business, the part of the country in which it is located, etc. Very subjective considerations can come into play in this decision, depending upon whether the immigration service feels the visa request is an abuse of the investor category. For example, purchases of motels are now often looked at with suspicion, as they have been too frequently used as vehicles to then try to obtain employment visas for extended families. Creativity and uniqueness in your proposal can make it much more difficult to challenge. To the immigration agent examining the application, there is a big difference between opening another motel or sandwich shop and opening a firm providing marketing advice to American computer companies planning to market their products in Europe. The first tends to look like the real purpose is just to get the visa; the second is much more convincing as to business being the primary purpose. Consulting with an expert may be advisable before the application is filed.

An E-2 Treaty Investor may not change the business or activity for which the visa is issued unless specifically authorized by the District Director of the US Immigration and Naturalization Service.

An E-2 visa is usually issued for a period of four years but must be renewed each year. E-2 visas may be renewed almost indefinitely as long as the holder can give sufficient evidence that his continued presence in the United States is necessary for the development and operation of the enterprise for which the visa was issued.

Family members of an alien qualified for E-1 or E-2 status are classified in the same sub-category as the principal alien; no separate sub-category is designated just for family members, as is the case with many other non-immigrant categories.

Countries having treaties providing for both trade and investment (E-1 and E-2 status) are: Argentina, Austria, Belgium, Canada, China (Taiwan only), Colombia, Costa Rica, Ethiopia, France, Germany, Honduras, Iran, Italy, Japan, Korea, Liberia, Luxembourg, Netherlands, Norway, Oman, Pakistan, Paraguay, Philippines, Spain, Suriname, Switzerland, Thailand, Togo, Turkey, and the United Kingdom.

Treaties providing only for trade (E-1 status) are in existence with: Bolivia, Brunei, Denmark, Estonia, Finland, Greece, Ireland, Israel, and Latvia. Treaties providing only for investment (E-w) status are in existence with: Bangladesh, Cameroon, Egypt, Grenada, Morocco, Senegal, and Zaire. (Treaties with Congo, Haiti, Panama, Poland and Tunisia have been negotiated but not yet implemented.)

Although a treaty alien must be a bona fide non-immigrant who intends to depart the United States when his stay is completed, the alien need not maintain a foreign residence (a requirement for many other non-immigrant categories) and does not need to specify a date by which he intends to depart the United States permanently. The alien can remain in the United States indefinitely, as long as the trade or investment enterprise continues to qualify for treaty classification. This makes the E category visas some of the most useful for prospective immigrants who do not want to obtain immigrant status. Of course, any children born in the United States gain automatic United States citizenship.

For an E-1 visa, application is made on Form I-129, accompanied by proof that the applicant qualifies as a Treaty Trader under and in conformance with the provisions of the pertinent treaty.

For an E-2 visa, application is also made on Form I-129, accompanied by proof that the applicant qualifies as a Treaty Investor under and in conformance with the provisions of the pertinent treaty; and proof of investment of a substantial amount of money.

CLASS F VISA: ACADEMIC STUDENT (SEE CLASS M FOR VOCATIONAL STUDENTS)

F-1 ISSUED TO:

– an alien with a permanent residence in a foreign country who is a bona fide student qualified to pursue a full-time academic course of study and who seeks to enter the United States temporarily for the sole purpose of pursuing such a course of study at a place in the United States recognized as a legitimate place of study.

F status is conferred only for academic programs, which include language training programs. Also included are elementary school, academic high school, college, university, seminary, and conservatory programs. In schools that offer both academic and vocational programs, such as many junior or community colleges, whether a student qualifies for F status depends on the specific program he is taking.

The school or place of study must be named by the applicant at the time of application for an F-1 visa and must be an institution approved by the US Immigration and Naturalization Service.

The applicant must be accepted for admission by the school of his choice before making application for an F-1 visa.

The applicant must be able to prove that he has the educational qualifications necessary to pursue the intended course of study. Such proof would include records from schools attended in the applicant's home country. Those records would have to show the courses the applicant had successfully completed and the grades received for those courses.

The applicant must be able to *speak and understand* English well enough to successfully do the work required by the US school. The consular office may require the applicant to take an English language comprehension test. If the applicant cannot meet this requirement, he must submit a statement from the US school that provisions have been made for special assistance or tutoring for the applicant or that the school offers the applicant's required courses in a language that the applicant can understand.

F-1 visa holders are not permitted to work in the United States except under special circumstances. (For exceptions to the non-employment regulation, see EMPLOYMENT AND TRAINING below.) The applicant must show proof that he is able to support himself without working while he is in the United States. The means of support may be funds held by the applicant or his family, or a certified document guaranteeing support by a sponsor.

An applicant for an F-1 visa must prove to the US consular office that he truly intends to return to his own country once his course of study and/or training is completed. If there is any doubt, the consular office may require the applicant to post a substantial cash bond with the United States Attorney General.

An F-1 visa is issued for the term reasonably necessary to complete the applicant's studies. An extension for practical training may be granted for up to one year.

F-2 ISSUED TO:

— the spouse and dependent children of an F-1 visa holder.

An F-2 visa is issued for the term of the F-1 visa holder's stay. Dependents are not permitted to remain in the United States after the F-1 sponsor has returned to his homeland.

Employment and Training

F-1 students are permitted to work in the United States in limited circumstances:

1. Under a pilot program ending 30 September 1994. a student may work off-campus for not more than 20 hours per week, if the employer obtains a labor condition approval with the Department of Labor, the student has completed one full academic year in F-1 status, be in good academic standing, and not work more than 20 hours per week when school is in session. (Full-time work is permissible during vacation periods.);
2. If the employment is considered necessary training in his chosen career field. (A medical student completing a required hospital internship could be included in this category.) Such training must be recommended by the school, which files the recommendation with the INS. Only after that has been done may the student apply for a work authorization using Form I-765;

3. An F-1 visa holder may secure on-campus employment at his school *without permission* from the US Immigration and Naturalization Service.

Holders of an F-2 visa are not permitted to work in the United States under any circumstances. F-2 visa holders who seek or accept employment are subject to deportation.

Employment For Training Or As Continuing Education

Once the holder of an F-1 visa has successfully completed the required course of study for which he was admitted to the US, he may apply for permission to receive additional practical training in his chosen field of study. Practical training is work which will prepare the alien to more successfully pursue his career outside the United States only, and not to prepare the alien for a permanent position in the US with the employer providing the training. In order to receive such permission, the applicant's school must recommend the extra training and certify that such training is not available in the applicant's country.

Creative Uses of a Student Visa

Don't be put off by the term "student." While the majority of student visa holders are college students under 25, there is no actual age limitation. And a student visa is relatively easy to obtain. So how does this help you?

Assuming you can afford it, pick a city you want to establish yourself in, and look for a short program – perhaps one academic year – leading to a certificate in business (or whatever subject), or an intensive English-as-a-Second-Language course. This gives you a year to both improve your skills and to build up your social and business connections, or perhaps make preliminary arrangements to open your own business later. Then you can either apply for a change of visa status, or return to your own country to organize your plans, and apply again under an investor or business category to return to the American city in a year or two.

For an F-1 visa, application is made on Form OF 156 – Non-immigrant Visa Application, accompanied by (1) Form I 20A-B – Certificate of Eligibility (For Non-immigrant F-1 Student Status); (2) documents to show proof of financial ability to provide support for applicant and any dependents or Form I 134 – Affidavit of Support; (3) school transcripts proving qualification to pursue the intended course of study or training; (4) proof of ability to speak and understand English well enough to pursue studies or documentation from the applicant's designated school that special tutoring has been arranged or that classes will be in a language the applicant understands; (5) proof that the applicant truly intends to return to his home country once the course of study or training is completed.

Exceptions to F-1 Visa Requirements

A passport is not required of a Canadian national if he is coming into the United States from a place in the Western Hemisphere. This exception also applies to any person residing in Canada or Bermuda who has a common nationality with Canadian nationals or with British subjects.

An F-1 visa is not required for any person having a common nationality with Canadian nationals or with British subjects who reside in Canada or Bermuda.

Countries whose citizens have a common nationality with Canadian nationals or British subjects are: Australia, Bahamas, Bangladesh, Barbados, Botswana, Cyprus, Fiji, Gambia, Ghana, Guyana, India, Ireland, Jamaica, Kenya, Lesotho, Malawi, Malaysia, Malta, Mauritius, New Zealand, Nigeria, Pakistan, Sierra Leone, Singapore, South Africa, Sri Lanka, Swaziland, Tanzania, Trinidad and Tobago, Uganda, United Kingdom (including colonies, territories and dependencies such as Hong Kong, Gibraltar, Cayman Islands, etc.), Western Samoa, Zambia. NOTE: These countries have also agreed with the United States that their passports will be accepted as valid for six months beyond the expiration date indicated on a passport.

For an F-2 visa, application is made on Form OF 156 – Non-immigrant Visa Application, accompanied by the marriage license (spouse) or the birth certificate (children).

CLASS G VISA: REPRESENTATIVES OF INTERNATIONAL ORGANIZATIONS

G-1 ISSUED TO:

- the designated principal resident representative of a recognized international organization from a foreign government legally and officially recognized by the United States if that government is a member of the represented organization;
- accredited members of the staff of the designated representative;

- members of their immediate families.

G-1 visas are issued for the duration of the holder's official assignment in the United States.

G-2 ISSUED TO:

- other accredited representatives of a recognized international organization from a recognized foreign government as stated above;
- members of their immediate families.

G-2 visas are issued for the duration of the holder's official assignment in the United States.

G-3 ISSUED TO:

- any accredited alien representing a foreign government not legally or officially recognized by the United States but which government is a member of a recognized international organization;
- an accredited alien observer to an international organization, whose government may or may not be recognized by the United States but which foreign government is not a member of the recognized international organization;
- members of their immediate families.

G-3 visas are issued for the duration of the holder's official assignment in the United States.

G-4 ISSUED TO:

- officers or employees of recognized international organizations and their immediate families

G-4 visas are issued for the duration of the holder's official assignment in the United States.

G-5 ISSUED TO:

- attendants, servants, and personal employees of G-1. G-2, G-3 and G-4 visa holders;

– members of their immediate families.

G-5 visas are issued for one year but may be renewed.

See the discussion under A-3 visas for possible creative uses of a G-5 visa.

For G-1, G-2 and G-3 visas, application is made on Form OF 156 – Non-immigrant Visa Application with proof of accreditation as either the designated principal resident, or other representative of a recognized international organization.

For the G-4 visa, application is made on Form OF 156 – Non-immigrant Visa Application, with proof of employment with the international organization.

For the G-5 visa, application is also made on Form OF 156 – Non-immigrant Visa Application, accompanied by proof of employment by a G-1, G-2, G-3 or G-4 visa holder.

CLASS H VISA: ALIENS OF DISTINGUISHED MERIT AND ABILITY/ TEMPORARY WORKERS AND TRAINEES

H-1A PROFESSIONAL NURSES
H-1A ISSUED TO:

– aliens who are professional nurses and whose US employers have filed attestation with the Department of Labor regarding their efforts to eliminate reliance on foreign workers.

This is a new category created by the Immigration Nursing Relief Act of 1989. It remains in effect only to 31 August 1995, unless Congress extends it further.

Eligible employers are not just hospitals, but also nursing homes and nursing contractors who employ nurses in order to provide their services to institutional facilities and private households.

The alien spouse and children of an H-1A non-immigrant are classified in the H-4 category. H-4 aliens are not authorized to work in the United States unless they qualify independently for a work-authorized non-immigrant status. H-4 aliens may study while maintaining valid status.

An approved H1-A petition is valid for up to three years. Extensions of stay are available up to a total of five years, with a sixth year available in extraordinary circumstances. A nurse who has spent five years in the H-1A classification cannot seek an extension, change status, or be readmitted to the United States in the H or L non-immigrant categories unless he or she has resided and been physically present outside the United States for the immediately preceding year.

H-1B SPECIALIZED OCCUPATIONS
H-1B ISSUED TO:

- an alien coming to the United States to perform services in "specialty occupations" for which the alien holds the requisite qualifications.

This category was created by the 1990 Act. Specialty occupation is defined to mean "an occupation that requires (A) theoretical and practical application of a body of highly specialized knowledge, and (B) attainment of a bachelor's or higher degree in the specific specialty (or the equivalent) as a minimum for entry into the occupation in the United States."

To provide evidence the alien's standing in the specialty occupation, at least one of the following types of evidence must also be submitted:

(1) recognition of standing in the occupation by at least two recognized authorities in the field;
(2) membership in a recognized foreign or US association or society in the field;
(3) published material by or about the alien in professional publications, books, or major newspapers;
(4) licensure or registration to practise the occupation in a foreign country; or
(5) achievements which a recognized authority has determined to be significant contributions to the field.

Fashion models were added by a special law in 1991. They do not need to meet the definition for specialty occupations but must have national or international renown, documented by such evidence as clippings showing modelling appearances in recognized and respected publications.

The employer must first file a petition with the Department of Labor, and the class is limited to 65,000 new H-1B workers per year.

Initial approval will be issued for up to three years. An extension up to a maximum of six years may be obtained if the employer obtains a new certification from the Department of Labor.

An alien who has remained in the United States for six years in the H-1B category may not be readmitted to the United States in the H or L categories until he has resided and been physically present outside of the United States for a full year. Time spent in the United States during the one-year period, such as a business visitor, cannot be counted toward fulfilling the requirement.

H-1B workers need not maintain a foreign residence abroad while on assignment to the United States.

H-2A TEMPORARY AGRICULTURAL WORKERS
H-2A ISSUED TO:

– aliens who will work on a temporary basis in agricultural positions of a temporary or seasonal nature.

The employer must demonstrate that it has only a temporary need for the type of services or labor to be performed by the aliens and it must demonstrate that United States workers are not available who are unemployed and qualified for the position. In addition, aliens must have a foreign residence that they have no intention of abandoning and must intend to depart from the United States at the end of their temporary stay.

The employer may seek H-2A status for any number of aliens at the same time but they must all obtain their visas at the same United States consulate abroad. When applications are filed by associations of which individual employers are members, temporary workers obtained in this manner can be transferred among any of the association's members during the authorized period of admission to the United States.

H-2B NON-AGRICULTURAL TEMPORARY WORKERS
H-2B ISSUED TO:

an alien who wishes to enter the United States temporarily to perform a service or job because unemployed US citizens or nationals are either not available, or are unwilling to perform the service or are unwilling to accept the job.

Visa applications in this category must be filed for the applicant by his prospective employer. There is a limit of 66,000 new H-2B admissions per year.

The work can be skilled or unskilled, thus differentiating this category from the H-1B specialized occupations category.

The employer must demonstrate that it has only a temporary need for the type of services or skills to be performed by the aliens, and it must demonstrate that US workers are not available who are unemployed and qualified to fill the position.

The aliens must have a foreign residence which they have no intention of abandoning and must intend to depart the United States at the end of their temporary stay.

The temporary nature of the need is important and there have been many cases of denial of the employer's petition because the firm has an ongoing need for the type of position being filled by the alien. Special projects, peak loads, a non-recurring large contract or seasonal needs such as a resort hotel, are the most likely to be approved.

H-3 TRAINEES
ISSUED TO:

– an alien who wishes to enter the United States temporarily as a trainee.

A trainee in this case is someone who is *invited* by an individual, organization, company, or other source of training to receive instruction in any field of endeavor – agriculture, commerce, communications, finance, government, a profession (legal, medical, etc.). industry, the arts, etc. If the designated place of training is a school, college, university, or some other institution recognized as a place of academic learning, the applicant must apply for a student visa, not an H-3 visa.

Visa applications in this category must be filed for the applicant by the prospective training source. The alien must have the intention to depart the United States upon completion of the training and must maintain a foreign residence which he or she has no intention of abandoning. The proposed training must not be available in the alien's home country and the training must benefit the alien in pursuing employment outside the United States.

An H-3 visa holder may receive support/salary from either abroad or domestically but must not be engaged in productive employment to receive the support/salary. Therefore the type of training the applicant will receive must be approved *in advance* by the United States Immigration and Naturalization Service.

The term of an H-3 visa is usually set for the amount of time necessary to complete the training described in the application, but will not exceed two years.

H-4 ISSUED TO:

- the spouse or dependent children of an H-1A, H-1B, H-2A, H-2B, or H-3 visa holder.

The term of an H-4 visa is limited to the term of the principal H visa. No employment is possible on an H-4 visa.

For all H visas, application is made on Form I 129 with H Supplement – Petition To Classify Non-immigrant As Temporary Worker or Trainee and Form OF 156 – Non-immigrant Visa Application

CLASS I VISA: REPRESENTATIVE OF FOREIGN INFORMATION MEDIA

ISSUED ON THE BASIS OF RECIPROCITY TO:

- an alien who is a certified representative of foreign press, radio, television, film or other information media who wishes to enter the United States temporarily solely to engage in such an occupation, and his spouse and any unmarried children under 21 years of age.

The holder of an I-class visa may not change the media *occupation* for which the visa is issued, nor may he change employers without specific permission from the United States Immigration and Naturalization Service.

Non-immigrants in the I category are admitted to the United States for the duration of employment. With regard to the usual requirement that a non-immigrant intends to remain in the United States temporarily, the I non-immigrant must only intend to leave the United States upon the expiration of his authorized stay, whenever that might be.

The employer of the alien must have its home office in a foreign country in order for the alien to qualify for I status. The alien must be engaged in production of informational or educational reports or films. Aliens involved in the production of commercial films or advertisements are not included in the I category. Entrepreneurs producing investment or business newsletters could easily use this category to base themselves in the US as long as their publication was issued from a foreign office.

Application for an I class visa is made on Form OF 156 – Non-immigrant Visa Application, accompanied by certification that the applicant is a bona fide representative of a foreign information media organization.

CLASS J VISA: EXCHANGE VISITOR

J-1 ISSUED TO:

– an alien who is a genuine student, scholar, trainee, teacher, professor, research assistant specialist, or leader in a field of specialized knowledge who wishes to enter the United States temporarily as a participant in a program *accredited by the United States Information Agency* for the purpose of teaching, instructing, lecturing, studying, observing, conducting research, consulting, demonstrating special skills, or receiving training in that program.

Application for a J-1 visa must be filed by *both* the program sponsor and the applicant.

The applicant must prove that he can speak and understand English well enough to participate in the proposed program or that the sponsoring organization knows of his language deficiency and has indicated its willingness to accept the applicant anyway.

Applicants for a J-1 visa who will be participating in a program financed either by the US Government or by the government of their home country or applicants who have an occupational skill listed on the "Skills List" issued by the United States Secretary of State as being necessary in the alien's home country must agree to a two-year foreign residency requirement before a visa will be issued. This requirement means that when the alien has completed the program for which the J-1 visa is issued, he must leave the United States and remain outside the United States for two years before he will be eligible to re-apply for admission under either an immigrant visa or a non-immigrant H or L classification. A waiver of the two-year foreign residency requirement may rarely be obtained only upon meeting one of the following grounds for waiver:

1. Upon formal request of a US government agency with a favorable recommendation by the US Department of State;
2. Upon showing proof that departure from the US would impose an exceptional hardship upon the J-1 holder's spouse or children, if the spouse or children are a US citizen or permanent resident aliens;
3. Upon showing that the alien cannot return to his country because he would be subject to persecution;
4. Upon issuance of a letter of "no objection" from the government of the foreign country that such government has no objection to the alien's not returning to his home country for the two year period, and with the favorable recommendation of the US Department of State.

A J-1 visa holder may accept employment and receive compensation/salary for employment if the program for which the visa is issued includes this authorization.

A J-1 visa is issued for the term of the program named in the application, but not to exceed one year.

J-2 ISSUED TO:

– the spouse and minor children of a J-1 visa holder.

The spouse of a J-1 visa holder may accept employment by applying for permission from the United States Immigration and Naturalization Service but that permission will be granted *only* if such employment is necessary for the support of the spouse and any accompanying minor children. The necessity for seeking employment may not be to support the J-1 visa holder.

The term of a J-2 visa will be limited to the term of the J-1 holder's visa.

For J-1 visas application is made on Form IAP 66 – Certificate of Eligibility of Exchange Visitor Status, accompanied by Form I 134 – Affidavit of Support and Form OF 156 – Non-immigrant Visa Application. Normally the sponsoring organization will be involved in preparing and presenting visa applications in this category.

For the J-2 visa application is made on Form OF 156 – Non-immigrant Visa Application.

CLASS K VISA: FIANCE OR FIANCEE

K-1 ISSUED TO:

– the fiance or fiancee of a United States citizen or national who wishes to enter the United States solely to marry.

The marriage must take place within 90 days of entry into the United States. If not, the alien must either leave the country or apply to the US Immigration and Naturalization Service for a change in visa classification.

Holders of a K visa are permitted to work within the 90-day period.

A K-1 visa is issued for 90 days only. No extensions are permitted.

K-2 ISSUED TO:

– the minor children of the K-1 visa holder.

A K-2 visa is issued for 90 days only. No extensions are permitted.

The petition must be accompanied with evidence documenting that the parties have met within the two years immediately preceding the filing of the petition and that both parties have the legal capacity to marry within the 90 days allowed.

Application for a K-1 visa is made on Form I 129F – Petition to Classify Status of Alien Fiance or Fiancee For Issuance of Non-immigrant Status, accompanied by Form G-325A, a biographical information form.

For the K-2 visas, add a Form OF 156 – Non-immigrant Visa Application for each child. The K-1 and K-2 applications should all be presented together.

CLASS L VISA: INTRA-COMPANY TRANSFEREES

L-1 ISSUED TO:

– an alien who wishes to enter the United States temporarily in order to continue to render services to the sane firm, corporation or other legal entity which employs him abroad.

To qualify for L-1 status, the alien must meet the following conditions:

1. Has been employed continuously for one year immediately preceding the time of his application by the employer transferring him;
2. The employer abroad must be an affiliate, branch office or subsidiary of the company in the United States;
3. The alien must be entering the US to serve in a capacity which is executive, managerial or involves specialized knowledge.

An application for an L-1 visa must be made for the applicant by his employer.

A new requirement added in 1987 is that the company must be doing business as an employer in the United States and at least one other country during the entire period of the alien's stay in the United States. Doing business is defined to cover the regular, systematic, and continuous provision of goods or services by an organization that has employees – it does not include the mere presence of an agent or office in the United States or abroad. The 1987 regulation was added to enforce the intent that the category be used by international organizations and not as a means for small investors to relocate themselves to the United States. Whether this regulation is sufficient to overturn earlier case law that permitted small business transfers remains to be seen.

It is not required that an L-1 applicant maintain a foreign residence but his intention to enter the US temporarily must be established.

The term of an L-1 visa is generally set for the amount of time necessary to fulfill the function described in the visa application. The initial approval cannot exceed three years. Extensions up to a total of seven years can be obtained for executives and managers and extensions up to a limit of five years can be obtained for specialized knowledge personnel.

L-2 ISSUED TO:

— the spouse and minor children of an L-1 visa holder.

The term of an L-2 visa is limited to the term of the L-1 holder's visa.

An application for a L-1 visa requires Form I 129 and L Supplement – Petition to Classify Alien As Non-immigrant Worker or Trainee, accompanied by a letter and supporting documentation from the employer explaining the relationship between the foreign and the US companies, the capacity in which the alien serves abroad and the capacity in which he will serve in the US, the nature of his specialized knowledge (where specialized knowledge is involved) and its importance to the applicant's job.

The L-2 visas are applied for on Form OF 156 – Non-immigrant Visa Application.

CLASS M VISA: VOCATIONAL STUDENTS

M-1 ISSUED TO:

– aliens coming to the US to engage in a program of vocational study at an educational institution approved by the Immigration & Naturalization Service.

The M category is similar to the F student category, except that the M category is limited to vocational and other non-academic educational programs (excluding language training programs which remain in the F category). As with the F category, M students are required to be engaged in a full-time course of study at an approved educational institution.

Employment even for unforeseen financial difficulties cannot be authorized by the Immigration & Naturalization Service. The student must also demonstrate that he has a residence abroad which he has no intention of abandoning.

M-2 visas are available for immediate family members of a M-1 visa holder but no employment is authorized on M-2 visas.

See the comments under the Class F student visa as to possible ways a student visa can help you get started in the US.

To apply as a vocational student, you need an INS Form I-20M-N from an authorized school, and Form OF 156 – Non-immigrant Visa Application.

An M-1 visa holder may obtain approval to change schools but not to change educational objectives.

CLASS N VISA: FAMILY MEMBERS OF G-4 SPECIAL IMMIGRANTS

This is a special category for former employees of international organizations who have resided in the United States for long periods of time in the G-4 non-immigrant category. It would apply in only very special situations, such as the family of a United Nations employee who had been in the US for perhaps 20 years and preferred to remain after the employee retired.

CLASS O VISA: EXTRAORDINARY ABILITY ENTERTAINERS, ATHLETES, AND OTHERS

O-1 ISSUED TO:

– aliens of extraordinary ability in the sciences, arts, education, business or athletics.

The O-1 category is for aliens with extraordinary ability. With regard to the arts, extraordinary ability means distinction. To qualify for such status, aliens must have sustained national or international acclaim as evidenced with extensive documentation of their achievements in their fields. They must be entering the United States to work in their fields. If an alien is seeking to enter the United States for a motion picture or television production, rather than sustained national or international acclaim, he must have a demonstrated record of extraordinary achievement.

O-2 ISSUED TO:

– certain aliens accompanying or assisting those aliens, and their family members.

The O-2 category for accompanying or assisting is reserved for those who are an integral part of the actual performance and have critical skills and experience with the principal alien which are not of a general nature and which cannot be performed by other individuals. For accompanying aliens on a movie or television production, they must have a pre-existing and longstanding working relationship with the principal alien or must be needed because of continuity caused by filming both inside and outside the United States. O-2 aliens must also have a foreign residence which they have no intention of abandoning. This requirement is not imposed for O-1 aliens.

For an O class visa, file Form I-129 with O Supplement and Form OF 156 – Nonimmigrant Visa Application.

CLASS P VISA: ENTERTAINERS AND ATHLETES

P-1 ISSUED TO:

– entertainers and athletes who cannot qualify under the extraordinary ability standard for the O category.

The P-1 category is for alien athletes who compete individually or as part of a team at an internationally recognized level and alien entertainers who perform as part of a group that has received international recognition as outstanding for a sustained and substantial period of time.

The P-1 athlete or entertainer must also be coming to the United States to perform in a specific athletic competition or performance.

Entertainers and performers must have a sustained and substantial relationship with the group over a period of at least one year and must provide functions integral to the performance of the group, but 25 per cent of the performers and entertainers are exempt from the one-year prior association requirement. Circus performers are entirely exempt from the prior association requirement.

P-2 ISSUED TO:

— artists and entertainers, including groups, who seek to be admitted through a reciprocal exchange program between foreign-based and US based organizations which are engaged in the temporary exchange of artists and entertainers.

The coverage of this category extends to those aliens who are an integral part of the performance of a group.

P-3 ISSUED TO:

— artists and entertainers, including groups and accompanying aliens who are an integral part of the performance of a group, who will perform, teach or coach under a commercial or non-commercial program that is culturally unique.

All P class visas require Form I-129 and P Supplement; accompanied by Form OF 156 – Non-immigrant Visa Application.

CLASS Q VISA: INTERNATIONAL CULTURAL EXCHANGE ALIENS

Q VISA ISSUED TO:

— aliens coming to the United States for business training pursuant to an international cultural exchange program designated by the Attorney General.

The designated program must provide practical training, employment, and the sharing of the history, culture, and traditions of the country of the alien's nationality, and the alien must receive the same wages and working conditions as US workers. The Q alien may not bring his spouse or children to the United States and must have a foreign residence that he has no intention of abandoning.

Business training as part of an exchange program is also authorized under the J category. The difference is that the Q category is intended to cover programs in which the principal goal is for the alien to share his culture with Americans, rather than the mutual exchange of the J-1 program which emphasizes the sharing of American culture with foreign nationals who can take that knowledge abroad and further US interests there.

The Q program is interpreted very narrowly and is not generally a useful category for readers of this book.

CLASS R VISA: MINISTERS AND RELIGIOUS WORKERS

R-1 ISSUED TO:

— aliens coming to the United States temporarily as religious workers.

The category is for ministers of religion and religious workers who will work for their denomination in a professional capacity in a religious vocation or occupation, or who will work for the denomination or a bona fide organization which is tax-exempt and affiliated with the denomination in a religious vocation or occupation (not necessarily in a professional capacity).

R-2 ISSUED TO:

— family members of minsters and religious workers

R-2 family members are not permitted to accept employment.

The R non-immigrant is not subject to a petition requirement. The applicant presents his case directly to a consular officer and must provide a copy of the US religious organization's tax-exempt certificate.

The R visa holder may be admitted for an initial period of three years, and is eligible for an extension of two years, up to a maximum stay of five years.

This used to be a highly useful category and an easy way to obtain a long term stay in the US with minimal review but a great many conspicuous abuses over the past decade have made it very difficult to qualify in this category for anyone other than a full-time dedicated religious worker. But it is not impossible, as America gives equal recognition to all religions, no mater how small.

The R-1 visa requires Form OF 156 – Non-immigrant Visa Petition accompanied by Form I-129 with R Supplement and

a letter from an authorized official of the specific organizational unit of the religious organization that will employ the alien in the United States. The letter must establish that:

(a) the religious denomination has a bona fide non-profit organization in the United States;

(b) the foreign religious organization of which the alien has been a member belongs to the same denomination as the US organization;

(c) the alien has been a member of that denomination for the two-year period immediately preceding the application for a visa;

(d) the alien, if a minister, has authorization to conduct the duties usually performed by a minister of that denomination;

(e) the alien, if a professional religious worker, has the required bachelor's degree and the position requires such a degree; and

(f) the alien, if a non-professional religious worker, is a monk, nun, or religious brother or will perform work relating to a traditional religious function. The letter must also indicate the arrangements for remuneration and the name and location of the specific organizational unit of the religious organization where the alien will work.

VISITING WITHOUT A VISA

Over ten million people have visited the US under the visa waiver program. Visitors must be from one of the countries listed (these have been selected on the basis of reciprocity) and can be admitted to the US for up to 90 days as B-1 or B-2 visitors. No extensions of stay are permitted.

To enter, you complete Form I-94W, which is provided by the airline, have a valid passport (which normally must be valid for at least six months beyond the end of the visit), have a round trip airline ticket, and have proof of ability to support yourself while in the US.

The program is currently available to citizens of Andorra, Austria, Belgium, Denmark, Finland, France, Germany, Iceland, Italy, Japan, Liechtenstein, Luxembourg, Monaco, The Netherlands, New Zealand, Norway, San Marino, Spain, Sweden, Switzerland, and the United Kingdom. The program is expected to have other countries added to the list.

When you enter the US under the visa waiver program, you will not be allowed to change your status to another non-immigrant classification without first leaving the country. Moreover, if you come to the US under this program and wish to apply for a green card, you will be limited to making your application at a US consulate abroad.

Participation in the visa waiver program is optional. Aliens from those countries qualifying for visa waivers can still get standard visitors' visas and come to the US conventionally. We advise you not to make use of this new program if you can avoid it. You will have more flexibility and rights once you enter the US if you come with a visa. The visa waiver is most useful if you are making a short holiday visit or coming as part of an organized sightseeing tour and have no possible reason to stay over. But if you are coming on business or visiting family you never know when extensions or changes might be necessary.

CANADIAN FREE TRADE AGREEMENT

Since 1989, when the US-Canadian Free Trade Agreement took effect, there have been special arrangements for Canadians under the treaty, separate from the normal visa rules in the immigration law.

B-1 visas may be applied for at the border, although it is helpful to have a letter from the company verifying the business trip. L-1 visas may also be applied for at the border but still require Form I-129 and the L supplement with supporting documents.

Canadian nationals who are qualified in one of the occupational fields listed in the United States-Canada Free Trade Agreement may enter the United States in the TC category established specifically for that purpose. The list of occupations includes accountants, engineers, registered nurses, architects, lawyers, hotel managers, librarians, and many science and medical professions. The TC non-immigrant is admitted for one year and can receive extensions of stay in one-year increments. The main advantages to using the TC category rather than the H-1B category are that prior petition approval is not required for admission, no visa is required for Canadian nationals, and there is no outer limited on the total period of stay, including extensions. TC visas can also be applied for at the border.

Canadians eligible for E category visas cannot apply at the border but must apply through the nearest US consulate in advance. With the exception of the B-1 visas for business visits, we really don't recommend applying at the border even though it is legally possible.

See also the Class F student visa section for special rules for Canadian students.

SPECIAL WORK PRIVILEGES FOR CANADIAN VISITORS

The United States-Canada Free Trade Agreement includes a program permitting Canadian visitors to do certain kinds of work in the United States without having work visas. There are no other countries whose citizens are afforded these privileges. To get them, you must show written proof that you are engaging in one of the occupations included in the program. A letter from your Canadian employer verifying the work to be done will serve this purpose. If relevant, you should also offer evidence that you are qualified for the job, such as copies of diplomas or licenses. These documents are presented to a US immigration officer on your entry to the United

States. No fee or special application is needed. The types of work that Canadians may do in the United States without work visas are:

* Perform research and design functions for a company located in Canada;
* Supervise a crew harvesting agricultural crops. Only the owner of the company qualifies;
* Purchase for a company located in Canada;
* Conduct other commercial transactions for a company located in Canada;
* Do market research for a company located in Canada;
* Attend trade fairs;
* Take sales orders and negotiate contracts for a company located in Canada;
* Transport goods or passengers into the United States;
* Pick up goods and passengers in the United States, only for direct transport back to Canada;
* Perform normal duties as a customs broker. The goods must be exports from the United States to Canada;
* Service equipment or machinery after sales;
* Perform any professional services, provided no salary is paid from within the United States;
* Perform financial services for a company located in Canada;
* Consult in the fields of public relations and advertising;
* Conduct tours that originate or have significant portions taking place in Canada;
* Perform language translation and act as interpreter for a company located in Canada.

IMMIGRANTS/PERMANENT RESIDENTS

GENERAL INFORMATION FOR IMMIGRANT VISAS

The 1990 changes in the US immigration law have changed the entire system for obtaining US resident visas for the first time since 1952. The changes in the non-immigrant categories were relatively minor, primarily adding some new types of visa. But for resident visas – the so-called "green card" – everything is different now. If you were unable to gain residence before because of long waiting lists, you may find that you have priority under the new laws.

In 1986, a law was passed providing for an amnesty for illegal immigrants who registered within certain time limits. That program is long over and it is too late to use this avenue to a resident status.

The 1990 law kept limits on the numbers of visas but because the priorities as to who is eligible have changed, the different situation may give you a chance that you didn't have before.

The major categories now are employment-based immigration, family-sponsored immigration, and an entirely new category called diversity immigration.

The United States has a world-wide quota of 700,000 persons for permanent residence visas. Beginning on 1 October 1994, this will be reduced to 675,000 per year. In any given category, applicants are considered on a first-come, first-served basis.

"Permanent resident" as an immigration status is a legal term defined as a person who has been granted a US residence visa and has the intention to reside in the United States permanently. The status does not require an actual dwelling place in the United States. Thus, a resident alien may be absent from the US for prolonged periods without abandoning residence, as long as he maintains the intention to remain a resident. Therefore, it can be useful to obtain the status before the quotas are reduced or other more restrictive immigration laws are introduced.

As long as you maintain an intention to remain a resident, that status cannot be taken from you except through a formal deportation or exclusion proceeding, which can only be for some serious cause, such as a criminal conviction. The burden is on the government to establish abandonment of residence.

If you do plan to be outside the US for extensive periods after obtaining residence status, it is helpful to document your intentions. Since this is a matter of proof, maintaining ties with the US (such as having an actual residence even though not required), having bank accounts, filing US resident income tax returns, or maintaining club memberships can all weigh heavily in your favor should your residence ever be disputed.

The one time limit that it is critical to meet is a four-month limit for arriving in the US after your immigrant visa is issued at a consulate. Once you have actually made that first landing in the US, you have permanent resident status and are free to come and go as often as you wish.

Many Europeans have maintained a US resident visa for decades, just in case they should ever need it. They consider it a security measure in case of another war in Europe, and since the income tax rates in most European countries are higher than in the US, the worldwide taxation of US permanent residents is not a concern to them. They simply file a US tax return every year and take the higher foreign taxes as a credit against US taxes, thus having no payment to make to the US Recent changes to the US tax law make all permanent resident visa holders subject to US tax. Prior to this, one could argue that although holding the resident visa, there was insufficient presence in the US to make one resident for tax purposes because the definition of resident in the tax and immigration laws was different. However, these prudent visa holders, realizing they wouldn't actually owe any money, found it beneficial to file US income tax returns even before the change of law because it helped them to document their intention to remain permanent residents of the United States. It also prevented any possibility of the US Internal Revenue Service charging them with failure to file a tax return. The continued filing of US resident income tax returns is considered to be particularly strong evidence of intent to maintain permanent residence. There is also an exclusion of $70,000 per year for working abroad so that even if you are working in a tax haven and not paying local income taxes, you can still file a US resident tax return and have nothing due. This is explained more fully in the tax tricks chapter.

Long-term absences are becoming more subject to challenge, as the immigration authorities attempt to enforce the requirement that the visa holder has an intent to reside permanently in the US Working abroad for a US employer is easy to justify but even this can become questionable after several years. Intention is still legally the dominant factor, and court cases have held that the intention exists if the alien's actions, at all times before and after his departure, indicate that the United States is the alien's "true and permanent home."

Some resident aliens hold the mistaken belief that permanent resident status can be preserved by simply returning to the US once each year for a few weeks. This mistaken belief apparently arises from the rule that one can return to the US on only the green card within one year. This rule has nothing to do with resident status and is simply a travel documentation rule that eliminates the need for papers such as re-entry permits for short trips abroad by a permanent resident.

If you have a green card, and know you will be outside the US, you should apply for a re-entry permit before leaving the US This document is valid for two years and can be obtained only while in the United States. It is applied for on INS Form I-131. Should you be gone more than two years, it is necessary to obtain a special visa at the nearest US consulate. These are 1991 regulations, which should show you how much tighter the situation is becoming, and the prevailing trend. The days of the indefinite, but unused, permanent residence status are ending.

If you plan to be out of the US for an extended period after you get your green card, you should maintain as many ties to the US as possible, such as real estate ownership, bank accounts, credit cards, club memberships, and a US driver's license.

In 1989, the regulations for the Alien Registration Card were revised. The card used to be valid as long as the alien remained a permanent resident. Now the card expires ten years after the date it was issued. The alien then will be required to obtain a new card.

If your card was issued before the age of 14, it must be updated to include fingerprints once you reach the age of 14. The card will contain new photos and the fingerprint.

There are two major exceptions to the numerical limits on resident visas. Refugees and asylees (those who are granted political asylum) have a separate limit set annually by Congress. This category can be 200,000 or more visas so it may have importance, depending upon your country of origin. And "special immigrants" – which will be discussed in detail later – are not subject to numerical limitations. The major group of special immigrants is spouses and minor children of US citizens so there are still circumstances in which marriage can help.

In general, however, marriage to a US citizen does not guarantee that a visa will be granted and marriages are looked at with a great deal of suspicion by the Immigration and

Naturalization Service. But a marriage can be helpful if you are kept out only because you are too far down the waiting list and it can reduce the period to obtain citizenship from five years to three years, if obtaining US citizenship is important to you.

Each category has its own limitations within the total 675,000 visas. Family-sponsored immigrants are limited to 480,000 beginning in 1995 (465,000 until then). This limit can be increased by the number of visas unused in the previous year from the employment-based allotment.

The annual limit for employment-based immigration is set at 140,000.

The diversity immigrant category is limited to 55,000, starting in 1995. Until then, there is a limit of 40,000 visas under a program with slightly different requirements. Until 1995, there are an additional 55,000 annual visas available for immediate families of aliens who have been granted amnesty under the earlier program to legalize illegal immigrants – so if you are a qualifying family member an immediate application is essential. We will discuss the diversity program in detail later.

There are various clauses in the law that automatically can change these numbers slightly in various circumstances but they are not relevant to discussion of the overall structure nor the procedures for your application.

All applicants in the permanent residence category are routinely fingerprinted and criminal record checks are made both in the US and with foreign governments.

Immediate relative applications may take two to six months to process. If you are not in the immediate relative category, then your priority date becomes important. The priority date is the date on which your relative files a petition for you or the date your employer filed an application for you. The immigration authorities keep careful record of this date and visas are granted in the order applications are filed in each preference and for each country, even though the wait may be many years.

For example, for Mexico there are over 60,000 brothers and sisters of US citizens on the waiting list and the wait is several years.

These long waits create a problem of which many are unaware. If, during these years, you want to go to the US as a non-immigrant – as a tourist, businessman, student or official of your government – it is improbable that the US Embassy in your country will approve your application for a non-immigrant visa.

Why? Because you already have an application on file for an immigrant visa! This is interpreted by the US government as a statement that you intend to live permanently in the US

You should be aware of this possibility. Of course, there is an exception to every rule. If you can convince the US consulate that you will not remain illegally in the United States waiting for your immigrant visa number to come up and that you will return to your country once the period of your non-immigrant stay is over, you may be granted a non-immigrant visa. However, people with temporary work status on H visas need not worry about this happening to them, as the 1990 law exempts them from this possibility.

EMPLOYMENT-BASED IMMIGRATION

Although the public in the United States is becoming somewhat against immigration – primarily because the alleged "taking of jobs" is always easy political rhetoric in a period of recession – the business community is strongly in favor of liberal immigration when businessmen find that they cannot readily hire the qualified people that they need.

The sad truth is that America has an increasing percentage of unqualified or underqualified workers and a failing state education system that is the subject of much talk but little reform. What this means to you is that there are more opportunities than ever for qualified immigrants who have skills to offer. Employers will welcome you and a move to America may well be your key to a fortune. The 1990 law changes *tripled* the number of employment-based visas available – which says plenty about what the business community wants.

The 1990 law created five preference categories for this employment-based immigration:

1) "priority workers";
2) members of professions holding advanced degrees and persons with exceptional ability in the sciences, arts, or business;
3) "skilled workers", entry-level professionals, and unskilled workers;
4) special immigrants; and
5) "employment creation" immigrants (investors in "new commercial enterprises").

Each year, 40,000 visas will be available in each of the first three of these preference classes. Visas unused in the first preference category may be used in the second, and visas unused in the first two may be used in the third preference. They do not carry down to the fourth and fifth preferences but it is not expected that there will be any unused visas after the third preference category. But unused visas in the fourth and fifth preferences go up to the first preference, where they can again come down to the second and third preferences if unused in the first preference.

The fourth and fifth preferences are limited to 10,000 visas per year each.

We will go into the details of each preference and how you might qualify but, first, a few generalities that apply to all of the employment-based categories.

All of the employment preferences require a petition to the Immigration and Naturalization Service to classify the alien in the specific preference and be filed before a visa application is filed at a US consulate.

LABOR CERTIFICATION FOR SECOND AND THIRD PREFERENCES

For the second and third preferences, before the petition can be filed there must be approval of an alien employment certification application, which is filed with the U. S. Department of Labor by the prospective employer. This certification is not required for the first, fourth, and fifth preferences.

The alien employment certification (commonly called a labor certification) is actually filed with the state employment service in the state where the alien will be employed – the law provides that the state employment service is the delegate of the US Department of Labor for this purpose. (The federal government pays the state agencies for the work involved.)

The certification is to the effect that US workers are unavailable and that the wages and working conditions offered to the alien will not adversely affect US workers. Upon filing the labor certification application, you receive a "priority date" which will be used to determine the date when an immigrant visa number will become available to you.

The employer has to show that it has made a recruitment campaign, usually by placing advertisements for the position in newspapers and by posting the opening at its work site. This proof is then attached to the certification application.

The certification application consists of two parts. Part A is the "Offer of Employment" and contains a description of the duties of the job, the salary that will be paid, the minimum education and experience requirements for the job and any other special requirements. You complete and sign Part B of the application, which consists of your biographical information, including education and work experience.

Obviously one of the best ways to "get through the system" in this preference category is to have a job description that will be nearly impossible to fill, and that US workers are unlikely to be applying for. Thus, some creative planning may be useful. If you are to accept a job as "export manager" there are probably many US workers with experience as an export manager who may apply. But if you are to be appointed as export manager for the company's new expansion into the former Soviet republics, even though that may constitute only 10 per cent of your export manager duties and you just happen to speak two or three relevant languages –

perhaps Russian, Ukrainian, and Estonian – in addition to English, you have created conditions in which the labor certification will almost certainly have to be granted.

Such a combination might also qualify you in one of the specialized skill categories – you wouldn't have to be that specialized in this category. We're giving the example to show a job description can be created that is unlikely to fill the position with a US worker. It is important that everything be clearly related to the job, so that the authorities cannot challenge it by saying the stated unique requirement is just a gimmick to avoid filling the job with somebody else.

It used to be that negative requirements also kept applicants away – in normal circumstances very few would have applied for a job as a sewer inspector. Unfortunately, the unemployment situation in America is now so bad for unskilled work that when the dog catcher in a rural city of 28,000 advertised for a half-time dog cage cleaner at minimum wage ($4.35 per hour) there were over 1000 applicants. Until the economy recovers from the prolonged recession, it is better that the job specifications be unique rather than merely unpleasant.

The Department of Labor is used to these tricks since they were used under the older immigration law as well. In reviewing the job duties, officials determine whether the position offered represents a combination of jobs because requiring that a combination of jobs be performed in one position affects the availability of US workers, since workers are not usually qualified to perform several jobs. Therefore, an employer is not allowed to seek a labor certification for a position involving a combination of job duties, unless the combination is common for the type of position offered or it can be justified on the basis of business necessity, such as the need to combine duties because of the small size of the company.

The minimum requirements for the job also are carefully examined because of their obvious impact on the availability of qualified US workers. The requirements imposed by the employer must be realistic minimum requirements, consistent with the employer's previous requirements in hiring similar workers and with the Department of Labor's investigation of minimum requirements for similar jobs with other employers. Restrictive requirements must be justified to the Department of Labor as a business necessity. Foreign language requirements and live-at-work requirements automatically are deemed to be restrictive and must be justified. The salary offered must be at the prevailing wage for the position in the area of intended employment, since otherwise US workers might be available but unwilling to accept the job at the pay offered. So offering the legal minimum wage for a simultaneous interpreter fluent in Arabic is not going to be approved. Working conditions are also checked for normality – split shifts or late hours will not be acceptable unless they are common for the position offered.

The Department of Labor will not issue the certification unless all US workers applying for the advertised position have been rejected for lawful, job-related reasons.

A major exception to the certification requirement is for fields in which the Department of Labor has predetermined that there is a chronic shortage of US workers. In these fields an individual labor certification is not necessary and the employer is not required to conduct a recruitment campaign. Since 1991, the list has consisted of only two groups. Group 1 is physical therapists and registered nurses, and Group 2 is "aliens of exceptional ability in the sciences and arts."

If the field of employment is listed, the employer files the preference petition directly with the Immigration and Naturalization Service, which will determine whether the alien meets the standards specified by the Department of Labor to qualify in the pre-certified occupation.

FILING THE PETITION AND OBTAINING THE VISA

The second step in an employment-based immigration application is the filing of a petition. In most cases, the employer must do this, but in certain cases involving "extraordinary ability" priority workers, the alien can file his own petition. Either way, the preference petition is filed with the Immigration and Naturalization Service Center having jurisdiction over the place of intended employment.

Acceptance of the preference petition constitutes a finding by the immigration authorities that the alien is qualified to apply for an immigrant visa. To proceed further, you must then file an application for an immigrant visa with a US consulate. However, you can make application only if the Department of State determines that an immigrant visa is "immediately available." Each month the Department of State publishes its *Visa Office Bulletin* which lists the latest priority date for which immigrant visas are available in each preference and for countries which are oversubscribed for allotted visas. In some cases a visa number will be immediately available on the date the petition is approved. Backlogs frequently develop, however, in some of the employment-based preferences or for some countries, due to high demand for available visas.

Under the former system, waits up to five years were not uncommon. Since the 1990 legislation, major delays are rare for employment-based visas.

If you are already in the US at the time an immigrant visa becomes available, you may apply to "adjust status" to permanent resident. This is useful if you entered on a business visa, found a job, and want to accept it without the expense of leaving the country and applying for a visa at a consulate. To do this, your status in the US must be legal and must have been legal at all times. It is not possible to "adjust status" from an expired visa or if there is a pending complaint that you have violated your visa, such as by working on a visitor's visa.

THE B LIST

In addition to the A list of occupations which do not require certification, the Department of Labor has a B list of jobs it has concluded have a chronic oversupply of qualified US workers. Most of the occupations on the list are menial or unskilled jobs. Certification applications will not be accepted for jobs on the B list. Although the list may change from time to time, this current list is probably typical of what the list will always be like:

assemblers;

attendants (amusement and recreation service);

attendants (services workers such as personal service);

attendants, parking lot;

automobile service station attendants;

bartenders;

bookkeepers II;

caretakers;

cashiers;

charworkers and cleaners;

chauffeurs and taxicab drivers;

cleaners, hotel and motel;

clerk typists;

clerks and checkers, grocery;

clerks, general;

clerks, hotel;

cooks, short order;

counter and fountain workers;

dining room attendants;

electric truck operators;

elevator operators;

floorworkers;

groundskeepers;

guards;

helpers, any industry;

household domestic service workers (but see below)

janitors;

keypunch operators;

kitchen workers;

laborers;

loppers and toppers;

material handlers;

nurses, aides and orderlies;

packers, markers and bottlers;

porters;

receptionists;

sailors and deck hands;

sales clerks, general;

sewing machine operators and handstitchers;

stock room and warehouse workers;

streetcar and bus conductors;

telephone operators;

truck drivers and tractor drivers;

typists (lesser skilled only);

ushers;

yard workers.

HOUSEHOLD DOMESTIC SERVICE WORKERS

"Household domestic service workers" – maids, butlers, child care, etc. – are on the B list BUT there are possible exceptions in this category.

To get around the restriction, the alien employee must have one year or more of full-time paid experience in the tasks to be performed and the employer must justify the need for somebody with one year of experience. This alone is not enough however as the Department of Labor will insist that there are many US workers who meet this requirement. The employer must also have a live-at-work requirement and justify the need for this working condition. Then a certification is available because US workers almost never will accept a live-at-work condition for a job.

SPECIAL EXCEPTIONS FOR COLLEGE TEACHERS

For labor certifications for college and university teachers and performing artists with exceptional ability, the employer need only show that the alien is more qualified than any US workers applying for the job, rather than that no US workers meet the employer's minimum requirements for the position.

The employer will be required to document the recruitment process that led to hiring of the alien. Usually this will require at least one advertisement in a suitable national professional journal.

THE FIRST EMPLOYMENT-BASED PREFERENCE FOR PRIORITY WORKERS

This category has 40,000 visas per year, probably more than will be used by the category. The labor certification requirement does not apply to this category and priority dates for immigrant visa processing are established by the filing of the preference petition directly with the Immigration and Naturalization Service.

Within this category are three sub-categories:

1) aliens with "extraordinary ability" in the sciences, arts, education, business, and athletics;
2) "outstanding" professors and researchers;
3) executives and managers of multi-national corporations who meet specific requirements. Each sub-category has equal access to the annual total of 40,000 visas.

ALIENS WITH EXTRAORDINARY ABILITY

Unlike most aliens who seek to immigrate to the US on the basis of employment, aliens in this category do not need a specific job offer as long as they are entering the US to continue work in their field. Letters from prospective employers are helpful however but, since an offer is not required, a group of letters from employers interested in interviewing you would be sufficient.

This is intended to be a very restrictive sub-category for aliens having "extraordinary ability" in the sciences, arts, education, business, or athletics and the Immigration and Naturalization Service has high standards for certification in this category. Obviously receiving the Nobel Prize or an Academy Award will instantly qualify you in this sub-category.

But the standards do allow for other proofs. By regulation, having at least three of the following types of evidence can be acceptable:

1) Documentation of the alien's receipt of lesser nationally or internationally recognized prizes or awards for excellence in the field of endeavor;
2) Documentation of the alien's membership in associations in the field for which classification is sought, which require outstanding achievements of their members, as judged by recognized national or international experts in their discipline or fields;
3) Published material about the alien, in any language, provided it has been translated into English, in professional or major trade publications or major newspapers about the alien. This evidence must include the title, date, and author of the material;
4) Evidence of the alien's original scientific, scholarly, artistic, athletic, or business-related contributions of major significance in the field;
5) Evidence of the alien's authorship of scholarly articles in the field, in professional or major trade publications or other major media;

6) Evidence of the display of the alien's work in the field at artistic exhibitions or showcases;

7) Evidence that the alien has performed in a leading or critical role for organizations or establishments that have a distinguished reputation;

8) Evidence that the alien has commanded a high salary or other significantly high remuneration for services, in relation to others in the field;

9) Evidence of commercial successes in the performing arts, as shown by box office receipts or record, cassette, compact disk, or video sales.

Under these criteria it might prove hard for business persons to document their "extraordinary ability." Recognizing this potential problem, the Immigration and Naturalization Service rules permit the petitioner to submit "comparable evidence" to establish the alien's eligibility. The term "comparable evidence" is undefined in the regulations or policies.

OUTSTANDING PROFESSORS AND RESEARCHERS

To qualify in this sub-category requires aliens to have three years' experience in teaching or research in their field, and to have achieved international recognition for their work. The regulations provide that a professor or researcher is eligible if:

1) the alien is recognized internationally as outstanding in a specific academic field;

2) the alien has at least three years of experience in teaching or research in the academic field;

3) the alien is offered a tenured or tenure-track teaching or research position at a university or a comparable research position with a private employer if the employer has at least three full-time researchers and documented accomplishments in the research field.

The employer must file the preference petition with the Immigration and Naturalization Service. The alien is not allowed to file the petition for qualification in this sub-category.

To qualify as recognized internationally as outstanding in the academic field, the Immigration Service requires at least two of the following:

1) Documentation of the alien's receipt of major prizes or awards for outstanding achievement in the academic field;

2) Documentation of the alien's membership of associations in the academic field, which require outstanding achievements of their members;

3) Published material, in any language, provided it is translated into English, in professional publications written by others about the alien's work in the academic field. This documentation must include the title, date, and author of the material;

4) Evidence of the alien's participation either individually or on a panel as the judge of the work of others in the same or an allied academic field;

5) Evidence of the alien's original scientific or scholarly research contributions to the academic field; or

6) Evidence of the alien's authorship of scholarly books or articles, in scholarly journals with international circulation, in the academic field.

To meet the three-year requirement, teaching and research can be combined. To meet the ability requirements, obviously an applicant is going to need a whole lot more than three years experience in the field but this rule keeps an applicant who has spent most of his career in research from being barred from a teaching position and vice versa.

In recognition that many research positions at universities are not tenured or tenure-track positions, the Immigration and Naturalization Service rules permit a job offer to qualify if the university is offering a "permanent research position" to the alien. A "permanent" position is one for a term of indefinite or unlimited duration and in which the employee ordinarily will have an expectation of continued employment unless there is a good cause for termination.

The immigration authorities do recognize that since private employers do not give tenure to employees, a "comparable" position would be one in which the job description and duties are analogous to those of a researcher in an academic setting and who is offered a permanent position.

Failure to achieve tenured status will not cause a loss of the visa, so you need not fear that university campus politics will hurt your residency.

INTERNATIONAL EXECUTIVES AND MANAGERS

The third group in the priority worker preference is likely to be the most used. This is an alternative to the non-resident visa class L, for those executives who seek permanent residence with their transfer to the US.

To qualify as a multinational company allowed to use this category, the employer must be conducting business in two or more countries, one of which is the US So looking for a job with an American company's foreign branch or affiliate can be a good way to begin arrangements for your move to the US.

To be included in this group, you must have been employed in a managerial or executive capacity for at least one continuous year in the preceding three years by the overseas affiliate, parent, subsidiary, or branch of the US employer, and must be coming to work in the United States in a managerial or executive capacity.

The definitions in the 1990 law are broader than the former immigration service regulations so if you tried this category before, it is worth taking a fresh look.

The definition of *managerial capacity* requires (1) management of an organization, department, component, or function; (2) supervision and control of other supervisory, managerial, or professional personnel or management of an essential function; (3) authority to make personnel decisions (hire-fire, etc.), or functioning at a senior level if a function is managed; and (4) exercise of discretion over operations or a function.

First-line supervisors are not included as qualifying managers. Staffing levels are to be considered only in relation to the reasonable needs of the business and its stage of development, thereby permitting the transfer of managers to recently-established offices. The major change in this category over prior immigration service definitions is the inclusion of managers who manage a function rather than other personnel.

The definition of *executive capacity* requires (1) management of an organization or major component or function; (2) authority to establish goals and policies; (3) wide latitude in discretionary decision making; and (4) only general supervision from higher executives, the board of directors, or stockholders. As in the case for managerial personnel, staffing levels are to be considered in relation to the reasonable needs of the business and its stage of development.

If you are already in the US on an L-1 visa and wish to change to permanent residence, it can be done in this category if you were employed by the same company for at least one year preceding entry as a non-immigrant.

The company must have been doing business in the US for at least one year, so it is not possible for the first executive hired for a new office to use this visa category.

The US employer must submit the petition under this category.

THE SECOND EMPLOYMENT-BASED CATEGORY FOR EXCEPTIONAL ABILITY ALIENS AND ADVANCED-DEGREE PROFESSIONALS

This category is allotted 40,000 annual visas, plus visas not used in the first employment-based preference. Each of the two groups in this category has equal access to the annual visa allotment. It is not expected that all of the visas in this category will be used, making immediate immigration possible for those in this category once their petitions have been approved.

The category has the same Department of Labor certification requirements as in the First Employment-Based Category, with the exception that some aliens with exceptional ability may be able to qualify without a specific job offer.

ALIENS WITH EXCEPTIONAL ABILITY

The first group in the second employment-based preference includes aliens with exceptional ability in the sciences, arts, or business. Inclusion in the exceptional ability group requires that the alien has a degree of expertise above that ordinarily encountered in his field. The Immigration and Naturalization Service has decreed that possession of a degree, diploma, certificate, or similar award from a college, university, school or other institution may not be considered sufficient by itself to evidence exceptional ability; nor may a license or certificate to practise a profession or occupation be considered sufficient.

Under the Immigration and Naturalization Service regulations, to establish exceptional ability, you must present at least three of the following:

(1) An official academic record showing that the alien has a degree, diploma, certificate, or similar award from a college, university, school, or other institution of learning relating to the area of exceptional ability;

(2) Evidence in the form of letters from current or former employers showing that the alien has at least ten years of full-time experience in the occupation for which he is being sought;

(3) A license to practise the profession or certification for a particular profession or occupation;

(4) Evidence that the alien has commanded a salary, or other remuneration for services, which demonstrates exceptional ability;

(5) Evidence of membership of professional associations; or

(6) Evidence of recognition for achievements and significant contributions to the industry or field by peers, governmental entities, or professional or business organizations.

As in the case of "extraordinary ability" aliens in the first preference, the regulations provide that in cases where these criteria do not readily apply to the alien's occupation, the petitioner will be permitted to submit "comparable evidence" to establish eligibility.

For business persons, probably it will be necessary to establish that the business requires the services of an exceptional business person due to the complexity of the business and the responsibilities required in the position.

ADVANCED-DEGREE PROFESSIONALS

In this sub-category, the alien must possess an advanced degree or its equivalent in his proposed field of professional employment in the United States. It must also be shown that the work you will be doing requires a professional holding an advanced degree or its equivalent.

The Immigration and Naturalization Service regulations define a profession to mean an occupation for which a US baccalaureate degree (or its foreign equivalent) is the minimum requirement for *entry* to the field.

An advanced degree is defined by the rules to mean any US academic or professional degree (or a foreign equivalent) above a bachelor's degree level.

The new law requires that a bachelor's degree plus at least five years of progressive experience in the specialty be considered the equivalent of a master's degree.

You must have the bachelor's degree, however, because the rules do not allow for the evaluation of education and experience to determine whether you have the equivalent of a bachelor's degree.

The rules also do not permit the revaluation of education and experience to determine the equivalent to a doctorate; if a doctorate is required for a field, you must have the doctorate.

Under the rules, the petition for an advanced-degree professional must be accompanied by either (1) an official academic record showing that the alien has a US advanced degree or a foreign equivalent degree or (2) an official academic record showing that the alien has a US bachelor's degree or a foreign equivalent degree and letters from current and former employers showing that the alien has at least five years of progressive post-baccalaureate experience in the specialty. The petition must be accompanied by a labor certification or proof of qualification in one of the shortage occupations which does not need a labor certification.

THE THIRD EMPLOYMENT-BASED PREFERENCE FOR SKILLED WORKERS, PROFESSIONALS, AND OTHER WORKERS

The third employment-based preference is a catch-all category for aliens with job offers in the United States. This preference is also allotted 40,000 visas annually, plus any visas unused in the second preference.

Labor certification, or a Department of Labor exemption of the particular occupation from individual labor certification, is required for all aliens in this category. A job offer is also required in *every* case, and the employer must file the preference petition.

There are three sub-categories in the third preference: (1) professionals with bachelor's degrees in their fields (but not necessarily any experience); (2) skilled workers, defined as aliens capable of performing a job requiring at least two years of training or experience; and (3) other workers, also referred to as "unskilled" workers, who are capable of filling positions requiring less than two years of training or experience.

The distinction between the three groups in the third preference is very important because the new law limits unskilled workers to only 10,000 of the 40,000 annual visas. This limitation will probably mean that sufficient visas maybe available immediately for skilled workers and professionals but a substantial waiting list is likely to develop for aliens classified as unskilled workers. This waiting list will include household workers, most specialty chefs, and other workers. This list is expected to grow to four or five years wait. So if you intend to obtain your "green card" in this category, we must stress the importance of applying as soon as possible.

PROFESSIONALS

The first group in the third employment-based preference consists of aliens who hold bachelor's degrees and who are members of the professions. The Immigration and Naturalization Service limits this category exclusively to those with the degree – equivalent experience is not acceptable. This difference may not be important in practice however, as such persons would be likely to qualify in the second sub-category as skilled workers.

In this sub-category the employer must file the petition which has to be accompanied by (1) an official college or university record showing the date the degree was granted and the area of concentration or study; (2) evidence that the occupation is a profession, on the basis that a bachelor's degree is required for entry; (3) evidence that the alien is a member of the professions by virtue of his education and experience (in the form of letters from trainers or employers with the name, address, and title of the trainer or employer, and a description of the training received or the experience of the alien); and (4) a labor certification or documentation to establish that the alien qualifies for one of the shortage occupations on Schedule A.

SKILLED WORKERS

The definition of this sub-category is aliens who are capable, at the time the petition is filed, of performing skilled labor requiring at least two years of training or experience. It is very important to note that it is the *position* that requires two years of training or experience. The fact that you have at least two years of training or experience in an occupation will not qualify you as a skilled worker if the occupation does not require two years of training or experience.

In the early years of the new law, it is likely that there will be many disputes between employers and the Department of Labor as to whether the occupation *requires* two years of training or experience, or whether the employer merely has a personal preference for two years' qualification.

You must have a permanent job offer and the preference petition must be filed by the employer.

OTHER WORKERS

This is the unskilled classification. Even if you have more than two years of training or experience, if the *position* you are being offered does not require that training or experience, you will be treated as an unskilled applicant – and may be placed on the long waiting list for the 10,000 annual visas in this sub-category.

The petition, with the labor certification, must be filed by the employer.

INFORMATION COMMON TO THE FIRST THREE EMPLOYMENT-BASED PREFERENCES

One particularly easy trap to fall into is the requirement that the alien be qualified for the position *when the petition is filed.* If your employer files a petition for you in April, because you are going to receive your bachelor's degree in June, it will be seen as an attempt to jump into an early position on the list, and the petition will be denied. You will then find yourself starting over after all the other June graduates already have been given dates, if the prospective employer is even willing to wait through all those months only to begin again.

It is also quite likely that your processing will be prejudiced by the attempt, even though nobody officially will admit to that. Bureaucrats are human too and if they feel you have been dishonest in your first attempt, your second attempt can be rejected on technicalities, mysteriously lost in processing, moved each day back to the bottom of the pile, or subject to years of verification investigations (requests for new certifications of records directly from each of your schools, etc.)

Be sure that you meet the published rules – in this or any other visa category – before you file an application. The authorities processing these applications do not care to have their time wasted by unqualified applicants who should have read the rules first, and they will have no sympathy. You are the one that is in the wrong. Almost qualified is not good enough. If you don't meet every single requirement listed for the particular visa, don't apply.

Anyone undertaking a matter as serious as a new future in a new country should be informed enough to know the requirements for the visa for which he is applying – and to file an unqualified application certainly will raise questions as to whether you are a suitable person to be allowed to immigrate to the US. Do it right the first time.

There is one exception to this general rule. It is legal to file multiple petitions in different classes if there is legitimate doubt as to whether the Immigration and Naturalization Service will certify a person in a higher category. This is to your advantage, as it saves the time of doing the petitions in sequence. But we are talking here of legitimate questions of Immigration and Naturalization Service discretion – will the officials consider you an "exceptional ability" case in the first preference or merely a "professional" in the second preference. In these cases the multiple petitions are filed together and quite openly because there can be a legitimate question as to how the immigration authorities will exercise their discretion in a particular case. That is an entirely different thing from filing a petition in a category for which one does not meet the published requirements, such as our example of filing before you actually have the required degree.

Meeting the requirements for the job offered is very important because the labor certification is issued on the assumption that the job can be filled only by a person meeting the specified qualifications. If an alien who falls short on some of the requirements can be accepted, then so could a US worker who doesn't meet the requirements and the labor certification will not be valid.

The Immigration and Naturalization Service also will evaluate the employer's ability to pay the alien being offered the job. Small companies will be especially closely scrutinized in this regard and will be asked to submit several years of tax return records, audited financial statements, and employment records. The immigration authorities can also ask for copies of bank records and other documentation if the first items do not satisfy them. This procedure is now being strictly followed to eliminate situations in which people create a company to hire themselves or have a friend simply print up a letterhead and then write an employment offer to get the visa. Both of these ploys have been common in the past and worked many times. But they won't work now.

Intent is another important area. The immigration authorities will consider whether they believe that there is a true intention to work in the offered position. Even if already working in the position and only seeking a change of status, this doubt can arise. What they are concerned with is people qualified for a particular type of visa using a job offer to get a preference and then do something else after they are a permanent resident.

Legally, there is no obligation to remain in any particular employment once you are a permanent resident and your residence is not conditional on remaining in that occupation.

Many immigration advisors will mislead you by pointing out this rule. What they do not tell you is that the Immigration and Naturalization Service can challenge your permanent residence status, and begin deportation proceedings, if there is a hasty departure from the qualifying job once the residence status is granted. They do this by charging that the sudden change is evidence that the application was made in bad faith and therefore the visa was procured by fraud.

Worse, if you are deported for fraud on a visa application, you can never again gain admission to the US in any category, not even as a visitor. Another common lie is that if you are deported you can re-enter again after five years. Not true and you could spend some time in prison for trying, especially if you physically entered the US as a tourist because you come from a country whose citizens are no longer required to have tourist visas. Not being required to have a visa and having a legal right to enter after deportation are two different things. When the immigration inspector sees your name come up on the computer as a prior deportee, he is going to take you into custody. Usually such a person will just be deported again after a few days or weeks but the authorities do like to choose a few miscreants of whom to make an example and you just might be one of them.

In processing the petition, the Immigration and Naturalization Service can require interviews with both the alien and the employer. It can also investigate anything it wants to and this includes overseas investigations into the claimed employment experience if the authorities have any suspicions. This is most likely in the cases of work experience claims in countries where the immigration authorities have had a particularly high incidence of fraud. India, Hong Kong, and Taiwan are high on the suspect list at the moment. On the other hand, many petitions are routinely approved by mail, with no interviews and not even a telephone call. A chartered accountant from western Europe, with several years experience at a world-class accounting firm, for example, is very likely to have his petition approved in this way.

THE FOURTH EMPLOYMENT-BASED PREFERENCE FOR SPECIAL IMMIGRANTS

Ten thousand annual visas are available in this category. The category includes religious workers, persons under the protection of a US juvenile court, certain medical doctors, and employees of the US mission in Hong Kong. This is a change from the old law in which religious workers were exempt from the numerical limitations.

RELIGIOUS WORKERS

There are three sub-categories of religious workers:

(1) aliens who will work as ministers;

(2) aliens who will work for a religious organization in a professional capacity in a religious vocation or occupation; and

(3) aliens who will be working for a *bona fide* religious organization in a religious vocation or occupation.

Religious workers in the latter two sub-categories are eligible for the fourth employment-based preference classification under a three-year pilot program which began on October 1, 1991. No more than 5,000 of the yearly total of fourth employment-based preference visas may be in these two sub-categories.

The qualification rules are very similar to those for non-immigrant religious worker visas. The alien must have been a member of a religious denomination which has a *bona fide* religious organization in the United States for at least two years immediately preceding the date of filing the immigration petition. The alien also must have worked in the religious vocation during this two-year period. And the alien must be seeking entry to the United States *solely* for the purpose of carrying on a religious vocation or occupation. All of this strictness has come about recently because there were a number of well-publicized large-scale abuses of the religious worker visa classification in the past couple of decades.

A minister does not require a university degree but the term does not include a lay preacher not authorized to perform the normal duties of the clergy.

Religious professionals are required to have the minimum of a baccalaureate degree – experience cannot be substituted. There is no degree requirement for other workers in a religious vocation or occupation. As a practical matter, since both types of religious workers are considered as one group for purposes of the annual limitation of 5,000 immigrant visas, there is no advantage to qualifying in one sub-category or the other.

Specifically excluded from the definition of religious workers are janitors, maintenance workers, clerks, fund raisers, or persons solely involved in the solicitation of donations.

Because this is a three-year program only, the petition must be filed by 30 September 1994. Use INS Form I-360, Petition for Classification as a Special Immigrant.

MISCELLANEOUS FOURTH PREFERENCE VISAS

In addition to religious visas, the fourth employment-based preference includes a variety of special sub-categories. These are: long-term US government employees abroad and their accompanying spouses and children; medical school graduates who have continuously practised medicine in the United States since 9 January 1978; certain unmarried sons or daughters of international organization employees; and children who have been declared dependent on a US juvenile court and have been deemed eligible by that court for long-term foster care.

THE FIFTH EMPLOYMENT-BASED PREFERENCE FOR IMMIGRANT INVESTORS

This new category is getting a lot of attention from prospective immigrants. Depending upon your personal goals and situation, one of the non-immigrant investor or trader categories may be both easier to obtain and more beneficial. If you are insistent that permanent resident status is what you really want, then the fifth preference is for you.

This category has 10,000 visas per year, 3,000 of which are set aside for "targeted employment areas," defined as rural areas and areas experiencing high unemployment rates. The fifth preference is for immigrant investors in new commercial enterprises but their spouses and children are also included in counting the 10,000 limit.

To qualify in this class, you must make an investment of at least $500,000 in "targeted employment areas" and at least $1 million in other "high unemployment areas." The investment must benefit the US economy and create full-time employment for at least ten "qualified employees." The investor, his family, and non-immigrant visa holders are not considered qualified employees.

The commercial enterprise must be a profit-making business. Specifically excluded are projects such as setting up a corporation to own a personal residence which employs a staff of ten! (If you have this kind of wealth, there are other categories you can more easily qualify in.)

The assets of the business may not be used to finance the business – an actual cash investment is required. And you must be prepared to document the legitimate sources of the money used. The Immigration and Naturalization Service is most likely to not only ask for copies of your tax returns for the last decade or so but also to contact your country's tax and police departments for verification of your legitimacy and the legitimacy of your money. Be prepared for a much more thorough investigation than you would expect even if your own country suspected you of a major crime! The immigration authorities have become absolutely paranoid that a drug dealer might use this category to buy his way into the United States.

Multiple investors in the same enterprise are allowed, provided that each investment meets the minimum requirements and creates ten jobs. So ten people could open a $10 million factory employing 100 people and obtain visas for each of the 10 partners.

Purchase of an existing business is permitted IF the purchase is part of a restructuring of the business that will increase the capital and the employment of the business. Taking over an existing concern alone is not sufficient because it is a mere change of ownership and does not create jobs. In general, a 40 per cent increase is considered acceptable, so investment of $1 million that only creates four additional jobs in a company already employing 10 will meet the requirements. But it is not wise to try to cut these requirements too close. The authorities want to be convinced that the purpose is the business investment, not the visa, and playing games with the very edge of the minimum requirements is not going to impress them.

To apply in this category, you must file INS Form I-526, Immigrant Petition by Alien Entrepreneur. The form is filed with the Immigration and Naturalization Service Center having jurisdiction over the location of the planned enterprise.

With the petition, you must include evidence that: (1) the new commercial enterprise has been legally established in the US (certified copies of incorporation documents or the partnership agreement); (2) the petitioner has invested the requisite capital (proven by bank records showing payment of the capital into the new enterprise and copies of the stock certificates); (3) proof that the capital was obtained by lawful means (all of your personal and business tax returns for the past five years, foreign business registration records, and records of all criminal, civil, or administrative proceedings you have been involved in during the past 15 years); (4) the new enterprise has created, or will create, 10 new jobs (payroll records or a copy of a comprehensive business plan covering the coming two years); (5) that the investor is an active, not a passive, investor who will be involved in the daily management of the business.

In addition, if the investment is in a "targeted employment area" then proof of that through copies of the official designations of the area.

The Immigration and Naturalization Service can ask for any additional data it wishes and most often will probe personal background and sources of income. If your personal tax returns for the five previous years do not show sufficient surplus income to have made the investment, you can expect a very thorough investigation, with notifications to the police and tax authorities in your country.

Unlike the other permanent residence visa categories, approval in this category results in only a conditional visa for the first two years, which requires continued involvement in the business and proof of its success. If the business fails during the two years, regardless of the reason, the visa will be revoked. There are no exceptions and proof of having made your best efforts doesn't count for anything.

With all these potential problems, we would seriously advise any sane businessperson to stay away from this category, as it is only inviting trouble. This is the category that many immigration lawyers are advertising heavily as well, which will mean a flood of applications and even more attention. (Remember, the lawyers don't care as it all just generates more fees for them. Especially when applications become bogged down in processing and inquiries from the immigration authorities, so that the lawyer has continuing reasons to go back to the client and request more money to deal with each inquiry from the authorities.)

FAMILY-SPONSORED IMMIGRATION

The 1990 law continues to place a high priority on family reunification, with special provisions for relatives of US citizens and permanent residents. There is no numerical limit on visas given to close family members of US citizens.

Verify anything you learned before 1990 – many of the categories and rules are now different. Visas allotted to the family-sponsored visa category now are completely separate from the visa allotment for employment-based immigration.

As under the old system, the first family-sponsored preference in the new system is for unmarried sons and daughters of citizens.

Second preference is divided into two sub-categories: the family 2A preference sub-category is for spouses or children (unmarried and under the age of 21) of permanent residents, and the family 2B preference covers adult unmarried sons and daughters of permanent residents. Seventy-five per cent of the family 2A immigrants are exempt from the normal per-country numerical limitations. What this means is that countries with long waiting lists in the second preference category (Mexico, the Philippines, and the Dominican Republic) will have their earliest registered cases receive the most annual visas until the backlogs for these countries are eliminated.

The new third family-sponsored preference, which includes married sons and daughters of US citizens, parallels the old fourth preference category.

Finally, brothers and sisters of adult US citizens, who were formerly included in the fifth preference category, now are covered by the fourth family-sponsored preference.

Under the new law, the preference classifications of beneficiaries of approved family-based petitions filed prior to 1 October 1991, have been automatically converted to the corresponding new family-sponsored categories. In many cases this will mean a faster, or even immediate, visa.

Visa availability in the family-sponsored visa preference categories varies widely depending on the prospective immigrant's country of origin. Natives of the Philippines, Mexico, India, and the Dominican Republic typically face the longest delays. First-preference visas for the Philippines currently are backlogged by more than five years; fourth-preference visas for the Philippines currently are backlogged for more than 14 years, and the waiting list for Mexicans is more than 12 years. So if you can possibly enter the US on an employment-based visa, you should most certainly pursue that route instead of the family option.

The most favored category of family members is that of immediate relatives of US citizens. There is no numerical restriction on the number of immediate relatives permitted to immigrate each year to the United States and, accordingly, none of the extended delays commonly faced by other family members of citizens and permanent residents in obtaining permanent residence.

The term "immediate relative" includes:
(1)   spouses and unmarried minor children of US citizens;
(2)   parents of citizens when the citizen is at least 21 years of age;
(3)   certain widows and widowers of citizens.

Number two in this list was designed to limit the ability of a pregnant woman to enter the US to have a child and then apply for permanent residence based on being the mother of a US citizen.

In most family-sponsored immigrant visa cases, the U. S. citizen or permanent resident must file an immigrant visa petition on INS Form I-130, Petition for Alien Relative, on behalf of the immediate relative or other family member. The citizen or resident is considered the petitioner and the alien is considered the beneficiary of the petition. The principal exception to this rule is in the case of an alien widow or widower of a deceased citizen; in that case the alien files the immigrant visa petition on INS Form I-360, Petition for Amerasian, Widow(er), or Special Immigrant.

THE ACCOMPANYING RELATIVES PROBLEM

If you get a green card as a preference relative and you are married or have unmarried children below the age of 21, your spouse and children automatically can get green cards as accompanying relatives simply by proving their family relationship with you. If, however, you qualify as an immediate relative, they cannot. The difference may create some real problems in cases involving parents with adult children or step-parents and step-children who wish to immigrate as a family.

Example 1: Suppose your child is over age 21 and is a US citizen. You are applying for a green card as an immediate relative with your US citizen child acting as petitioner. If you are married, your spouse can't get a green card automatically as an accompanying relative because accompanying relatives are included only with preference relatives, not immediate relatives. Any other children you may have, even if they are minors, cannot be accompanying relatives either, for the same reason.

Of course, if your US citizen child is the offspring of your spouse as well, he may file petitions for each parent at the same time but the two filings will be completely separate. The marriage between you and your spouse will not be relevant when the Immigration and Naturalization Service considers your cases. Likewise, your US citizen child may also sponsor his or her brothers and sisters under the Family Fourth Preference but, again, the fact that you qualify for a green card will not help your children. There is a wait of many years under the quota for Family Fourth Preference applicants, while there is no wait at all for immediate relatives. In this manner, members of the same family can be forced to immigrate on different time schedules.

Example 2: Again, suppose you are the parent of a US citizen child who is over age 21. You are applying for a green card as an immediate relative with your US citizen child acting as petitioner. You are married but your present spouse is not the other parent of your US citizen child. Clearly, you have a problem. Your spouse cannot get a green card automatically as an accompanying relative because accompanying relatives are included only with preference relatives, not immediate relatives. Neither can your spouse be sponsored separately by your US citizen child because your spouse is not the child's parent.

If your present marriage took place before your US child reached the age of 18, your problem is solved, because your spouse is, according to immigration law, a step-parent. Likewise, if your spouse adopted your child before the child's birthday, he qualifies as an adopting parent. Step-parents and adopting parents can qualify as the immediate relatives of a US citizen. Your child can petition for a step-parent or adopting parent just as if he or she were a natural parent.

What if your marriage took place after the petitioning child's 18th birthday? Now your spouse is not considered a step-parent for immigration purposes and so you will have to wait until you get your own green card before anything can be done for your spouse. Once you get your own green card, your spouse will qualify under the family second preference as the relative of a green card holder. Unfortunately, this category is currently subject to a quota wait of several years, so your spouse will have to wait even longer before getting a green card.

The same sort of problem also comes up when the US citizen petitioner is the step-parent. The US step-parent may easily petition for the non-American spouse. If the non-American spouse has children by a previous marriage, however, unless those children were under age 18 when the present marriage took place, they will not qualify for a green card. They will have to wait until their natural parent gets a green card. Then they will qualify under the family second preference, again subject to the quota wait of several years.

Example 3: Suppose you are unmarried and under age 21. Your parent is a US citizen and you are applying for a green card with your parent acting as petitioner. You are in the unique situation of being able to choose between classifications. You qualify either as an immediate relative or in the family first preference category. It would seem logical for you to choose the immediate relative category because preference relatives are limited by quota while immediate relatives are not.

Let us further suppose that you have a child of your own. It now seems logical to place yourself in the preference category rather than the immediate relative category because then your child could automatically get a green card as an accompanying relative. On the other hand, preference relatives, limited by quotas, usually wait longer for green cards than immediate relatives. At present, the family first preference has waiting lists only for people born in Mexico and the Philippines so, for everyone else, there is no difference between the waiting periods for family first preference and immediate relative applicants. The waiting period for Mexicans is about one year but the waiting period for Filipinos is nearly seven years. Faced with a choice, would you elect to get your green card quickly and leave your child behind or wait out the family first preference quota? The splitting up of families is sometimes a surprising and unpleasant consequence of US immigration. This is also one of the reasons the author of this book so strongly favors non-immigrant categories unless there is a genuine need for a permanent residence visa.

AUTOMATIC CONVERSION IN THE FAMILY CATEGORY

Suppose you belong in the family preference category and some event (marriage, divorce, death of spouse, or the simple passage of time) places you in a different preference category.

Your original priority date remains unchanged, even if you have become eligible for a different preference category.

For example, suppose you are a beneficiary of a family second preference petition as the unmarried son of a lawful permanent resident, your mother. But recently she has been naturalized as an American citizen, so you could now move into the family first preference category as the unmarried son of a US citizen. If the waiting list for the family first preference category is shorter than the waiting list for the family second preference category, you are eligible to receive your immigration visa more quickly than if you remained in your second preference status.

The same advantage is available to someone in the immediate relative category; for example, the unmarried child under 21 years of age of a US citizen. When the child turns 21 and has not yet arrived as an immigrant in the United States, the child moves into the first preference category but keeps the priority date assigned to the immediate relative petition filed by the US parent. Since this could result in a longer wait, if the child expects to immigrate soon, it may be beneficial to make a trip to the US and obtain the actual entry and permanent resident status before the 21st birthday.

A beneficiary of the family third preference category (married son or daughter of a US citizen), whose marriage is annulled or ends in divorce, becomes eligible as a beneficiary of the family first preference category after the annulment or divorce. The priority date of the previous preference petition is applied to the new petition for an immigrant visa in the family first preference category.

You must always call to the attention of the US embassy, or the Immigration and Naturalization Service, this conversion of your preference category and your right to keep your old priority date. Either write a letter, with copies of the documents to prove your change of preference category, or file a new petition. In either case, always enclose a copy of your previously approved petition to show your old priority date.

This rule on the conversion of preference categories applies *only* to family-sponsored immigrant visas.

LEGAL DEFINITIONS OF "CHILD" – MORE OPENINGS THAN YOU MIGHT THINK

The terms "child" and "parent" are broader than you might expect and it is important to look at them closely in case you qualify. The term child can cover legitimate children, step-children, legitimated children, illegitimate children sponsored by their natural mothers or by natural fathers who have a "bona fide parent-child relationship" with them, adopted children, and orphans who will be adopted by US citizens. In all of these cases, to be considered a "child" for immigration purposes, the alien must be unmarried and under 21 years of age.

The term "parent" does not include the natural father of a child if he has disappeared or has abandoned or deserted the child or has irrevocably given the child up for adoption to a US citizen or citizens. So you can't let your child be adopted by a US citizen and then use the original relationship to enter the US as a parent of a citizen. Adoption is a legal process which substitutes the adoptive parents for the natural parents so after the adoption proceeding the natural parents are legally strangers to the child and have no special rights – for immigration or any other purpose.

The parent-child relationship can create some interesting visa-obtaining possibilities, and some traps. For example, if the widowed parent of a 17-year-old, unmarried alien marries a US citizen, the child becomes the step-child of the citizen, and therefore is a "child" of a citizen for immigration purposes.

But, if the 17-year-old child in this example is already married at the time of his or her parent's remarriage to a US citizen, and remains married through his or her eighteenth birthday, he or she will not qualify as a "step-child" under the immigration laws and, therefore, never will be able to qualify as a "son" of "daughter" for immigration purposes. This is important because to qualify in other family-sponsored preference categories, it is necessary to prove that the son or daughter was classifiable at one time as a child. So in this second example family-sponsored immigration as an adult married child of the US citizen would never be possible.

Sons and daughters of citizens who do not qualify as children because they are married or are over the age of 21, or both, must qualify for immigration in one of the family-sponsored immigrant preference categories, which are subject to numerical limitations, or on another basis, such as employment-based or diversity immigration.

The immigration law gives six sub-categories of child:

(1) legitimate children;

(2) step-children, whether born in or out of wedlock, if the marriage creating the step relationship occurs before the child turns 18;

(3) children legitimated by the age of 18, if the legitimation occurs under the law of the child's or father's residence;

(4) illegitimate children of a natural mother, or of a natural father, if there exists a bona fide parent-child relationship between the father and child;

(5) children who are adopted before the age of 16, if the child has been in the legal custody of, and has resided with, the adopting parents for at least two years; and

(6) orphans under the age of 16 on whose behalf an immediate relative petition has been filed, provided that a number of conditions have been met and procedures followed by the citizen parent or parents.

Whether a child is legitimate for immigration purposes is determined by the law of the child's place of birth. Because all children born in wedlock are considered legitimate under the immigration law, the issue of legitimacy arises only in cases involving children born out of wedlock.

A child born out of wedlock may be considered legitimate if the country where the child was born has eliminated all legal distinctions between legitimate and illegitimate children. Children born after the effective date of the abolition therefore are legitimate and are children for immigration purposes. So a close study of the law of the country of birth may be necessary in these situations.

Under the second sub-category, some children who were illegitimate at birth may qualify as "children" if they are legitimated before their 18th birthdays. Legitimation can occur in one of two ways: (1) the law of the jurisdiction where the child was born can retroactively eliminate all distinctions between legitimate and illegitimate children prior to the time the alien reaches the age of 18; or (2) the father can legitimate the child under the law of the child's or father's place of residence, again if done prior to the time the child turns 18.

For example, in some jurisdictions, a child can be legitimated by the marriage of his or her parents. If the marriage occurs before the child turns 18, the child will be deemed legitimated for immigration purposes as well.

Legitimation for purposes of making an alien a "child" under the immigration law can also occur by judicial decree or through acknowledgment of the child by the natural father, as long as the act of acknowledgment erases all disabilities of illegitimacy under the law of the place of birth.

An alien can also qualify as a "child" for immigration purposes if a step relationship is created with a parent before the child reaches the age of 18. For example, under this rule, an illegitimate child whose father marries a US citizen before the child turns 18 can be sponsored for immigration by the citizen step-parent, to whom the alien is a "child", even if the illegitimate child could not be sponsored by the father because of the lack of a bona fide parent-child relationship.

Aliens who have been adopted before they reached the age of 16 also are considered "children" for immigration purposes. Such children must have been legally adopted under the law of the place of adoption and must have been in the legal custody of, and residing with, the adopting parent(s) for at least two years. This two-year period can be either before or after the formal adoption.

The final statutory sub-category of children consists of alien orphans under the age of 16 who will be adopted by US citizens. The child must either be adopted abroad or be coming to the United States for adoption.

In addition to the six sub-categories established in the immigration law, a special law in 1982 created a special immigration category for Amerasian children. To qualify under this law, the alien must establish that he or she was fathered by an American citizen in either Korea, Vietnam, Kampuchea, or Thailand between the years 1950 and 1982. An Amerasian child of a US citizen may file a petition on his or her own behalf, or if under the age of 18, he or she may be sponsored by a US citizen or permanent resident who will assume legal custody over the child after his or her arrival in the United States. This ability to file one's own petition is a special concession to Amerasian children which does not apply to the other categories of children.

The immigration authorities can require blood tests of the mother, father and child to verify a relationship of which they are suspicious.

In the case of adoption of an orphan child, the state where the child is to live must conduct a home study to verify that the prospective adoptive parents are suitable and the immigration authorities will require that both adopting parents be fingerprinted.

THE MARRIAGE GAME

Spouses of citizens qualify as immediate relatives who can immigrate regardless of any numerical limitation, while spouses of permanent residents can qualify as immigrants in the 2A preference sub-category.

There are three determining factors as to whether an alien qualifies as a spouse: (1) the validity of the marriage under the law of the jurisdiction where it was performed; (2) whether the marriage was entered into in order to confer an immigration benefit on the alien (a sham marriage or marriage of convenience); and (3) the current status of the marriage.

The only legally-sanctioned marriage defined by the law to be invalid for immigration purposes is one in which the two parties were not physically in the presence of each other at the time of the marriage ceremony, unless the marriage was subsequently consummated. This was written into the law to eliminate proxy marriages connected with the mail-order bride business.

Other marriages may be considered invalid, however, because one of the parties lacked legal capacity or because the marriage is against the law of the jurisdiction where it was performed. Thus a marriage between cousins that might be legal in one jurisdiction might not be legal in another jurisdiction. The most common question of the validity of an apparently legal marriage is the objection that one of the parties could not legally marry because of the invalidity of a prior divorce. Any prior divorce must meet the legal standards of the jurisdiction where the divorce decree is entered and must be recognized in the jurisdiction where the subsequent marriage occurs. While the immigration service is required to consider all US divorce decrees as valid, it may not accept a foreign divorce decree and is entitled to conduct its own investigation. Thus a mail-order, or a one-day, divorce which is valid in the country that issued it, may not be accepted by the immigration authorities if it is not recognized by the laws of the country where the new marriage took place.

The marriage route is both one of the easiest and one of the hardest ways to gain entry to the US Easy because there is no waiting list since there is no numerical limitation; but hard because the authorities have become so suspicious of marriages that might be for immigration purposes that every case is examined very carefully. Congress has become so concerned that special laws on the subject have been passed, which we will discuss in detail. The Immigration and Naturalization Service has become infamous for its investigation of marriage-based immigration requests and frequently proceeds in an aggressive and antagonistic manner. Investigative techniques frequently involve actions such as questioning the spouses in separate rooms at the same time, asking such detailed questions as who sleeps on which side of the bed, what color is the wallpaper, how often do you have sex, what do you usually have for dinner – all to try to catch inconsistent statements to try to prove the marriage is a sham. It is not that officials care what the answers are – only that the answers match. After several hundred such questions, it is unlikely that a married couple who were only faking a relationship for immigration purposes could be totally consistent.

Even if a marriage is legally valid, it may be considered a sham for immigration purposes if it was entered into to confer an immigration benefit on the alien and this is the underlying purpose of this detailed investigation. It is quite possible to have the immigration authorities refuse to recognize a marriage on these grounds, even though the couple is still legally married for all purposes in their own country.

In 1986 Congress enacted the Immigration Marriage Fraud Amendments Act – the mere title should give you a clue as to the hostile feelings that were behind its passage. This law says that aliens who obtain an immigration benefit on the basis of a marriage entered into within two years of the time the benefit is conferred will be granted only *conditional* resident status for a period of two years. Before this period ends, the couple must file a joint petition to remove the conditional basis of the alien's residence. Failure to file this joint petition by the deadline results in automatic termination of the alien's resident status.

There is one exception allowed here. When the alien-conditional resident is unable to obtain the co-operation of the citizen spouse, a waiver of the joint petition requirement can be applied for. The basic requirement for obtaining this will be whether the parties entered into the marriage sharing the intention to establish a life together. Thus, the fact that the couple is presently divorced or separated does not necessarily negate the validity of the marriage for immigration purposes – but you can imagine the questions that such circumstances will raise. If a viable marriage is subject to such heavy scrutiny by the immigration authorities, a terminated marriage is next to impossible to get approved for permanent resident status. Waivers sometimes have been granted in cases of severe physical abuse by a spouse.

There is no requirement that a marriage currently be viable for conversion to permanent resident status. So long as the couple entered into a *bona fide* marriage and have neither divorced nor legally separated pursuant to a formal written separation agreement, they will be considered spouses for immigration purposes. This is the clause that most marriages of convenience rely on and the parties agree to co-operate in the filing of the petition, even if they are no longer living together. But it will still raise questions and investigation.

Far better are the spouses who claim a viable marriage is still functional and they are merely temporarily living apart for career reasons (such as working in different cities). Better yet are those who share a home or apartment, even with separate bedrooms, and claim that they have separate rooms because of conflicting working hours, not because of incompatibility.

Co-operation and creativity can go a long way in making such deals work but there really has to be some benefit for both parties to have a successful marriage of convenience that can also be legally viable. The best ones are often based on a business relationship, enhanced by marriage for mutual immigration benefits. For example, an Irish lawyer and an American lawyer set up an international law partnership to refer clients to each other, get married, and at the end of the three years each gets the citizenship of the other spouse as a bonus, with no loss of the original nationality. This is the kind of deal that can work nicely for everyone concerned and with the shared business there is a reason to keep it going for at least the three years – and perhaps much longer if neither spouse has any urgent need to get divorced for a re-marriage. Such relationships can often create tax benefits for both spouses. They may also create opportunities for children (whether of the marriage or children that one or both spouses had before the marriage, or even mutually adopted children) to qualify for government-aided tuition at universities in the other country.

By the time a relationship this complex has been created, it is likely to survive, even if it isn't a traditional marriage with a romantic love between the parties. And because of the many family relationships created, it is more likely to survive scrutiny by the immigration authorities.

Of course if one isn't in a hurry, the marriage can be allowed to exist for two years before the permanent resident visa is even applied for, which again adds a great deal of credibility to the application, and avoids the initial conditional visa requirements of the Immigration Marriage Fraud Act. So in marriage-based immigration, patience is a virtue.

Note that these rules apply only to a marriage-based immigration application. If the alien immigrates in some other category and marries a US citizen – whether before or after the date of the immigration – the special two-year conditional residence rule is not involved, and of course the marriage is reducing the waiting period for US citizenship.

An interesting loophole in this is that alien spouses who immigrate "derivatively" – as part of the family unit when the other spouse is the principal immigrant – are not covered by the Immigration Marriage Fraud Act. Thus one could arrange a marriage of convenience with a person who is about to apply for a US resident visa, enter the US as a permanent resident on that basis, and then divorce or separate.

Note that children of a spouse who is covered by the Immigration Marriage Fraud Act also obtain only a two-year conditional residence visa. But there are some loopholes in this as well and, if exploited properly, the children may be able to immigrate without the two-year conditional status. For example, if the alien's spouse is a US citizen, and the child has not yet reached the age of 18, the child will be able to immigrate as an immediate relative step-child. Alternatively, the child may be admitted as an immediate relative child of a US citizen if the citizen adopts him and if the legal custody and residence requirements are met. Because the child's immigrant status is not dependent on the marriage in either of these cases, there will be no condition placed on the child's residence.

In determining whether an alien is subject to the conditional residence rules, the date of actual admission to the US controls. So if you have been married for one year and ten months at the time of the visa processing, but actually arrive in the US three months later, you will be admitted unconditionally as a permanent resident, provided of course that the marriage is *bona fide*. What counts is that the marriage was over two years old at the time of your admission to the US There is a trap here as well – if you arrive in the US even one day prior to your second wedding anniversary, the two-year conditional residence period will be imposed. So it may often be advisable to delay the actual first entry into the US for a few weeks, to avoid this conditional residence requirement.

Even though the two-year period is called "conditional", you will possess the same rights, privileges, responsibilities, and duties as all other immigrants. You can work freely, travel freely, and file preference petitions on behalf of close relatives. And once the conditional part is removed, the two years count fully towards the residence requirements for naturalization.

Within the three months *prior* to the *second anniversary of entry to the US* the couple must jointly file INS Form I-751, Petition to Remove the Conditions on Residence, with the Immigration and Naturalization Service Center having jurisdiction over the couple's place of residence. In completing the joint petition, the couple must declare, under penalty of perjury, that: (1) the marriage was valid in the jurisdiction where it took place; (2) the marriage has not been judicially annulled or terminated; (3) it was not entered into to procure immigration benefits; and (4) no fee or other consideration was paid in return for filing the immigrant visa petition.

Among other details, the couple is required to state on the petition all of their places of residence and employment since the alien was admitted as a conditional resident. This gives the immigration authorities a starting point for an investigation. If the neighbors say that to their knowledge a person was single and they never saw any sign of a spouse, a very thorough investigation is going to start very quickly. Likewise, if the employer says that the employment record shows the person was single and no spouse was mentioned in connection with tax deductions, health insurance, or pension benefits, for example, there is going to be a major presumption that something is wrong and a fraud investigation will begin. Should this happen, remember that not only is the alien spouse facing possible deportation but both parties are facing possible prison sentences for immigration fraud. And such sentences are not uncommon. If it is a marriage of convenience, and you haven't had the good sense to be consistent, you are in about the same position as a bank robber who doesn't wear a mask even though he knows he is being videotaped by the bank's security cameras. There is nobody to blame but yourself for the resulting prison sentences.

The joint petition must be supported by evidence establishing that the marriage is not a sham entered into to evade the immigration laws. Among the types of documentary proof you should submit with the petition are evidence of joint ownership of property, such as a deed or mortgage; a lease showing that you are living together in the same residence; financial records showing common financial resources, such as in a joint checking account; birth certificates of children born to the marriage; affidavits from people who know you.

And the record should be consistent – a joint checking account on which only one spouse has ever signed checks is suspicious. Even if one spouse habitually pays the bills, it would be unlikely that in the entire two years the other spouse would never write out a check. Some people trying to document a marriage that is really a sham have the spouse sign a checking account application on the day of the marriage – but the spouse doesn't know where the bank account is and has never signed a check. It isn't going to work. Little things can trap you too – the checks are all in the same handwriting but every now and then the spouse has signed one for appearances' sake. Or perhaps an occasional check has been completely written out by the spouse but the check register is all in one handwriting. It is unlikely that the person writing out the check would not also enter it in the register and this is likely to make the investigator suspect that perhaps the spouse was handed the register already complete and told to write out a check to match the entry. If the immigration authorities are suspicious, these are the little clues that they are going to seek.

If you are the subject of an investigation that has started to turn nasty, you should probably consult a lawyer. At least, he *may* be able to head off a prison sentence through some plea bargain arrangement that includes deportation and a fine or probation for the remaining spouse. Or if the marriage is legitimate but still under attack by the immigration authorities, then legal help to defend the marriage and the immigrant visa may be very important. This is a far different situation than our earlier advice to avoid hiring a lawyer to process an initial visa application. When you are defending yourself in possible legal proceedings, whether civil or criminal, legal representation is normal, proper, and prudent.

RELATIVES OF FORMER ILLEGAL IMMIGRANTS – SPECIAL CATEGORY AVAILABLE ONLY UNTIL 30 SEPTEMBER 1994

For each year until this cut-off date, 55,000 visas are available on a first-come, first-served basis to the spouses and minor children of the more than 3 million permanent residents who acquired that status through one of the amnesty programs for illegal immigrants which existed during the 1980s. For this special category, the petitioning legalized resident must have been married to, or be the parent of, the alien seeking to immigrate under the program, *at the time he or she obtained permanent residence through legalization.*

Application is made for a standard 2A preference petition. Only if a visa number is not available under that program will the petition be considered for this special program so, in effect, applicants in this category have two chances to get a visa.

But because of the large number of illegal immigrants who received amnesty in the 1980s, already there is a waiting list for visas in this special category, and the 55,000 is not likely to cover the demand.

DIVERSITY IMMIGRATION

An entirely new category, created by the 1990 law, is "diversity" immigration. There is both a transitional program, until 30 September 1994, and a permanent program which starts on 1 October 1994. Both of these programs involve a lottery for qualified applicants, and are heavily promoted.

Our advice is to enter one of these programs if you are eligible and on a long waiting list but it makes more sense to look for other categories in which you can apply and particularly through some of the non-immigrant visa categories. Your odds of being successful are about the same as in any other lottery.

If you are eligible, there is nothing to lose by trying, especially if you prepare your own application and don't spend money on legal fees. There are some advantages, in particular that you do not need to have relatives in the US, do not need to have labor certification, and do not need to be a highly skilled professional.

And if you are Irish, you should especially give the diversity program a try because of the high number of visas set aside for Irish citizens.

THE TRANSITIONAL AA-1 PROGRAM

This is the program that lasts until 1994. It has 40,000 visas per year and 40 per cent of them must be made available to natives of Ireland. To be eligible, an applicant must have a firm offer of employment for at least one year from the date of admission to the US. The job offer must be presented before the visa is granted but it does not have to be available at the time the application is made.

There is no pre-printed application form for the AA-1 program. Instead, an application can be submitted on a sheet of paper which contains the following information (typed or printed):

1) applicant's name;
2) the applicant's date and place of birth;
3) the names and dates and places of birth of the alien's spouse and children;
4) a current mailing address;

5) the location of the consular office nearest to the alien's current residence, or, if the alien is in the United States, the consular office nearest to the last foreign residence of the alien prior to entry into the US.

Even if the applicant fails to list his spouse or children in the application, they are included automatically in the application, provided the marriage takes place before the applicant is actually admitted to the US for permanent residence (the children may be born after the alien's admission to residence if the marriage is entered into before such admission).

This program is sometimes called the "lottery" program because the notice is suddenly published in the Federal Register and applicants who are natives of designated countries only have a short time to file. For example, in 1992 applications were only accepted between 14 October and 20 October and had to be mailed to a post office box designated in the notice.

Because of the way this program is handled, no book can deal with it adequately and you should check with the US Embassy in your country to see when the filing period will be. The countries for which this program is in effect until 30 September 1994 are:

Albania;	Indonesia
Algeria;	Ireland
Argentina;	Italy
Austria;	Japan
Belgium;	Latvia
Bermuda;	Liechtenstein
Canada;	Lithuania
Czechoslovakia;	Luxembourg
Denmark;	Monaco
Estonia;	Netherlands
Finland;	New Caledonia
France;	Norway
Germany;	Poland
Gibraltar;	San Marino
Great Britain (including Northern Ireland);	Sweden
Guadeloupe;	Switzerland
Hungary;	Tunisia
Iceland;	

THE PERMANENT DIVERSITY PROGRAM

This program begins on 1 October 1994, and provides for 55,000 visas per year. To be eligible, an alien must: (1) be a native of a "low admission" country, as designated by the Attorney General and; (2) have at least a high school education or its equivalent, or at least two years of training or experience in a skilled occupation (one requiring at least that much training or experience), gained within five years of the date of application for a diversity visa. Unlike the transitional diversity program, it is not necessary to have a firm job offer in the US.

Because the designated list of countries is going to be changing throughout the program, this is another one on which it is necessary for you to check with the US Embassy to see if your country is included at that time. The initial list under the permanent program is likely to be fairly similar to the transitional list above. As with the temporary program, it is expected to be operated as a short term lottery with applications taken only during a few days of the year.

For this program, and only for this program, Northern Ireland is treated as a separate country.

SPECIAL IMMIGRANT VISAS FOR NATIVES OF HONG KONG

A special section of the 1990 immigration law provides a program that allows the issuance of 12,000 immigrant visas to Hong Kong natives working for US companies in Hong Kong. The 12,000 limit includes spouses and children. The program began in late 1990 and runs for three years.

In order to qualify, both the alien and the employer must meet certain standards. The alien must: (1) have been employed for at least one year by the company in Hong Kong; (2) have been employed in Hong Kong in an executive, managerial, or specialized knowledge capacity, or be a supervisor or an officer; and (3) must have a comparable offer of employment from the company in the US.

The company must: (1) have at least 100 employees in the US and at least 50 outside the US; (2) be owned or organized in the US; (3) have a gross annual income of at least $50 million; and (4) be offering the alien a position in the US that provides salary and benefits which are not different from those offered to other employees in similar positions in the US.

Aliens who qualify can opt to immigrate to the US immediately or to delay their immigration until 1 January 2002.

The initial visa petition is filed with the Immigration and Naturalization Service on Form I-140-Immigrant Petition for Foreign Worker, accompanied by Form ETA 750B-Statement of Qualifications of Alien, and a company letter of support.

Once the petition is approved, it is forwarded to the US Consulate in Hong Kong. The consul will notify the intending immigrant, who can then immediately proceed with the completion of the application, or delay it, as described above. Note, however, that the US job offer must still be documented, even if the alien chooses to delay his immigrant visa application.

REFUGEES AND ASYLUM

There may be circumstances in which you can gain US residence as a refugee or asylee. But our general recommendation is that if you can possibly fit into any other visa category, you should do so. Refugee and asylee status is as politically controversial in the US as it currently is in many European countries. Applications of this type are subject to a lot of scrutiny and active opposition by the immigration authorities. The exception is every now and then when some special status is created for refugees from a known war zone – and it has sometimes taken a long time for Congress to act, with those trying to get asylum or refugee status before that recognition taking a huge risk because, if rejected, they face deportation to the very country they were trying to avoid. But if you fit into a clearly established category, then this might be worth pursuing.

You may feel that you have a well-documented case but if the immigration authorities decide that you are not in danger of being killed or tortured upon return to the country from which you are fleeing, you may not have the opportunity to write and say "I told you so" when you get back home.

The important criteria to bear in mind here is that economic refugees are most unwelcome, and 90 per cent of applicants are rejected on this grounds. This is particularly so with the current flood of Haitian "refugees" who are shipped back to Haiti in most cases, usually after spending some time in an American prison or refugee camp awaiting processing of their refugee application.

A similar situation has applied to thousands of Cuban refugees who have been in US federal prisons since the *Mariel* "boat lift", in 1980, during President Carter's administration. Many of the refugees who arrived from Cuba were unwelcome in the US and have been in prison ever since because Cuba won't take them back and the US won't allow them loose in the country. It is all too easy to get oneself into this kind of mess with a refugee or asylum application.

The harsh attitude of the US is historical – in the 1930s Congress refused to enact statutes allowing entry of refugees from Nazi terror, including even proposed exceptions for groups of Jewish orphans. In fact, the first refugees were not allowed in the US until 1948. But even after that, the United States refused to accede to the 1951 United Nations Convention Relating to the Status of Refugees, which defines "refugee" and sets standards for the acceptance of refugees by nations acceding to the Convention. The US did not ratify the Convention until 1968 but with such strong reservations that it was practically meaningless. The accession simply let the US say that it had signed the Convention, with an exception to its provisions so broad that in effect the Convention does not apply in the US.

Despite all these negatives, the US still accepts more refugees per year than any other country in the world, so let's take a look at the circumstances in which it might be beneficial for you to pursue this route.

Generally, the pattern was that during some crisis the Attorney General or the President permitted a special class of refugees from that country to enter the US on a temporary basis and later Congress has legalized their status and made them permanent residents. This happened with Hungarians in 1956, Cubans in the early 1960s, Chinese and Czechs in the middle and late 1960s, and Indo-chinese in the 1970s.

Only in 1980 did Congress finally enact the Refugee Act, which adopted the definition of refugee from the United Nations Convention and established rules and procedures for dealing with refugees.

But to avoid using the law, and giving the refugees the legal rights it provided, the Immigration and Naturalization Service created a special category (without any statutory authority to do so) called "Cuban/Haitian Entrants." Only in 1986 were the Cuban refugees given permanent resident status.

The same thing happened later with Soviet Jews and several other groups – the Refugee Act was ignored and the immigration authorities refused to classify them as refugees.

By now, this history should be showing you why we are saying that the US is the one country in the world in which you want to avoid pursuing refugee or asylee status. But there's more.

Refugee status normally lasts for one year, after which you receive a green card. Political asylum is granted in one-year increments, renewable indefinitely until either a green card is issued or the conditions in your home country no longer justify a grant of asylum.

To qualify as a refugee, you must be fleeing from your home country because you experienced persecution in the past or have a well-founded fear of persecution in the future. To apply for refugee status, you must be physically outside the US And even qualified refugees often wind up on a waiting list. As a refugee applicant, you must have a financial sponsor inside the US before your application can be approved. You must also show that you have not been permanently resettled in another country.

Political asylees apply after arrival in the US but must otherwise meet the same basic requirements as refugees. Since they are already in the US, they don't need financial sponsors to be granted asylum.

The persecution must be based on race, religion, nationality, membership in a particular social group or political opinion. Note also that the persecution must be by your government. There have been several cases in which refugee status was denied because the persecution was by rebel force and not a recognized government.

The immigration authorities also have the legal right to determine that a person may be in danger if deported to a particular country and order their deportation to any other country that will accept them. This is what has happened to the Cubans who have been held in prison since 1980 – the US recognizes that their lives are in danger in Cuba but no other country will accept them, so they remain in prison. The United States Supreme Court ruled a few years ago that Cubans had no right to bring court cases challenging their detention. The perverted legal reasoning involved was that they were not legally persons because they had never been legally admitted to the United States, despite their physical presence in American federal prisons for more than 12 years now.

Refugee law is one area in which legal help is appropriate, frequently there are volunteer legal aid groups taking up the cause of particular classes of refugees. Without legal help your chances of obtaining refugee status are close to zero. It is also an area in which dishonest immigration lawyers make their fortunes out of others' misfortune. For genuine refugees, there are plenty of volunteer groups ready to help without charge. Beware of high-priced immigration lawyers who are ready to help the wealthy from a particular war zone. They know that in the area of refugee law they can create a controversy that can drag through the court system for years, generating huge legal fees but doing little good for the refugee. But to one unfamiliar with the process, it will appear that the lawyer is carrying on a major battle on your behalf.

Whole books have been written about refugee law, should you have an interest in pursuing the subject, but in terms of practical immigration help for the average reader, we can only stress that as far as the US is concerned, this is one category you don't want to get anywhere near.

As a last word, you should be aware that conviction for a serious crime is a mandatory barrier to being granted asylum or refugee status in the US This provision was used against many of the still-detained Cubans, since they were deported from Cuban prisons.

WHO CANNOT ENTER THE US

There are a number of categories of persons prohibited from entering the US, as immigrants or non-immigrants. These laws even apply to tourists. Just because citizens of a country are able to enter the US as tourists without a visa does not mean that there has been a waiver of the requirements. Should the immigration authorities find out that a person who has entered the US as a tourist without a visa is in a prohibited category, he can be deported. He also can be sentenced to prison for illegal entry but normally deportation is the only remedy, unless there is some evidence that the person wilfully and knowingly violated the immigration law.

The 1990 immigration law did change the exclusion grounds somewhat from the prior law, so if you were excluded before you should look at the current list to see if it still applies to you.

MEDICAL GROUNDS FOR EXCLUSION

The 1990 law now lists four medical-related grounds for exclusion:

(1) aliens determined to have "a communicable disease of public health significance";
(2) aliens who are determined to *have* a physical or mental disorder, and behavior associated with the disorder that may pose, or has posed, a threat to the alien or others;
(3) aliens who *have had* a physical or mental disorder, and behavior associated with the disorder which has posed a threat to the alien or others and which is likely to recur;
(4) aliens determined to be drug abusers or addicts.

There has been considerable controversy over whether AIDS or HIV infection is a communicable disease but it is being used as a basis for exclusion and in 1993 Congress passed special legislation making it clear that this is to be a ground for exclusion.

Questions about drug use will be asked during the required medical examination. Any indication of as little as one prior use of drugs formerly resulted in exclusion but the current practice appears to be that only use within the prior three years will be used as a ground for exclusion. This is a matter of interpretation by the medical examiners, not a regulation or statute, so it is subject to change.

Two major changes from the law prior to 1990 are that homosexuality is no longer a grounds for exclusion and physical disability is no longer a ground for exclusion if the alien can demonstrate means of financial support. This has been of great help in many family reunification situations where the family is quite willing to support a disabled relative, or the person has independent financial means, but under prior law they could not enter the US.

CRIMINAL ACTIVITY GROUNDS FOR EXCLUSION

The criminal and related grounds for exclusion are broad and almost continuously being amended to toughen the provisions and provide for not only exclusion but mandatory deportation after conviction for many types of crime in the US. It is likely that this trend will continue for some time.

The official grounds for exclusion in this category are:

(1) conviction or commission of crimes involving moral turpitude;
(2) violation of laws relating to controlled substances (drugs);
(3) conviction of two or more offenses;
(4) engaging in illicit trafficking in a controlled substance (not requiring a conviction);
(5) engaging in prostitution (or recent past prostitution activities);
(6) commission of a serious criminal offense for which diplomatic immunity has been asserted.

Note that several of these grounds specifically do not require a conviction. If US drug agents in your country send back a report saying that you are suspected of being one of the biggest drug kingpins in Bolivia, you are not going to get a visa. Or if the village policeman in Italy answers a letter from the US Embassy by saying that he thinks you might be in the Mafia, you can forget the visa.

Some of these categories call for a bit of explanation.

Conviction for a crime involving moral turpitude can be very confusing to someone not familiar with US legal terminology. A sub-ground here, although rarely used because it hardly ever comes up, is admission to having committed a crime involving moral turpitude or to having committed acts which constitute the essential elements of such a crime. It rarely comes up, because not many people are confessing crimes they weren't even convicted of to an immigration inspector – but it has happened. Sometimes something has come up in another context, perhaps in testimony given in a civil proceeding, or as a witness in a criminal case. An example of this would be somebody who was granted immunity from prosecution in exchange for his testimony and in his testimony admitted to having committed a crime. This has happened in drug cases, particularly where somebody might have testified that he bought a small quantity of narcotics from a larger dealer. During the background investigation the US immigration authorities obtain a copy of the court records of the testimony and the legal requirement of confession to a criminal act has been met, even though there was no conviction of the person who gave the evidence.

Note that the sections on drugs do not require a conviction. This came into the law specifically to deal with cases where a person was caught at the border with a small quantity of drugs but the prosecutor decided not to prosecute the case. The new wording prevented the person from being able to be admitted to the US at some future time.

There are possibilities to overcome the barrier of a criminal record if it can be demonstrated that the crime was a *purely* political one. Convictions for distribution of literature against a Communist regime have been overlooked, as have convictions for participating in political demonstrations in such countries. But the assassination of the Soviet ambassador to Poland was held to have been motivated in part by personal animosity and was not just an attempt to strike at the ambassador in his official capacity and, therefore, was held by the US immigration authorities not to be a purely political offense.

Sometimes a waiver can be obtained for a minor offense if it was committed under the age of 18 and at least five years before the application for immigration. Certain adult petty offenses, with a minor punishment, also can be waived.

Generally the crime must be a crime in the US before it becomes a bar to immigration.

The term "moral turpitude" is not defined in the law but in legal practice covers most crimes. Fraud has long been included in the definition, and generally almost all offenses against the person or property of others involve moral turpitude. Even some crimes that involve only reckless conduct have been included, although negligence is *probably* insufficient. In general the term "moral turpitude" identifies offenses that are considered morally wrong independent of any particular governmental policy or prohibition. Thus murder is a crime of moral turpitude but smuggling is not generally considered to be a crime of moral turpitude.

A later expungement or pardon for the crime does not waive the grounds for exclusion (with the exception of a pardon that was granted *on the grounds of innocence* in a country which does not have a procedure for reversing an erroneous conviction).

The prostitution bar to entry is a separate sub-section within the criminal exclusions. It includes anyone who has engaged in prostitution within ten years of the date of application. It also covers persons who have sought to procure prostitutes or have made a living from the proceeds of prostitution. Because prostitution is a separate sub-section of the immigration law and not part of the general criminal section, the waiver for petty crimes does not apply. Thus, paying a $5 fine for prostitution or having purchased a prostitute's license in a country where prostitution is legal will be sufficient for this ground for exclusion to apply. Even if the license was bought for a joke and was never used, it may be very difficult to prove that the section should apply and that no prostitution was committed. Some jokes can come back to haunt one years later.

SECURITY GROUNDS FOR EXCLUSION

Another broad set of exclusions applies under the category of "security and related grounds." This whole section was substantially liberalized by the 1990 law and again if you were excluded before, it is worth seeing if that is still the case. We won't go into detail about the obvious ones such as terrorism or espionage – if you fit in these categories you know who you are, and aren't likely to be applying for a US visa.

The immigration law now contains five basic security-related grounds for exclusion from the US:

(1) seeking entry to engage in espionage, sabotage, export of prohibited technology, activities with a purpose of violent overthrow of the US government, "or any other unlawful activity";

(2) past terrorist activity or the likelihood of engaging in such activity after entry (including fund-raising or other support activities for terrorist groups, which has been used to block some Irish visitors raising funds for charities alleged to be fronts for the Irish Republican Army);

(3) a potentially serious adverse foreign policy consequence would result from the alien's entry or proposed activity (usually not a concern unless you are a recent deposed head of state);

(4) membership by immigrant aliens of the Communist or other totalitarian party (non-immigrants are not excludable on this basis)

(5) participation in Nazi-era persecution or other activity meeting international definitions of genocide.

Each of these grounds is defined in detail in the statute and some are carefully circumscribed with qualifications and exceptions to limit their coverage. They don't apply to very many of our readers and we would suggest that if you are in one of these categories you either need legal advice or shouldn't be applying to enter the US in the first place.

In many of these security cases, the alien may be summarily excluded without the exclusion hearing normally provided to other aliens. The alien also need not be informed of the evidence against him, the reasons for exclusion, or even the statutory section under which excludability has been found. We do know that security grounds were used to exclude Libyan nationals seeking entry to train as pilots and in cases involving persons associated with organized crime.

Membership of the Palestine Liberation Organization is automatically deemed to be involvement in terrorist activity and therefore excludable, regardless of the individual's activities, or lack of activity. Exceptions are provided for PLO members on official business at the United Nations.

The foreign policy ground for exclusion has been used to bar the foreign minister of the Sandinista government in Nicaragua and the widow of assassinated President Allende of Chile. This clause has been made even more restrictive since those cases and the government now can use it pretty much as it wishes.

SPECIAL RULES FOR FORMER COMMUNIST PARTY MEMBERS

The one security section that could legitimately concern a number of our readers is the one about membership of a totalitarian party, which traditionally was used to bar anyone who was a member of the Communist party or an organization affiliated with it. Note that this ground applies only to immigrant visas, not to non-immigrant visas.

For those applying for immigrant visas, some exceptions to this membership rule apply: membership ending by age 16; automatic membership by operation of law; or membership for purposes of obtaining employment or other "essentials of living." Service in the armed forces of a country does not constitute or establish the alien's membership of the Communist party or an affiliate. Court cases have also held that "non-meaningful membership" is also a basis for exemption from this ground for exclusion.

Most immigrants from Eastern Europe and the former Soviet Union can enter under an exception that provides that the exclusion ground does not apply if the alien has terminated his membership at least two years before the application for a visa and the alien is determined not to be a threat to the security of the United States. (So if you were a KGB official the latter part of the clause might still keep you out.) A different time period applies, however, to aliens who are nationals of countries still controlled by a totalitarian party at the time of application for a visa. In that case, membership of the party must have been terminated at least five years before the date of application. The longer time period currently applies to nationals from Cuba, the People's Republic of China, Laos, North Korea, and Vietnam.

Another exception applies to Communist party members seeking to immigrate based on a relationship to a close US citizen or permanent resident family member. In the case of a party member who is the parent, spouse, son, or daughter of a permanent resident, the Attorney General may exercise his discretion to waive the exclusion ground for humanitarian purposes, to assure family unity. or when it is otherwise in the public interest. This waiver possibility applies even in the case of current Communist party members.

Although the 1990 law liberalized the exemptions and waivers available to former and present Communist party members in order to permit them to become US permanent residents, the bar to naturalization for persons engaging in activities associated with the Communist party within the preceding ten years has not been revised. This could place a person in the position of waiting ten years instead of five years after entry as a permanent resident to be able to apply for US citizenship.

THE IMMIGRATION FRAUD GROUND FOR EXCLUSION

A person involved in fraud or misrepresentation on a visa application or entry to the US is generally excludable. This ground also applies to assisting others in immigration-related crimes. Thus, smuggling a family member across the border in the trunk of your car is going to result in a ban from the US.

THE "PUBLIC CHARGE" GROUND FOR EXCLUSION

This exclusion has been in existence since 1882. It provides broad discretion to the immigration authorities to bar entry to anyone whom they believe may become a "public charge." The discretion is broad, since the basis for exclusion is speculative and can depend on the opinion of the consular officer or the immigration officer at the border. Job offers and affidavits of support from sponsors (not necessarily family members) are usually sufficient to overcome objections under this section. Alternatively, a bond may be posted to ensure that the alien will not become a public charge.

Aliens who become a public charge within five years of admission are deportable. So if you make a welfare application while in the US, expect a deportation to follow shortly thereafter. A lesser known danger is aliens who become public charges after the five-year period may be subjected to this ground for exclusion if they depart the United States and seek re-admission because the grounds for exclusion apply to each re-entry by an alien, even long-time residents. Some families who have collected welfare in the US for years and then made a Christmas visit to their home country have been quite surprised to find that re-entry was denied them upon arriving at the airport.

DEPORTATION AND APPEALS

There are extensive appeal procedures in the immigration law for all sorts of things – deportation, exclusion, etc. If you become involved in any of these matters, you are way beyond the realm of do-it-yourself law and should seek prompt legal help.

However, if you are about to be deported because of a criminal conviction in the US, you should be wary of lawyers who will take your money even when they know you cannot win the case.

In this regard, it is important to note that the deportation after a conviction will generally be upheld. There are provisions to apply for a waiver of deportation on the grounds of *extreme hardship to US citizens or permanent residents*. This waiver of deportation is in the discretion of the immigration judge hearing the case and in deportations based on criminal convictions it is rarely granted. In other cases it might be and legal advice could be helpful. But if the deportation is the result of a criminal conviction, you may be wasting your money on a lawyer if you are going to be deported anyway. In particular, note that the hardship must be to *US citizens or permanent residents*. Permanent resident status is revoked by law upon conviction, so you are no longer a permanent resident for purposes of this clause. Thus a criminal can never obtain this waiver based on hardship to himself, even after 30 or 40 years in the US Many a person convicted of a drug offense, who was brought to the US as a small child, has found himself suddenly deported to a country of birth of which he had no knowledge.

The hardship can be either emotional or financial but it must be to others. And the grant of the waiver is always discretionary. In serious crimes it is almost impossible to obtain. The "extreme hardship" showing is usually based on the economic reliance of the citizen or resident relative on the alien; emotional hardship caused by the separation of the alien and citizen or resident is usually not enough standing alone to demonstrate extreme hardship. Even if extreme hardship can be shown, it is also necessary to demonstrate the alien's rehabilitation; an alien who is still in jail or on parole is unlikely to show that he has undergone sufficient rehabilitation to justify approval of the waiver request. And since the alien will nearly always be in jail in these cases, they are normally impossible to win.

The law specifically defines drug-related offenses, including money laundering, as major crimes for which deportation is normally mandatory. So arguing that a minor possession of marijuana for personal use is a trivial matter does not have any legal basis.

Many dishonest lawyers prey upon people with drug convictions, telling them that they will apply for the hardship waiver, even though the lawyer knows perfectly well that it cannot be granted because there is no hardship to US citizens or permanent residents. But by then he has your money – usually $5,000 to $10,000 – and he knows you can't come back to the US to sue him for it, even if you could prove that he acted improperly in advising you.

So if you fall into this situation, you are probably better off saving your money to start life over in another country and face the reality of the deportation. In other circumstances, particularly non-criminal deportations, it might be worth spending money to try to get a hardship waiver.

RIGHTS AND OBLIGATIONS OF ALIENS

Most of the protective clauses in the US constitution refer to persons rather than citizens. For example, all persons are guaranteed equal protection of the laws.

This does not mean, however, that all rights of aliens are identical to those of citizens. There are often limitations but they are usually in specialized areas, such as certain types of government jobs, voting, and holding public office. But for most everyday purposes there are no legal distinctions between a legal resident alien and a citizen.

Many of these distinctions have been the subject of litigation in the US court system. In recent years the courts have permitted restrictions on employing aliens as police officers, public school teachers and probation officers. But the courts have prohibited restrictions on the licensing of lawyers, engineers, notary publics, physicians, and dentists. Note that even in categories where the courts have permitted restrictions, this does not mean that every state has such restrictions – it merely means that such restrictions are permitted if a state wishes to enact them. There is a prohibition on aliens in federal government employment.

Since the 1986 immigration law, private employers have generally been prohibited from discriminating against legal aliens.

Permanent resident aliens who have been in the US for a period of time (which varies from state to state and from program to program) generally are eligible for welfare and medical care benefits.

Licenses to run radio and television stations are not issued to aliens but licenses to sell liquor are.

BECOMING A CITIZEN

THE REQUIREMENTS FOR CITIZENSHIP

The goal for many aliens in coming to the United States is to become a US citizen. There is no requirement that an alien apply for citizenship, no matter how long he intends to reside permanently in the US Some aliens, even after becoming permanent residents, have no interest in becoming US citizens, often because they would have to relinquish their foreign citizenship under the law of their home country.

The actual legal requirements for citizenship are:

(1) Lawful admission as a permanent resident of the US;

(2) Continuous residence (not to be confused with physical presence) in the US for at least five years immediately preceding the filing of the naturalization application (three years for spouses of US citizens);

(3) Physical presence within the US for a total of at least one half of the period of residence;

(4) Residence for at least three months in the state in which the naturalization application is filed;

(5) Ability to read, write, and speak ordinary English;

(6) Knowledge and understanding of the fundamentals of the history and government of the US;

(7) Good moral character, attachment to the principles of the Constitution and proper disposition to the good order and happiness of the US;

(8) Continuous residence (again, not to be equated with physical presence) in the US from the date of filing the naturalization application until actual admission to citizenship;

(9) The intention to reside permanently in the US This requirement is not stated specifically in the law, but is implied in a separate section which permits the denaturalization of a naturalized citizen based on actions which are deemed to presumptively indicate a lack of intent to reside permanently in the US at the time of naturalization;

(10) Attainment of 18 years of age at the time of filing the naturalization application (with certain exceptions when a child is naturalized with his parents).

If the citizen spouse dies, the surviving spouse must meet the five-year requirement instead of the three-year requirement.

To use the three-year term for a spouse, instead of the normal five years, the alien must have been married to the US citizen for three years, and the citizen spouse must have been a US citizen for the entire three years.

Two possible exceptions that may be of interest are:

(1) Permanent resident seamen who serve on a US government ship, a ship with a US home port that is owned by US nationals or a US flag vessel can count time spent on duty outside of the US toward the physical presence and continuous residence requirements;

(2) Permanent resident aliens who have served in the US military service for three years, provided the naturalization application is filed while the alien is still in the service or within six months of discharge. Periods spent in military service count toward the physical presence and continuous residence requirements, even if the alien was stationed outside of the US If the application is not made within the six month deadline after leaving the service, these periods will still count towards the five-year requirement but the special three-year benefit cannot be claimed.

The "good moral character" requirement can delay a person from naturalization even though he has obtained a waiver from deportation. For example, a minor criminal conviction, or a conviction for prostitution, after an alien was in the US for four years, may have been waived on hardship grounds *for residence purposes*. But for citizenship purposes he needs a five-year period of clean conduct, so he will have to wait a total of nine years.

There are discretionary issues in the "good moral character" clause in addition to the statutory list. For example, a parent who is in default on court-ordered child support payments is likely to be found to lack good moral character.

Failure to register for military service, even though there is no active military draft at present, is a bar to naturalization, even if one is then too old to be required to register. It is important to be prepared to present your military registration card or other proof (such as a record from the military authorities) that you did register during the period you were legally required to do so. This requirement catches many people by surprise when it is too late to ever resolve it. It is also important to warn your US citizen children not to fall into this trap and risk possible prosecution for failure to register. The lack of an active draft has caused many to overlook the requirement.

THE CITIZENSHIP TEST

The Immigration and Naturalization Service is now using a standardized test and there are courses available everywhere to help one prepare for it. You aren't going to have to worry about this until some years after you have arrived in the US but to give you some idea of the questions you will eventually face, here are some samples from the current test:

When did the United States declare its independence from England?

What do the stripes on the US flag represent?

What is the name of the form of government used in the United States?

What are the three branches of the US government and the function of each?

What special name is given to the first ten amendments to the US Constitution and what are some of the special rights granted by these amendments?

How many members are there in the US House of Representatives and in the US Senate? How long are each of their terms of office?

Who are the US Senators from your state?

Who is the Secretary of State?

Where is the capital of your state?

Who is the Governor of your state?

Who is the US representative from your congressional district?

Who elects the President of the United States?

How long is the term of office of the President?

If both the President and Vice President should die in office, who becomes President?

How many Justices sit on the Supreme Court?

What is the name of the National Anthem and who wrote it?

What were some of the reasons for the American Civil War?

If you do not pass the examination, you will be given an opportunity to take it again a few months later.

DENATURALIZATION

Even after obtaining citizenship it can be lost if the US authorities later discover fraud in either the citizenship application or the underlying permanent resident visa application. Such cases have been on the increase in recent years, a reflection of the US crackdown on immigration in general. Since one of the requirements for naturalization is legal permanent residence, if the visa was procured by fraud or mis-statement, then there was never a legal basis for the naturalization and it can be revoked. Even an issue of immoral conduct, which the applicant was not intentionally concealing, can come to light years later and cause a denaturalization proceeding to begin. For example, a divorce case in which the spouse alleges sexual abuse of the children prior to the naturalization, and the court accepts the testimony as true, could then create a cause for denaturalization on the grounds that good moral character did not actually exist at the time of the naturalization. With the increase in allegations of sexual or physical abuse of children in US child custody proceedings, the risk of something like this happening is great.

The law also creates a rebuttable presumption that an alien who takes up residence outside the US within one year of naturalization misrepresented his intention to reside permanently in the US Factors considered are disposition of US property, location of family ties, involvement in business interests abroad and the purpose of the stay abroad. The government will ask the nearest US consulate to begin an investigation and the new citizen can present evidence on the issue, such as employment transfer at the order of the employer or illness of family members located abroad. After the investigation is completed, the reports are presented to the US Department of Justice for its decision as to whether it wishes to begin a denaturalization proceeding in a US court.

There is no statute of limitations on the government's ability to bring a denaturalization case.

DUAL NATIONALITY

The Supreme Court of the United States has stated that dual nationality is "a status long recognized in the law" and that "a person may have and exercise rights of nationality in two countries and be subject to the responsibilities of both. The mere fact that he asserts the rights of one citizenship does not without more mean that he renounces the other", *Kawakita v. US, 343 U,S.717 (1952)*.

Dual nationality results from the fact that there is no uniform rule of international law relating to the acquisition of nationality. Each country has its own laws on the subject and its nationality is conferred upon individuals on the basis of its own domestic policy. Individuals may have dual nationality not by choice but by automatic operation of these different and sometimes conflicting laws. Although US law requires a renunciation of former nationality as part of the naturalization process, this may not be meaningful under the laws of the country of birth. Many countries have formal requirements for the loss of their nationality and the mere inclusion in the US citizenship oath of a statement of renunciation most often does not meet those requirements. So if you are lucky enough to be a citizen of one of those countries, you still have your original nationality, regardless of the impression you might have been given that you lost it upon becoming a US citizen.

The laws of the United States, no less than those of other countries, contribute to the situation because they provide for acquisition of US citizenship by birth in the United States and by birth abroad to an American, regardless of the other nationalities which a person might acquire at birth. For example, a child born abroad to US citizens may acquire at birth not only American citizenship but also the nationality of the country in which it was born. Similarly, a child born in the United States to foreigners may acquire at birth both US citizenship and a foreign nationality.

The laws of some countries provide for automatic acquisition of citizenship after birth, for example, by marriage. In addition, some countries do not recognize naturalization in a foreign state as grounds for loss of citizenship. A person from one of those countries who is naturalized in the United States keeps the nationality of the country of origin, despite the fact that one of the requirements for US naturalization is a renunciation of other nationalities.

The current nationality laws of the United States do not specifically refer to dual nationality.

The automatic acquisition or retention of a foreign nationality does not affect US citizenship; however, the acquisition of a foreign nationality upon one's own application or the application of a duly authorized agent may cause loss of US citizenship under Section 349(a)(1) of the Immigration and Nationality Act (8 USC 1481(a)(1).)

In order for loss of nationality to occur under Section 349(a)(1), it must be established that the naturalization was obtained voluntarily by a person 18 years of age or older with the intention of relinquishing US citizenship. Such an intention may be shown by the person's statements or conduct, *Vance v. Terrazas, 444 US 252 (1980)*. If the US government is unable to prove that the person had such an intention when applying for and obtaining the foreign citizenship, the person will have both nationalities.

United States law does not contain any provisions requiring US citizens who are born with dual nationality to choose one nationality or the other when they become adults. This is a popular misconception.

Section 215 of the Immigration and Nationality Act (8 USC 1185) requires US citizens to use US passports when entering or leaving the United States unless one of the exceptions listed in Section 53.2 of Title 22 of the Code of Federal Regulations applies. Dual nationals may be required by the other country of which they are citizens to enter and leave that country using its passport but do not endanger their US citizenship by complying with such a requirement.

The Department of State is responsible for determining the citizenship status of a person who is located outside the United States or who applies for a US passport while in the United States.

Section 349 of the Immigration and Nationality Act (INA), as amended, states that US citizens are subject to loss of citizenship if they perform certain acts *voluntarily and with the intention to relinquish US citizenship*. Briefly stated, these acts include:

1) Obtaining naturalization in a foreign state
   Sec. 349(a)(1) (INA);

2) Taking an oath, affirmation, or other formal declaration to a foreign state or its political sub-division
   Sec. 349(a)(2);

3) Entering or serving in the armed forces of a foreign state engaged in hostilities against the US or serving as a commissioned or non-commissioned officer in the armed forces of a foreign state
   Sec. 349(a)(3);

4) Accepting employment with a foreign government if a) one has the nationality of that foreign state or b) a declaration of allegiance is required in accepting the position
Sec. 349(a)(4);

5) Formally renouncing US citizenship before a US Consular Officer outside the United States
Sec. 349(a)(5);

6) Formally renouncing US citizenship within the US (but only in time of war)
Sec. 349(a)(6);

7) Conviction for an act of treason
Sec. 349(a)(7).

The actions listed above can cause loss of US citizenship only if performed voluntarily and with the intention of relinquishing US citizenship. The Department of State has a uniform administrative standard of evidence based on the premise that US citizens intend to retain US citizenship when they obtain naturalization in a foreign state, subscribe to routine declarations of allegiance to a foreign state, or accept non-policy level employment with a foreign government.

Because of this administrative premise, a person who:

1) is naturalized in a foreign country;
2) takes a routine oath of allegiance; or
3) accepts non-policy level employment with a foreign government

and in so doing wishes to retain US citizenship need not submit prior to the commission of a potentially expatriating act a statement or evidence of his or her intent to retain US citizenship since such intent will be presumed.

When such cases come to the attention of a US Consular Officer, the person concerned will be asked to complete a questionnaire to ascertain his or her intent toward US citizenship. Unless the person affirmatively asserts in the questionnaire that it was his or her intention to relinquish US citizenship, the consular officer will certify that it was not the person's intent to relinquish US citizenship and, consequently, find that the person has retained US citizenship.

An individual who has performed any of the acts made potentially expatriating by statute and who wishes to lose US citizenship may do so by affirming in writing to a US Consular

Officer that the act was performed with an intent to relinquish US citizenship. Of course, a person always has the option of seeking to formally renounce US citizenship in accordance with Section 349(a)(5).

The premises established by the administrative standard of evidence are applicable to cases previously adjudicated by the Department of State. Persons who previously lost US citizenship may wish to have their cases reconsidered in light of this policy. A person may initiate such reconsideration by submitting a request to the nearest US Consular Office or by writing directly to:

Director, Office of Citizens Consular Services

Department of State

Washington DC 20520-4818

Each case will be reviewed on its own merits taking into consideration, for example, statements made by the person at the time of the potentially expatriating act.

Most (but not all) countries have laws which specify how a citizen may lose or divest citizenship. Generally, persons who do not wish to maintain dual nationality may renounce the citizenship which they do not want. Americans may renounce their US citizenship abroad pursuant to Section 349(a)(5) of the Immigration and Nationality Act (8 USC 1481(a)(5).

RENOUNCING US CITIZENSHIP AND WHY YOU MIGHT WANT TO

Having gone through years of effort to become a US citizen, you might wonder why we would be talking about renouncing citizenship. In fact, several thousand people per year do renounce their US citizenship, and the majority of them are naturalized US citizens. The reason is quite simple – having spent perhaps 20 or 30 years making their fortune in the US, they decide to retire to their original country and do not wish to retain the burdens (especially the tax burdens) of continuing to be citizens of the US when they know they will never return to the US.

You should be aware, however, that former US citizens are subject to US taxes *on US source income* for ten years after renouncing citizenship, unless it can be proven that the renunciation was not for tax purposes. Generally if you will pay less tax without the US citizenship, this will be impossible to prove. Leaving investments in the US would subject you to US tax on the earnings and selling your US business would still subject you to US capital gains tax on the profits under these rules.

Because of this taxation of former citizens, many immigrants to the US, particularly those who are wealthy or who are coming to establish a business, always retain their permanent resident status but deliberately do not apply for US citizenship. In this way, whenever they have made their fortune and are ready to leave, they can simply go. Upon surrendering the visa and stating that they have abandoned residence in the US, they will immediately be subject to tax in the same way as any other non-resident alien. This means that earnings from many investments will be tax-free. It also means that they will not be subject to US estate taxes upon their death.

Renouncing US citizenship does not cancel the right to a Social Security pension based on payments made to the US Social Security system. See the section on getting a pension from the US for more details.

United States citizens have the right to remain citizens until they intend to give up citizenship. It is also the right of every citizen to relinquish United States citizenship. Section 349(a) of the Immigration and Nationality Act (8 USC 1481) states:

"a person who is a national of the United States whether by birth or naturalization, shall lose his nationality by voluntarily performing any of the following acts with the intention of relinquishing United States nationality: . . .

(5) making a formal renunciation of nationality before a diplomatic or consular officer of the United States in a foreign state, in such form as may be prescribed by the Secretary of State; or

(6) making in the United States a formal written renunciation of nationality in such form as may be prescribed by, and before such officer as may be designated by, the Attorney General, whenever the United States shall be in a state of war and the Attorney General shall approve such renunciation as not contrary to the interests of national defense . . . ''

Renunciation is the most unequivocal way in which a person can manifest an intention to relinquish US citizenship. In order for a renunciation under Section 349(a)(5) to be effective, all of the conditions of the statute must be met. In other words, a person wishing to renounce American citizenship must appear in person and sign an oath of renunciation before a US consular or diplomatic officer abroad, generally at an American Embassy or Consulate.

Renunciations which are not in the form prescribed by the Secretary of State have no legal effect. Because of the way in which Section 349(a)(5) is written and interpreted, Americans cannot effectively renounce their citizenship by mail, through an agent, or while in the United States.

Section 349(a)(6) provides for renunciation of United States citizenship under certain circumstances in the United States when the United States is in a state of war. Such a state does not currently exist.

Once a renunciation is made before an American diplomatic or consular officer abroad, all documents are referred to the Department of State. The Director of the Office of Overseas Citizens Services reviews them to ensure all the criteria under the act have been met. It is not true that the renunciation can be refused on a discretionary basis – the right to renounce is absolute.

Parents cannot renounce United States citizenship on behalf of their children. Before an oath of renunciation will be administered under Section 349(a)(5), persons under the age of 18 must convince a US diplomatic or consular officer that they fully understand the nature and consequences of the oath of renunciation and are voluntarily seeking to renounce their citizenship. United States common law establishes an arbitrary limit of age 14 under which a child's understanding must be established by substantial evidence.

Under Section 351(b) of the Immigration and Nationality Act (8 USC 1483(b)), a person who renounced US citizenship before the age of 18 years and "who within six months after attaining the age of 18 years asserts his claim to United States nationality in such manner as the Secretary of State shall by regulation prescribe, shall not be deemed to have expatriated himself . . . " The relevant regulation is Section 50.20(b) of Title 22 of the Code of Federal Regulations which requires that the person take an oath of allegiance to the United States before a diplomatic or consular officer in order to retain US citizenship.

Persons who contemplate renunciation of US nationality should be aware that, unless they already possess a foreign nationality or are assured of acquiring another nationality shortly after completing their renunciation, severe hardship to them could result. In the absence of a second nationality, those individuals would become stateless. As stateless persons, they would not be entitled to the protection of any government. They might also find it difficult or impossible to travel as they would probably not be entitled to a passport from any country. Further, a person who has renounced US nationality will be required to apply for a visa to travel to the United States, just as other aliens do. If found ineligible for a visa, a renunciant could be permanently barred from the United States. Renunciation of American citizenship does not necessarily prevent a former citizen's deportation from a foreign country to the United States.

Persons considering renunciation should also be aware that the fact that they have renounced US nationality may have no effect whatsoever on their US tax or military service obligations. Nor will it allow them to escape possible prosecution for crimes which they may have committed in the United States or repayment of financial obligations previously incurred in the United States.

Finally, those contemplating a renunciation of US citizenship should understand that renunciation is irrevocable, except as provided in Section 351 of the Immigration and Nationality Act, and cannot be cancelled or set aside except with a successful administrative or judicial appeal (which is wildly unlikely).

LEGITIMATE TAX TRICKS FOR IMMIGRANTS

CHOOSING YOUR ARRIVAL DATE

For tax purposes, you become a US resident when you actually arrive in the US. So if you are about to receive a large capital gain, perhaps from the sale of a home or business, it would be best in many cases to receive this payment before becoming subject to US taxes.

If you have substantial foreign income that will continue while you are in the US for only a few years, it can be beneficial to create a trust or a holding company to accumulate that income for you until after you cease to be a US taxpayer. Matters of this nature need to be planned well in advance as once you are a resident of the US for tax purposes, it is too late and you should consult a US certified public accountant who is an expert in the US tax laws that relate to such matters. The best way to find one overseas is to contact some of the world-wide accounting firms – this is a specialized area in which you want to have the best available talent and their fees are normally very modest in relation to the savings to be achieved. Most certified public accountants practicing in the US are not going to be experienced in these special areas of tax law, which is why we are suggesting that you approach one of the major firms which has such specialists available. Even they will not have them in all offices but will be able to call on somebody appropriate within the firm.

TAX TREATY EXEMPTIONS

Tax treaties with about two dozen countries provide for exemption of US taxation for teachers temporarily employed in the US Normally the tax exemption period is limited to two years. But since other countries only tax on residence, this usually means that the earnings in the US will be totally tax free. So a temporary teaching assignment in the US can be a wonderful tax-free way to gain experience and a position that may enhance your future employment prospects in countries other than the US. It will also let you gain a US social security card, which can have some amazing benefits, as we discuss in a later section.

THE $70,000 EXCLUSION

This loophole is known as the foreign-earned-income-exclusion or the "$70,000 exclusion." It can let you maintain your US permanent resident visa while working outside the US, and still owe no US taxes. It allows for US citizens and residents who live and work outside the US to exclude from gross income up to $70,000 of foreign-earned income. In addition, an employer-provided housing allowance can be excluded from income. There are other tax breaks available: a married couple working overseas, for example, each can exclude salary of up to $70,000. That's a total of $140,000, *plus* housing allowances.

It is important to note that this is not a deduction, credit, or deferral. *It is an outright exclusion of the income from gross income.*

Naturally, to get these benefits you have to meet certain requirements:

* You must establish a tax home in a foreign country;
* You must pass either the "foreign-residence test" or the "physical-presence test";
* You must have earned income;

In the rest of this section, we'll discuss these tests and give some tips on maximizing tax-free income.

In the tax collector's view of the world, your tax home is the location of your regular or principal place of business. That is, the tax home is where you work, not where you live.

Take a look at what happened recently to one taxpayer who did not check the rules carefully. He is a flight engineer who lives in the Bahamas but all his flights originate from Kennedy Airport in New York. The Tax Court ruled, not surprisingly, that his tax home is in New York, not in the Bahamas. The flight engineer does not qualify for the $70,000 exclusion.

But the definition goes further for the foreign-earned-income exclusion. This is a trap that catches many Americans overseas who think they are earning tax-free income. If you work overseas and maintain a place of residence in the United States, your tax home is not outside the US. In other words, to qualify for the foreign-earned-income exclusion you have to establish both your principal place of business and your residence outside the United States. But since residence for immigration purposes and temporary residence for tax law purposes are different, it is possible to do both.

This trap catches a number of construction and oil workers. These workers generally work on a construction site or oil platform for three to six months. They get a few weeks or months off. Many of them make the mistake of leaving their family and personal possessions at their US home and visiting this home during their vacations. They can't use the offshore loophole because they never establish a tax home outside the United States. They maintained a place of residence in the United States. You need to sell or rent your US home and establish a primary residence outside the United States, which has to be handled very delicately to avoid conflict with the visa status.

After establishing your tax home, you must pass one of two additional tests.

The more straightforward test is the physical presence test. To pass the test, you must be outside of the United States for 330 days out of any 12 consecutive months. The days, of course, do not have to be consecutive. That sounds very simple but there are a number of smaller rules that can complicate it. Few people begin their foreign assignments on 1 January and end them on 31 December. Thus for most people, the first and last 12 months of their overseas stay will occupy two tax years. This requires them to prorate their income and the $70,000 exclusion for those tax years.

In addition, to count a day as one spent outside of the United States, you must be out of the United States for the entire day. There are exceptions for traveling days and days spent flying over the United States if the flight did not originate there. The IRS has a number of rules on counting days. If you are going to travel back and forth between the United States and foreign countries and if you want to try to pass this test, you'll have to learn the rules and count days very carefully.

The subjective test, known as the foreign-residence test, is probably easier for most taxpayers to pass but more dangerous if you are trying to simultaneously maintain your permanent resident visa, although it is not impossible to walk this tightrope without falling off. You must establish yourself as a *bona fide* resident of a foreign country or countries for an uninterrupted period that includes an entire taxable year and you must intend to stay there indefinitely. If you do not pass this test, you are considered by the Internal Revenue Service as a transient, or sojourner, instead of a foreign resident, and will not qualify as a foreign resident.

According to the tax law, your residence is a state of mind. It is where you intend to be domiciled indefinitely. To determine your state of mind, the IRS looks at the degree of your attachment to the country in question. A number of factors, none of them decisive or significantly more important than the others, are examined. The bottom line is that you establish yourself as a member of a foreign community and this can get dangerous if you do it for too long, since it then raises questions about your intent to maintain your US resident visa status.

Foreign countries (except for the Philippines) tax on the basis of residence. If you claim exemption from local taxes because you are not resident in that country, the IRS will conclude that you are a US resident and do not qualify for the foreign-earned-income exclusion under the foreign-residence test. Thus some people prefer to qualify under the physical-presence test rather than under the foreign residence test. With the physical-presence test, you might be able to claim that you are not a resident of the foreign country and thereby exempt from their taxes. At the same time, you can claim exemption from US taxes.

Because of the delicacy of maintaining permanent residence for your "green card" at the same time, we would recommend only using the physical presence test.

Once you have qualified for the offshore loophole, you must identify the kind of income that qualifies. Not all income qualifies for the exclusion – only foreign-earned income.

Foreign-earned income is income paid for services you have performed in a foreign country. This includes salaries, professional fees, tips, and similar compensation. Interest, dividends, and capital gains do not qualify.

Self-employed people must adhere to some additional rules. Professionals who do not make material use of capital in performing their services can qualify all of their net income for the loophole. But when both personal services and capital are used to generate income, no more than 30 per cent of net profits will be considered eligible for the exclusion. Note that for self-employed individuals and for partners, the *net income* is the amount that is applied toward the exclusion limit, not the gross income.

Other types of income that do *not* qualify for the loophole include the following: employer-provided meals and lodging on the business premises, pension and annuity payments, income paid to employees of the US government or its agencies, non-qualified deferred compensation, disallowed moving expense reimbursements, and income received two years or more after you earn it. But some of these payments – such as employer-provided meals and lodging on the business premises – are tax-free under regular US tax rules and retain that status. This is one way you can earn *more* than $70,000 tax-free.

The $70,000 limit on the offshore loophole applies to individual taxpayers. So if you are married, you and your spouse potentially can exclude up to $140,000 of foreign-earned income. But you cannot share each other's limit. For example, if one of you earns $80,000 and the other earns $30,000, you exclude only $100,000 on the return ($70,000 plus $30,000).

Too many people inadvertently close the offshore loophole. There are several ways of doing this.

One way is not to realize that the provision has requirements that must be met. Many assume that since they are living overseas, everything they do is free from US tax. That's not so. You've seen some examples of that in this section already and there are other regulations for taxpayers in different situations. Special situations include not being overseas for the full year and receiving advance or deferred payments of income, bonuses, and other special income items. It is well worth your while to discuss the matter with a tax attorney or accountant who understands the offshore loophole. Go over your situation and your plans in detail *before* leaving the United States. That way, you'll be sure to qualify for and make maximum use of this loophole.

Another way people close this loophole is by not filing tax returns. To get the exemption, *you must file a tax return and claim the exemption on Form 2555*. The IRS has had success in recent years contending that anyone who does not file the return loses the loophole, even if he meets all the requirements. Be sure you file the return and properly claim the loophole. The loophole exempts your foreign-earned income from tax but it does not exempt you from the filing requirement.

Instead of excluding income from taxes, you can take a deduction for foreign taxes paid on the income. But the foreign tax credit can get complicated and, in almost all cases, you'll find that it makes more sense to exclude income than it does to take the credit. But if your foreign-earned income exceeds the $70,000 limit, look into taking the credit for taxes paid on the income that exceeds the exclusion amount.

The disappointing part of the $70,000 exclusion is that it applies only to federal income taxes. The Social Security tax might still apply to salaried employees and the self-employment tax might still apply to self-employed individuals. (But see the next section on how you can turn this into a benefit.) The self-employed, for example, still figure their net self-employment income on Schedule C. The net income up to $70,000 still is excluded from gross income. But it also is used on Schedule SE to compute the self-employment tax. For salaried workers with US-based employers, the employer is supposed to withhold Social Security taxes.

The $70,000 offshore loophole is generous but savvy taxpayers know how to make it even more generous. In many situations you can exclude or deduct foreign housing costs.

You have an option here. You can deduct your housing costs to the extent that they exceed a base amount. Or if your employer reimburses you for the excess, the reimbursement can be excluded from income.

To get the write-off or exclusion, you must meet the same tests as for the foreign-earned income exclusion. That means either establishing a foreign residence or meeting the physical-presence test as well as establishing a foreign tax home. The rules for calculating this are very complex, and you will need to get a tax manual for the current year to do it correctly.

THE PUERTO RICO LOOPHOLE

Some US taxpayers find tax benefits by establishing residence in Puerto Rico. Since Puerto Rico is a commonwealth of the United States and has a similar tax system, the United States exempts income earned in Puerto Rico if you establish a *bona fide* residence there. For immigration purposes, Puerto Rico is part of the United States.

Provided that you are resident in Puerto Rico for the entire calendar year, you file a Puerto Rico tax return instead of a US tax return. Puerto Rico taxes all income on a worldwide basis. You should check out the Puerto Rican tax situation before trying to qualify for this provision. You will be subject to Puerto Rican taxes and Puerto Rico is not a tax haven. You might, in fact, find the country a tax liability, as its rates are now generally higher than in the US.

The one particularly interesting exception, however, is that dividends paid from a Puerto Rican company that has a tax holiday (such as the ten-year exemption granted to new factories) is free of Puerto Rican tax. One US couple owned a small manufacturing business in Puerto Rico. In the tenth year, they sold the business, but not the corporation, and paid a liquidating dividend from the corporation. Just before the tenth year, they established residence in Puerto Rico, and maintained it for the entire calendar year in which the liquidating dividend was paid. Total exemption from tax on the final payout!.

Since the dominant language and culture in Puerto Rico are Spanish, if you are immigrating to the US from a Spanish-speaking country, you may find it preferable to make your base in Puerto Rico instead of the mainland and have the tax advantages as well. In this case you could be continuously living on tax-free profits from the business. Salary payments would be subject to the Puerto Rican income tax rates but dividends from the ongoing business would not be.

There are some older tax holiday laws on the books in Puerto Rico that are often overlooked. For example, a ten year exemption from tax for companies engaged in export of a locally made or assembled product. This is often a more useful exemption than some of the manufacturing exemptions which give only a partial exemption in urbanized areas.

Another way to play a different Puerto Rico tax angle is if you are entering the US to operate your own business, and intend to eventually leave the US A foreign corporation with a branch in Puerto Rico is only taxed on Puerto Rico source income. If you create a Panamanian corporation, open a branch for it in Puerto Rico and accumulate the profits in the corporation, you can then take the money out of the corporation once you are no longer a US (or Puerto Rican) taxpayer. In this situation you would be taxed on the salary you pay yourself out of the corporation, which you would keep as low as possible, and then let most of the money stay as profits.

This angle works particularly well for a consulting or other service business or for a mail order or publishing business. Since Puerto Rico is within US domestic mail and telephone systems, it can be used as a base for such enterprises very easily. It also works the other way – the Puerto Rican branch office could be a business engaged in export representation of products to Latin America, since transportation from San Juan, Puerto Rico, to most points in Latin America is very easy with good flight schedules. Some major American corporations have done exactly this – they created Panamanian sales subsidiaries for their Latin American business and operate the subsidiaries out of Puerto Rico, from where the sales representatives can easily call on clients throughout the hemisphere.

For more information on the uses of tax havens, you should consult *The Complete Guide to Tax Havens* by Adam Starchild available at most major bookstores and on-line booksellers.

A PENSION FROM THE US GOVERNMENT (EVEN IF YOU ARE NOT AN AMERICAN)

If you have ever worked in the United States, and held an American social security card, you contributed social security taxes during the years you were there. Perhaps then you returned to your own country and forgot all about the taxes you paid in those early years of your career.

Well, don't forget about it. Dig up the records and find out how much you paid. If you contributed for ten years, you are considered "fully insured" and become eligible for a pension when you reach retirement age. The pension is based on your American earnings and is paid regardless of citizenship or residence.

Didn't work quite long enough? That's why you need to check this early. Perhaps you only contributed for seven years. You can achieve the fully-insured status, and thus a future pension, simply by paying in the minimum tax for another three years. That is only about $200 a year! All you need is a minimal amount of what the American tax law calls "self-employment" income from US sources. Approximately $2200 a year, which perhaps you earn from a consulting fee or selling some of your travel photographs, is all you need to owe the $200 tax for social security. The income tax on this amount will be small or negligible. What you are trying to accomplish is a situation in which you voluntarily file and pay the extra few hundred dollars to achieve fully-insured status.

The rules are complex, and we can't possibly begin to explain them all here, and the exact dollar amounts vary at the whim of Congress. Suffice it to say that the minimum pension is now around $650 a month, so if there is a chance that you are eligible, you want to qualify as soon as possible. Once your ten years' contributions, of at least the minimum rate, are paid and you have the status, you don't have to pay in another cent to get the pension. (Higher amounts of taxable earnings result in a higher pension but not at a rate that is going to gain you anything. The value of this idea is in meeting the minimum requirements to receive the minimum statutory pension.)

Unlike many other countries, the US does not have any provision for voluntary payments into the pension fund – so you must create a situation where you have to pay the social security tax.

Intention is an open-ended question, so if you have worked in the US for seven or eight years, there is nothing to prevent you from filing US tax returns as a resident for another few years, until you discover that you no longer have the intent to maintain your resident visa. Generally there will be little or no additional tax cost to do this, either because of the tax treaties or because the US income tax has an exclusion for earning up to $70,000 per year while living abroad.

Most US embassies have, at least, the basic social security information pamphlets. After you have read them, you can explore the specifics of your situation.

Social security payments are subject to 30 per cent withholding tax to some countries and totally exempt to some because of treaties. This is something to check at the time you start collecting because you may want to be a resident of a country covered by such a treaty – particularly if it is a country that does not tax foreign pension payments, and many do not.

UNDERSTANDING AMERICA

With the earlier brief explanation of the rights and obligations of aliens resident in the US, it should be perfectly clear that in all instances the "liberty and justice for all" which Americans profess in the Pledge of Allegiance to their flag is more than just lip service to an ideal.

Americans devoutly believe that they are born to freedom but, more importantly, they believe just as devoutly that it is the inalienable right of every person to be free from oppression in any form. Americans as a nation value nothing more than individual freedom, the freedom of each man . . . not of some privileged few but of all men. This precept is the guiding passion which, when threatened, from time to time impels Americans to put aside the luxury and safety of their isolated nation-fortress and sally forth to defend it. They fight not to assure a high standard of living but to assure the concept from which the bounty flows.

The American system is not perfect, of course. Far from it. But the important point to recognize is that Americans themselves are aware of the imperfections and are constantly making a conscious effort to rectify the imperfections and inequities.

Plunging into a free-wheeling open society such as America has can be frightening and confusing, especially for people who may have always lived in a rigidly-structured society. But, as it would for Americans anywhere else in the world, the rule is "When in Rome, do as the Romans". The burden always falls on the foreigner to adapt and conform. The adjustment to American behavior and customs can be a disturbing experience for the uninitiated.

Association with persons of other cultural groups can cause problems. A particular action can mean entirely different things in different cultures. Some cultures, such as the Arabs for example, touch a lot during conversation and stand very close to the person being addressed. Americans, on the other hand, rarely touch and prefer several feet of space between themselves and others. They will continually back away from people who get too close.

Newcomers to a different culture are constantly faced with the problem of how to act and speak correctly. What to do about giving and receiving gifts? What are the rules of buying and selling? How should one dress for a business meeting? A social occasion? How does one deal with a person of the opposite sex without causing offense? Does polite use of the language, designed to please the listener, constitute courtesy or will it be construed as a deliberate attempt to lie? What sort of behavior will indicate honor and integrity and which will convey the opposite meaning? There are so many patterns of acceptable behavior to learn that it is small wonder the foreigner feels completely overwhelmed.

Language can be a formidable barrier contributing much to confusion and misunderstanding. It is one thing to learn textbook English but quite another to understand all its subtleties.

In our native language, we learn vocabulary, correct grammar, and the mechanics of writing a language. But only in day-to-day practice do we learn the art of using a language. Such usage is called conversation, and conversation may have little to do with proper grammar.

Conversation involves not just using the correct word to convey a meaning but also using the proper tone of voice and vocal emphasis as well as proper hand gestures and facial expressions. In our native tongue all these conversational parts are known from childhood. But when we begin to speak in a different language, each part must be learned before we can either be understood or speak easily. Thus the trick to learning a foreign language is not just how many words one memorizes but learning how the natives use those words.

Unfortunately, of necessity, foreigners must learn to speak American English if they are going to live in the United States for an extended period of time because so few Americans can speak a second language.

American English is one of the most flexible languages on earth. It is especially easy for a foreigner to misunderstand an ordinary statement if he is not versed in the slang words and jargon for which Americans have a special fondness. The fact is slang and jargon are so much a part of American speech that most Americans are not aware they are using it.

Slang and jargon will be the hardest part of American English to understand because it is constantly changing. For example, Americans may call children: munchkins, house-apes, dwarfs, rug-rats or ankle-biters. A person who is mentally ill may be said to be: bananas, off his rocker, psycho, flipped out, a weirdo or a flake. The emotion of fear or extreme nervousness may be referred to as: feeling antsy, becoming unwound or apart at the seams or unglued, a bad case of butterflies in the stomach, or the jitters. And so on.

And in American English one parks the car in a driveway but drives on a parkway.

A valuable aid to learning conversational American English is the television. Watching and imitating what you hear is a good way to learn how Americans use their language.

Only time, patience and, most of all, practice will bring fluency in American English. NEVER be afraid or embarrassed to say, "I do not understand. What do you mean?"

Another common problem in switching from one language to another is the way people address each other. Many foreigners have great difficulty accepting the American disregard for using formal titles. Formal titles in other parts of the world are used to define class distinctions or business or professional rank. Americans, on the other hand, have little or no regard for class distinctions of any kind. They don't like using a formal title, even Mister or Mrs., preferring instead to be addressed by their first name or even a nickname. While this may seem offensive to foreigners, it is simply that Americans do not like any hint of social differences or class distinctions and the immediate movement to a first-name basis is one way they employ to break down the barriers.

If Americans define class at all, it is in terms of personal achievement. Americans tend to judge people on the basis of what they do rather than who they are, so occupational titles may be regarded as more important in some instances; although, about the only people in the United States who use and are addressed by their titles are top government officials, judges, military officers, medical doctors, clergy, and ranking university professors.

In most other countries class roles are very strictly defined. Strict rules of etiquette and protocol are a way of defining and protecting social position, business rank, and sometimes even age. The rules governing behavior at each level are rigidly followed by all members of the society. Formality is the rule.

There are, of course, social, economic and business class levels in America but the lines between one level and another are blurred and extremely fluid. In a manner that is often offensive to foreigners, Americans exhibit an airy lack of respect or concern for the social conventions that are so important elsewhere in the world. The American attitude toward the rituals of etiquette and protocol is definitely informal.

Americans are notorious for their casualness. They have origins in every part of the world but old world customs are generally practised only at home for the observance of some particular social or religious ceremony within the family or within a neighborhood where the families have a common ethnic background.

For example, in social situations American women never shake hands but in the last decade they have generally done so in business situations. Neither do Americans circulate around at social gatherings shaking hands when they prepare to leave. A thank you to the host and hostess and perhaps a general good-bye from the door to the other guests is the usual procedure. Americans don't take flowers when making social calls (although persons who are invited to small dinner parties do frequently take a bottle of wine).

Likewise, there is little regard among Americans for the amenities of protocol. Americans do not bow to each other, the guest of honor or highest-ranked person seldom occupies a special seat in a room, nor does the ranking person always go through a door first. American men do not always rise when new arrivals enter a room, especially if those new arrivals are known acquaintances. Young people, in particular, exhibit very few formal manners in the presence of elders.

Other "badges" of rank, wealth and privilege are not often acknowledged in the United States simply because in America even the poorest can own the same luxuries the wealthy and privileged enjoy.

Few people have personal servants. Even the most important people usually drive their own cars and take care of themselves at home. America is truly a do-it-yourself country and most Americans are extremely uncomfortable being waited upon by personal servants. In addition, the cost of personal service is very expensive and most Americans prefer to spend their dollars on travel, luxuries and hobbies.

In America, all people can own cars, color televisions, refrigerators, freezers, washing machines, dryers, boats, cars, furs and jewelry, and enjoy other luxuries that elsewhere in the world might be the exclusive perquisites of the elite classes. The wealthy in America can afford more luxuries and more expensive luxuries of course but anyone can acquire anything if he chooses to do so. The "magic" that makes this overall affluence possible is called credit.

The United States economic system is based on mass distribution of goods and services. The lowest-paid workers, even people on welfare, can and do own cars, appliances, houses and property; goods that represent great wealth in many other parts of the world. Credit makes it all possible.

In America, anything can be bought on credit. Many department stores, oil companies, banks, airlines and other businesses issue cards called credit or charge cards. These are plastic cards slightly larger than a business card, with the owner's name and special identifying number stamped on them. With a charge card, a person can go into any establishment which accepts the card, select any product or service he desires, sign a purchase ticket, and leave with the goods or having used the service without paying out one cent in cash. All charges (purchases) are totaled at the end of each month and a single bill is sent to the card holder. Generally, the card holder is not required to pay the bill in full on receipt but is allowed to pay a percentage of the total each month. This arrangement is called revolving credit.

Very expensive items such as cars and boats, houses and property, similarly can be paid for in monthly payments over a long period of time . . . usually three or more years on luxury items and 20 to 30 years on houses and property. In this instance, a cash down-payment (usually 5-10 per cent of the total price, plus any tax and other selling charges which may be due by law at the time of a sale) is required before possession can be taken by the buyer. This type of credit is called instalment buying.

Obviously, such a system allows people to have a great deal more than they could if each item had to be paid for in full at the time of purchase. Credit buying gives every person great purchasing power. The practice of buy-now--pay-for-it-later has allowed Americans to enjoy the highest standard of living in the world.

As in social situations, there is the same lack of regard for the amenities of status in American work situations. Misunderstanding and conflict may occur because foreign employees are accustomed to completely different work habits and attitudes.

American executives enjoy great flexibility in their work schedules. They may arrive late by foreign standards; that is around 10.00 a.m . . . usually exhibiting a great deal of lethargy and a seeming unwillingness to "get to work" . . . and then, at noon leaving for a lunch that may last well into the afternoon. But these same executives often work late into the night and on weekends. In addition, a great deal of business may have been conducted during that long lunch break. In spite of their slowness in getting started in the morning and their tendency to take long breaks, most American executives work many more hours without extra pay than do their eight-to-five subordinates.

Lower echelon workers usually maintain fixed schedules. They take regular controlled break periods and leave promptly at quitting time. Most work only five days a week. Their jobs may he rigidly defined, controlled and protected by union demands, contracts and any extra work = extra pay. But the price for all the protection and job security is usually very little opportunity to learn new skills or to advance to positions of greater authority and responsibility.

Many foreigners are uncomfortable with the casual friendliness between subordinates and superiors. Almost always everyone is on a first-name basis. For foreign workers who have always had a clear sense of their "place" in an organization, the lack of formality and protocol can be very upsetting. Americans prefer to keep the outward signs of authority and power to a minimum, barely visible. Public acknowledgement of status is felt to be pretentious and, therefore, undesirable. But in spite of the deliberately cultivated relaxed atmosphere, where men usually work in their shirt-sleeves and may put their feet on their desks, where radios may be playing, and where people may wander in and out of offices and indulge in idle chatter, the people in the organization know very well who is superior to whom and who THE BOSS is.

Foreigners from some parts of the world may also be surprised to learn how differently business is conducted in the United States. Using family connections, or buying or selling influence is regarded by Americans as immoral and not to be condoned, as well as being illegal. This is not to say that corruption does not exist in American businesses. Of course there are always people who will try to acquire more money and power any way they can. The difference is that in America corruption is not tolerated and so is the exception rather than the rule.

In many countries family and business are closely tied. Nepotism is a way of life. For example, a government official's wife may own a business that gets special favors such as tax breaks or lower duty fees or no duty fees. Or many of his relatives may control other businesses that get government concessions or contracts. Or many members of a family may draw salaries from a business whether they actually work in the business or not.

Similarly, in many countries corruption in the form of patronage, bribery and kickbacks is rampant. People must pay clerks a "fee" to secure permits or to expedite paper work. The clerk "donates" to his superior to ensure he does not get fired and so on up to the very top officials. Customs men are bribed to overlook goods being brought into the country. Businessmen bidding on contracts make "gifts" to the officials responsible for awarding the contracts. Payrolls are padded with non-existent people and the boss pockets the pay. Judges are bribed to hand down favorable decisions in court cases. Policemen are bribed to look the other way when crimes are being committed. And so on.

In America such corrupt practices will cause serious repercussions for the person caught attempting to employ them. In the case of foreigners, this usually means irrevocable deportation in addition to a jail sentence.

Workers in America have legal protection against unfair harassment on the job or unjust firing. Of course, any worker can be fired for due cause but if he does his job well and conscientiously and makes a genuine effort to get along with his fellow workers, his job will be secure. American employers know it is easier and less costly to retain good workers than to be constantly hiring and training new ones.

Americans seem to be constantly rushing headlong to nowhere. They seem to have no time for the small amenities of life, no time for leisurely meals, no time for friendly conversation on the street, no time to wait in line for goods and services. Americans seem always to be late, late, late . . . rushing pell-mell from home to job to somewhere else. They even seem to rush through their leisure activities. Hurry, hurry, hurry. Their manner may appear to be abrupt and rude.

One of the basic causes of this trait is the sheer complexity of American life. There are so many things to do! The variety is literally endless and there just aren't enough hours in the day to accomplish everything. But, undaunted, Americans keep trying to compress more and more activity into each day. Thus, there is in Americans an underlying unspoken urgency to finish whatever they are currently doing and to get on to the next thing. Their pace is intense and totally absorbed.

America is a highly mobile society always on the move . . . changing jobs, changing homes, changing friends. Americans think nothing of driving 75 to 100 miles to dine in a favorite restaurant or for an evening's entertainment. Young people often deliberately choose colleges as far from home as their parents can afford to send them for the sheer difference between the locale of college and home. Such mobility is possible in part because there are no government restrictions to moving or traveling within the United States. Such things as travel permits and identification papers are unheard of. Americans constantly flow from one place to another, from one job to another, from one home to another, and from one social level to another.

America is not only a do-it-yourself country, it is also a do-your-own-thing country. Strict uniformity and conformity are regarded as undesirable; individualism is encouraged. This freedom to achieve self-expression takes many forms, such as the way people dress, the way they criticize authority, and the lack of social restrictions, to name a few.

America has been called a rootless society and there is much truth in that label. Most Americans do not put down roots, nor is there an ancestral home *per se* for most American families. Many families move from one house to another every few years. Every child in a family may have been born in a different city. Different generations of a family seldom live in the same house.

There is no standard uniformity of dress. People wear the clothing that best expresses the way each individual feels about himself. It is not uncommon to see guests invited to a formal party appearing in anything from blue jeans to tuxedos and evening gowns. In all situations, women wearing pants (trousers) are completely acceptable.

Women in America enjoy a great deal more freedom than women in many other countries. American women may go anywhere unescorted, drive cars, and hold jobs that in some other countries might be reserved exclusively for men. They choose the men they wish to associate with and are accustomed to dealing with unknown men in both business and social situations. This independence may be confusing to foreign man who may be accustomed to strictly chaperoned "good" women, as opposed to uncontrolled "bad" women. But just because they are independent and have full control of their lives does not mean American women are immoral. American women may choose to indulge in premarital sex without social stigma because, as with everything else in America, morality is a matter of personal rather than community standards.

One of the Americans' favorite pastimes is criticizing authority. No person or institution is safe; no one is too rich or too important or too highly placed to be immune to criticism; no idea or dogma is too sacred to be questioned,

America is constantly undergoing a renewing and revitalizing process. The country was founded on the principles of dissent and self-determination. From early childhood, Americans are taught to explore new ideas, to analyze, to question and to argue . . . to learn to think for themselves. Social, political and religious ideas are continually subject to examination and change.

Peaceful demonstrations for or against a person, an institution or an idea is an accepted way of life in America. Even foreigners in America can, within the same legal limits as a citizen, freely criticize the United States Government as well as their own governments.

Americans love to argue. They argue about sports, religion, politics, educational systems, television programs, social issues . . . anything and everything! Foreigners may be surprised at these frequently-heated exchanges but should bear in mind that Americans are taught not to accept anything at face value. They tend to examine an idea in detail, "pick it apart", bluntly ask for proof, then challenge the proof and advance ideas and opinions of their own. The right to criticize and disagree is every American's birthright and they constantly take full advantage of the privilege.

The American ideals of personal initiative, personal freedom and free enterprise seem to many foreigners to be completely out of control; they wonder that anarchy is not rampant in the land. But the constant ferment and change is the way America grows. The system works for Americans because that is the way they want it and they work very hard to protect the system. Americans may disagree violently with each other but they quickly close ranks against any who would deprive them of their precious freedoms. Open and free competition and exchange of ideas and the constant movement of the people keep the nation free, strong and healthy.

America is a country which will demand that newcomers examine their old beliefs and old ways of behavior closely and, perhaps, modify or change them altogether. That some change will definitely occur can be assured. Exposed to the endless variety of American life, the newcomer will become a different person. Becoming a part of the American milieu can be an exciting and stimulating experience for those who are willing to make the effort. America has something to offer everyone. It is there for the taking by the determined and industrious. Making the adjustment will not be so difficult if the newcomer is willing to be open and sensitive to new people and new ideas.

It is normal for strangers in a foreign place to feel lonely and estranged. The lack of support of family and friends, familiar surroundings and a common language can be the source of great stress and unhappiness.

One of the best ways to overcome such feelings is to seek out the help and support of new friends who will share the same background, language, or interests. Many such sources are available to the new arrival in the United States.

There are many international social or professional groups which have world-wide branches, such as the YMCA or YWCA, Lions Club, Rotary International, or university alumni groups, sports clubs or professional organizations. Joining such a group or organization before immigrating will give one a ready contact with persons of similar interests in the United States.

Another good source of friendly welcome is the church. In smaller communities in particular, the church is often the center of a great deal of social activity. A place of worship can truly be a tie to one of the strongest sources of support for the new immigrant. Churches of all the world's major religions can usually be found in most of the large cities in the United States.

People generally feel more comfortable and happier with neighbors who have the same ethnic or religious background. Large American cities often have enclaves of people who share a common ethnic heritage. It is a simple matter to locate neighborhoods almost exclusively populated by various European, Oriental, Hispanic or African families. Those who have immigrated earlier can offer invaluable help and support to the new immigrant.

But if all else fails, or the newcomer finds himself in a place where there are no other immigrants to turn to for assistance, one simple rule can help assure a successful transition into American life: NEVER be afraid to ask. Ask questions about things you do not understand, ask for advice. ask for help. Ask, ask, ask again and again and again.

Most Americans are open and friendly. They are flattered when people express an interest in the way they live and the work they do. More importantly, Americans do not consider questions rude. On the contrary, most Americans enjoy the idea of helping a foreigner "get settled in" to the American scene. But you must make them aware that you need help by asking for it.

To make the decision to leave one's native land, where all is known and where the circumstances of one's life, even if terrible, are at least predictable, is a monumental act of courage. The first step is the hardest and the entire process can be very difficult. But the rewards can be many.

America is still the land of opportunity. The golden door is still open to the ambitious as well as the oppressed. Give America your best and she will give you hers.

APPENDIX

THIS FORM IS SUPPLIED GRATIS

NONIMMIGRANT VISA INFORMATION

WHO MAY TRAVEL WITHOUT A VISA

Travelers who meet ALL of the following requirements NO LONGER NEED A VISA FOR TRAVEL TO THE UNITED STATES:

- The traveler is a CITIZEN of one of he following countries: the United Kingdom, Japan, France, Switzerland, Germany, Italy, Sweden, Netherlands, Spain, Austria, New Zealand, Finland, Belgium, Denmark, Norway, Iceland, Luxembourg, San Marino, Andorra, Monaco and Leichtenstein;

- The traveler holds an unexpired passport (for UK nationals the passport must indicate that the bearer is a British "citizen"; a passport indicating that the bearer is only a British Subject, British Dependent Territories Citizen, British Overseas Citizen, or British National (Overseas) Citizen does not qualify for travel without a visa);

- The trip is for a holiday or business visit or in transit;

- The trip is for 90 days or less;

- If entering by air or sea, the traveler must have a return or onward ticket and must enter aboard an air or sea carrier that is participating in the Visa Waiver Program; if entering overland from Canada or Mexico no onward ticket is required.

- Travelers entering initially under the Visa Waiver Program may make side trips to countries adjacent to the U.S. (including the Caribbean Islands) and reenter the U.S. by any means of transport provided that the total trip is no longer than 90 days.

TRAVELERS WHO MEET THE ABOVE CRITERIA ARE ENCOURAGED TO TRAVEL WITHOUT A VISA AS PROCESSING TIME FOR VISA APPLICATIONS IS AT LEAST THREE WEEKS AND, DURING PEAK TRAVEL PERIODS, POSSIBLY CONSIDERABLY LONGER.

WHO STILL NEEDS A VISA

If ANY of the following circumstances apply, the traveler MUST APPLY FOR A VISA:

- The traveler is a citizen of a country other than those listed above;

- The trip is for any purpose other than holiday, business or transit (e.g. government officials traveling on official business, students undertaking a course of study in the U.S., temporary workers, immigrants, journalists on assignment, exchange visitors, treaty traders and investors, intra-company transferees, fiance(e)s of U.S. citizens, and crew members require visas);

- The trip is for more than 90 days;

- If the traveler has been refused a visa or previously denied admission to the U.S. or required to leave by the U.S. Immigration and Naturalization Service, he or she should contact the Embassy prior to attempting to travel without a visa;

    IMPORTANT: Under United States law, some people are ineligible to enter the U.S. unless they first obtain a waiver of ineligibility. If any of the conditions noted in Item 34 of the application form applies to you, you should submit a visa application BEFORE you make final travel plans. The U.S. government cannot accept responsibility for any charges you incur if we are unable to issue you a visa or if you are not admitted to the U.S.

VISA VALIDITY

A United States visa is only valid for the purpose for which it is issued. For example, a student visa cannot be used for entry as a temporary worker.

The validity period shown on a nonimmigrant visa refers only to the period during which it may be used to make application to enter the United States. It does not indicate the length of time the traveler may remain in the U.S.

ADMISSION

A VISA IS NOT A GUARANTEE OF ENTRY INTO THE UNITED STATES. When a traveler reaches the United States, an Immigration and Naturalization Service Officer determines whether or not the traveler qualifies under the law to enter the U.S. This applies whether or not the traveler has a visa. Therefore, travelers should carry with them evidence of the purpose of the trip, evidence of funds to support themselves during the stay in the U.S., and evidence of plans to depart the U.S. after a reasonable stay.

WORKING IN THE UNITED STATES

Only holders of special work visas may work in the United States. Holders of other types of visas may not accept employment, even informal work in a household as a "nanny," "au-pair," or "Mother's Helper."

HOW TO APPLY FOR A VISA

THOSE WHO ARE ELIGIBLE TO TRAVEL WITHOUT A VISA ARE STRONGLY ENCOURAGED TO DO SO, AS PROCESSING TIMES FOR VISA APPLICATIONS WILL BE AT LEAST THREE WEEKS AND, DURING PEAK TRAVEL PERIODS, MAY BE CONSIDERABLY LONGER. IF YOUR TRIP REQUIRES A VISA, PLEASE SUBMIT THE FOLLOWING:

1) A completed application form (attached) for each person travelling, even babies. Complete both sides of the attached application form, printing clearly. Sign the application.

2) A valid PASSPORT.

3) Photograph. Staple a small photograph to the back of the application.

4) Submit evidence substantiating the purpose of your trip and your intention to depart from the United States after a temporary visit. Examples of such evidence are: in cases of business trips, a letter from your employer; in cases of pleasure trips, documents outlining your plans while in the United States and explaining the reasons why you would depart the United States after a short stay, such as family ties, employment, or similar binding obligations in your home country; for students, a completed form I-20A/B; for exchange visitors, a form IAP-66, and for temporary workers and intra-company transferee, evidence of an approved petition.

If you are a British Citizen, a citizen of an E.C. country, or have indefinite leave to remain in the U.K., you may post your completed application form along with your PASSPORT (British Visitors Passports are not acceptable), any supporting documents and a STAMPED, SELF-ADDRESSED ENVELOPE TO:

VISA BRANCH, UNITED STATES EMBASSY
5 UPPER GROSVENOR STREET, LONDON W1A 2JB

Residents of Northern Ireland should apply to:

UNITED STATES CONSULATE GENERAL
QUEEN'S HOUSE, QUEEN STREET, BELFAST BT1 6EQ

Allow AT LEAST THREE WEEKS for return of your passport. Your passport will be returned to you in the stamped, addressed envelope you provide. If you fail to provide a stamped addressed envelope, your visa application will be subject to considerable delay.

APPLICANTS WHO ARE NEITHER BRITISH CITIZENS, CITIZENS OF AN EC COUNTRY, NOR HAVE INDEFINITE LEAVE TO REMAIN IN THE UK MUST APPLY IN PERSON.

Those applying in person in London should schedule an appointment in advance by phoning 0891-200-290.
Calls cost 36p/min cheap rate, 48p/min other times.

Applicants who qualify for visa-free travel, but who wish to apply for a visa anyhow, may only apply through the post; they may not apply in person.

Those holding an *UNEXPIRED VISA*, such as a multiple indefinite B-1/B-2 visa, in an *EXPIRED PASSPORT* may still use that visa provided that they also carry an unexpired passport of the same nationality as the expired passport.

VISA INFORMATION

THE EMBASSY'S VISA INFORMATION LINE, PROVIDING A VARIETY OF TAPE RECORDED MESSAGES ON BOTH NONIMMIGRNAT AND IMMIGRANT VISAS IS: 0891-200-290. Calls cost 36p/min cheap rate, 48p/min other times. Additional information can also be obtained by writing to the above addresses.

FEES FOR VISAS

There is no charge for most visas for British citizens. If your type of visa requires a fee, you will be notified of the amount and of how to pay it.

HOLIDAY NOTICE

U.S. consular offices are closed on British and American Holidays. If a holiday falls on a Saturday, the consular office will close on the preceding Friday. If a holiday falls on a Sunday, the office will close on the following Monday. We suggest you do not apply the day after an American holiday, as it is always busier than usual. The following are American holidays:

January 1	-New Years Day	First Monday of September	-Labor Day
Third Monday of January	-Martin Luther King Day	Second Monday of October	-Columbus Day
Third Monday of February	-Presidents' Day	November 11	-Veterans Day
Last Monday of May	-Memorial Day	Fourth Thursday of November	-Thanksgiving Day
July 4	-Independence Day	December 25	-Christmas Day

MEDICAL CARE IN THE UNITED STATES

Medical care in the United States is expensive and must be paid for, even in the cases of emergency. Serious injury or major illness requiring specialized treatment and/or prolonged hospitalization will incur substantial costs. Since provision for meeting such costs is the responsibility of the individual, you may wish to consider obtaining health insurance sufficient to cover such eventualities occurring during your visit. Your travel agent or insurance broker will be able to advise you.

THIS FORM IS SUPPLIED GRATIS

PLEASE TYPE OR PRINT YOUR ANSWERS IN THE SPACE PROVIDED BELOW EACH ITEM

1. SURNAMES OR FAMILY NAMES (Exactly as in Passport)

2. FIRST NAME AND MIDDLE NAME (Exactly as in Passport)

DO NOT WRITE IN THIS SPACE

3. OTHER NAMES (Maiden, Religious, Professional, Aliases)

4. DATE OF BIRTH (Day, Month, Year) | 8. PASSPORT NUMBER

5. PLACE OF BIRTH
City, Province   Country | DATE PASSPORT ISSUED (Day, Month, Year)

6. NATIONALITY | 7. SEX ☐ Male ☐ Female | DATE PASSPORT EXPIRES (Day, Month, Year)

9. HOME ADDRESS (include apartment no., street, city, province and postal zone)

10. NAME AND STREET ADDRESS OF PRESENT EMPLOYER OR SCHOOL (Postal Box number unacceptable)

11. HOME TELEPHONE NO. | 12. BUSINESS TELEPHONE NO.

13. COLOR OF HAIR | 14. COLOR OF EYES | 15. COMPLEXION

16. HEIGHT | 17. MARKS OF IDENTIFICATION

24. PRESENT OCCUPATION (If retired state past occupation)

18. MARITAL STATUS
☐ Married ☐ Single ☐ Widowed ☐ Divorced ☐ Separated
If married, give name and nationality of spouse

25. WHO WILL FURNISH FINANCIAL SUPPORT, INCLUDING TICKETS ?

19. NAMES AND RELATIONSHIPS OF PERSONS TRAVELING WITH YOU
(NOTE: A separate application must be made for each visa traveler, regardless of age.)

26. AT WHAT ADDRESS WILL YOU STAY IN THE USA ?

20. HAVE YOU EVER APPLIED FOR A U.S. VISA BEFORE, WHETHER IMMIGRANT OR NON-IMMIGRANT?
☐ No ☐ Yes Where ? _____
When ? _____ Type of Visa ? _____
☐ Visa was issued   ☐ Visa was refused

27. WHAT IS THE PURPOSE OF YOUR TRIP ?

28. WHEN DO YOU INTEND TO ARRIVE IN THE USA ?

21. HAS YOUR U.S. VISA EVER BEEN CANCELED?
☐ No ☐ Yes Where ? _____
When ? _____ By Whom ? _____

29. HOW LONG DO YOU PLAN TO STAY IN THE USA ?

22. Bearers of visitors visas may generally not work or study in the U.S.
DO YOU INTEND TO WORK IN THE U.S.? ☐ No ☐ Yes
If YES, explain

30. HAVE YOU EVER BEEN IN THE USA ?
☐ No ☐ Yes When? _____
For How long ? _____

23. DO YOU INTEND TO STUDY IN THE U.S. ? ☐ No ☐ Yes
If YES, write name and address of school as it appears on form I-20.

NONIMMIGRANT VISA APPLICATION

COMPLETE ALL QUESTIONS ON REVERSE OF FORM

OPTIONAL FORM 156 (Rev 4-81) PAGE 1 50156-106
Department of State

NSN 7540-00-139-0053

31 (a) HAVE YOU OR ANYONE ACTING FOR YOU EVER INDICATED TO A U S CONSULAR OR IMMIGRATION EMPLOYEE A DESIRE TO IMMIGRATE TO THE U S ? (b) HAS ANYONE EVER FILED AN IMMIGRANT VISA PETITION ON YOUR BEHALF? (C) HAS LABOR CERTIFICATION FOR EMPLOYMENT IN THE U.S EVER BEEN REQUESTED BY YOU OR ON YOUR BEHALF?

(a) ☐No ☐Yes   (b) ☐No ☐Yes   (c) ☐No ☐Yes

32 ARE ANY OF THE FOLLOWING IN THE U.S.? (If YES, circle appropriate relationship and indicate that person's status in the U.S , ie studying, working, U S permanent resident, U S citizen, etc)

HUSBAND/WIFE _____   FIANCE/FIANCEE _____   BROTHER/SISTER _____

FATHER/MOTHER _____   SON/DAUGHTER _____

33. PLEASE LIST THE COUNTRIES WHERE YOU HAVE LIVED FOR MORE THAN 6 MONTHS DURING THE PAST 5 YEARS BEGIN WITH YOUR PRESENT RESIDENCE

Countries   Cities   Approximate Dates

34 IMPORTANT ALL APPLICANTS MUST READ AND CHECK THE APPROPRIATE BOX FOR EACH ITEM:

A visa may not be issued to persons who are within specific categories defined by law as inadmissable to the United States (except when a waiver is obtained in advance). Are any of the following applicable to you?

- Have you ever been afflicted with a communicable disease of public health significance, a dangerous physical or mental disorder, or been a drug abuser or addict? .... ☐Yes ☐No

- Have you ever been arrested or convicted for any offense or crime, even through subject of a pardon, amnesty, or other such legal action? .... ☐Yes ☐No

- Have you ever been a controlled substance (drug) trafficker, or a prostitute or procurer? .... ☐Yes ☐No

- Have you ever sought to obtain, or assist others to obtain a visa, entry into the U.S., or any U.S immigration benefit by fraud or willful misrepresentation? .... ☐Yes ☐No

- Were you deported from the U.S.A. within the last 5 years? .... ☐Yes ☐No

- Do you seek to enter the United States to engage in export control violations, subversive or terrorist activities or any unlawful purpose? .... ☐Yes ☐No

- Have you ever ordered, incited, assisted, or otherwise participated in the persecution of any person because of race, religion, national origin, or political opinion under the control, direct or indirect, of the Nazi Government of Germany, or of the government of any area occupied by, or allied with, the Nazi Government of Germany, or have you ever participated in genocide? .... ☐Yes ☐No

A YES answer does not automatically signify ineligibility for a visa, but if you answered YES to any of the above, or if you have any question in this regard, personal appearance at this office is recommended. If appearance is not possible at this time, attach a statement of facts in your case to this application.

35. I certify that I have read and understood all the questions set forth in this application and the answers I have furnished on this form are true and correct to the best of my knowledge and belief. I understand that any false or misleading statement may result in the permanent refusal of a visa or denial of entry into the United States. I understand that possession of a visa does not entitle the bearer to enter the United States of America upon arrival at port of entry if he or she is found inadmissable.

DATE OF APPLICATION _____

APPLICANT'S SIGNATURE _____

If this application has been prepared by a travel agency or another person on your behalf, the agent should indicate name and address of agency or person with appropriate signature of individual preparing form.

SIGNATURE OF PERSON PREPARING FORM _____
(If other than the applicant)

DO NOT WRITE IN THIS SPACE

37mm x 37mm
PHOTO
Glue or Staple photo here

Optional Form 156 (Rev. 4-91) PAGE 2
Department of State

U. S. Department of Justice
Immigration and Naturalization Service

Application for Employment Authorization

How to File:
A separate application must be filed by each applicant. Applications must be typewritten or clearly printed in ink and completed in full. If extra space is needed to answer any item, attach a continuation sheet and indicate your name, A-number (if any) and the item number.

Note: It is recommended that you retain a complete copy of your application for your records

Who should file this application?
Certain aliens temporarily in the United States are eligible for employment authorization. Please refer to the ELIGIBILITY SECTION of this application which is found on page three. Carefully review the classes of aliens described in Group A and Group C to determine if you are eligible to apply.

This application should not be filed by lawful permanent resident aliens or by lawful temporary resident aliens.

What is the fee?
Applicants must pay a fee of $35.00 to file this form <u>unless</u> otherwise noted on the reverse of the form. Please refer to page 3. If required, the fee will not be refunded. Pay by cash, check, or money order in the exact amount. All checks and money orders must be payable in U.S. currency in the United States. Make check or money order payable to "Immigration and Naturalization Service." However, if you live in Guam make it payable to "Treasurer, Guam," or if you live in the U.S. Virgin Islands make it payable to "Commissioner of Finance of the Virgin Islands." If the check is not honored the INS will charge you $5.00.

Where should you file this application?
Applications must be filed with the nearest Immigration and Naturalization Service (INS) office that processes employment authorization applications which has jurisdiction over your place of residence. You must appear in person to receive an employment authorization document. **Please bring your INS Form I-94 and any document issued to you by the INS granting you previous employment authorization.**

What is our authority for collecting this information?
The authority to require you to file Form I-765, Application for Employment Authorization, is contained in the "Immigration Reform and Control Act of 1986." This information is necessary to determine whether you are eligible for employment authorization and for the preparation of your Employment Authorization Document if you are found eligible. Failure to provide all information as requested may result in the denial or rejection of this application

The information you provide may also be disclosed to other federal, state, local and foreign law enforcement and regulatory agencies during the course of the investigation required by this Service

Basic Criteria to Establish Economic Necessity:
Title 45 - Public Welfare, Poverty Guidelines, 45 CFR 1060.2 may be used as the basic criteria to establish eligibility for employment authorization when the applicant's economic necessity is identified as a factor. If you are an applicant who must show economic necessity, you should include a statement listing all of your assets, income, and expenses as evidence of your economic need to work

Note: Not all applicants are required to establish economic necessity. Carefully review the ELIGIBILITY SECTION of the application. Only aliens who are filing for employment authorization under Group C, items (c)(3) (i), (c)(13), (c)(14) and (c)(18) are required to furnish information on economic need. This information must be furnished on attached sheet(s) and submitted with this application.

What are the penalties for submitting false information?
Title 18, United States Code, Section 1001 states that whoever willfully and knowingly falsifies a material fact, makes a false statement, or makes use of a false document will be fined up to $10,000 or imprisoned up to five years, or both

Title 18, United States Code, Section 1546(a) states that whoever makes any false statement with respect to a material fact in any document required by the immigration laws or regulations, or presents an application containing any false statement shall be fined or imprisoned or both

Please Complete Both Sides of Form.

Reporting Burden: Public reporting burden for this collection of information is estimated to average sixty (60) minutes per response, including the time for reviewing instructions, searching existing data sources, gathering and maintaining the data needed, and completing and reviewing the collection of information. Send comments regarding this burden estimate or any other aspect of this collection of information, including suggestions for reducing this burden, to U S Department of Justice, Immigration and Naturalization Service, Room 2011, Washington, D C 20536, and to the Office of Management and Budget, Paperwork Reduction Project. OMB No 1115-0163, Washington, D C 20503

Form I-765 (Rev. 12/7/90)N Page 1

U. S. Department of Justice
Immigration and Naturalization Service

OMB # 1115-0163
Application for Employment Authorization

Do Not Write in This Block — **Please Complete Both Sides of Form**

Remarks	Action Stamp	Fee Stamp
A#		
Applicant is filing under 274a 12 _____		

☐ Application Approved. Employment Authorized / Extended (Circle One) _____ (Date).
   until _____ (Date).
   Subject to the following conditions: _____
☐ Application Denied.
   ☐ Failed to establish eligibility under 8 CFR 274a.12 (a) or (c).
   ☐ Failed to establish economic necessity as required in 8 CFR 274a 12(c) (13) (14) (18) and 8 CFR 214.2(f)

I am applying for:
☐ Permission to accept employment
☐ Replacement (of lost employment authorization document)
☐ Extension of my permission to accept employment (attach previous employment authorization document)

1. Name (Family Name in CAPS)   (First)   (Middle)
2. Other Names Used (Include Maiden Name)
3. Address in the United States (Number and Street)   (Apt Number)
   (Town or City)   (State/Country)   (ZIP Code)
4. Country of Citizenship/Nationality
5. Place of Birth (Town or City) (State/Province)   (Country)
6. Date of Birth (Month/Day/Year)   7 Sex   ☐ Male ☐ Female
8. Marital Status   ☐ Married   ☐ Single
                    ☐ Widowed   ☐ Divorced
9. Social Security Number (Include all Numbers you have ever used)
10. Alien Registration Number (A-Number) or I-94 Number (if any)

11. Have you ever before applied for employment authorization from INS?
    ☐ Yes (If yes, complete below)   ☐ No
    Which INS Office?   Date(s)
    Results (Granted or Denied - attach all documentation)
12. Date of Last Entry into the U S (Month/Day/Year)
13. Place of Last Entry into the U S
14. Manner of Last Entry (Visitor, Student, etc)
15. Current Immigration Status (Visitor, Student, etc)
16. Go to the Eligibility Section on the reverse of this form and check the box which applies to you In the space below, place the letter and number of the box you selected from the reverse side
    Eligibility under 8 CFR 274a 12
    (   ) (   ) (   )

Complete the reverse of this form before signature.

Your Certification: I certify, under penalty of perjury under the laws of the United States of America, that the foregoing is true and correct. Furthermore, I authorize the release of any information which the Immigration and Naturalization Service needs to determine eligibility for the benefit I am seeking. I have read the reverse of this form and have checked the appropriate block, which is identified in item #16, above.

Signature   Telephone Number   Date

Signature of Person Preparing Form if Other Than Above: I declare that this document was prepared by me at the request of the applicant and is based on all information of which I have any knowledge

Print Name   Address   Signature   Date

Initial Receipt	Resubmitted	Relocated		Completed		
		Rec'd	Sent	Approved	Denied	Returned

Form I-765 (Rev. 12/7/90) N Page 2

Eligibility

GROUP A

The current immigration laws and regulations permit certain classes of aliens to work in the United States. If you are an alien described below, you do not need to request that employment authorization be granted to you, but you do need to request a document to show that you are able to work in the United States. For aliens in classes (a) (3) through (a) (11), **NO FEE** will be required for the original card or for extension cards. A **FEE** will be required if a replacement employment authorization document is needed. A **FEE IS REQUIRED** for aliens in item (a) (12) who are over the age of 14 years and under the age of 65 years.

Place an X in the box next to the number which applies to you

- ☐ (a) (3) - I have been admitted to the United States as a refugee
- ☐ (a) (4) - I have been paroled into the United States as a refugee
- ☐ (a) (5) - My application for asylum has been granted.
- ☐ (a) (6) - I am the fiance(e) of a United States citizen and I have K-1 nonimmigrant status, OR I am the dependent of a fiance(e) of a United States citizen and I have K-2 nonimmigrant status
- ☐ (a) (7) - I have N-8 or N-9 nonimmigrant status in the United States
- ☐ (a) (8) - I am a citizen of the Federated States of Micronesia or of the Marshall Islands
- ☐ (a) (10) - I have been granted withholding of deportation
- ☐ (a) (11) - I have been granted extended voluntary departure by the Attorney General
- ☐ (a) (12) - I am an alien who has been registered for Temporary Protected Status (TPS) and I want an employment authorization document **FEE REQUIRED**

GROUP C

The immigration law and regulations allow certain aliens to apply for employment authorization. If you are an alien described in one of the classes below you may request employment authorization from the INS and, if granted, you will receive an employment authorization document. The instruction FEE REQUIRED printed below refers to your initial document, replacement, and extension.

Place an X in the box next to the number which applies to you

- ☐ (c) (1) - I am the dependent of a foreign government official (A-1 or A-2) I have attached certification from the Department of State recommending employment **NO FEE**
- ☐ (c) (2) - I am the dependent of an employee of the Coordination Council of North American Affairs and I have E-1 nonimmigrant status. I have attached certification of my status from the American Institute of Taiwan **FEE REQUIRED**
- ☐ (c) (3) (i) - I am a foreign student (F-1). I have attached certification from the designated school official recommending employment for economic necessity. I have also attached my INS Form I-20 ID copy **FEE REQUIRED**
- ☐ (c) (3) (ii) - I am a foreign student (F-1). I have attached certification from the designated school official recommending employment for practical training. I have also attached my INS Form I-20 ID copy **FEE REQUIRED**
- ☐ (c) (3) (iii) - I am a foreign student (F-1). I have attached certification from my designated school official and I have been offered employment under the sponsorship of an international organization within the meaning of the International Organization Immunities Act. I have certification from this sponsor and I have also attached my INS Form I-20 ID copy **FEE REQUIRED**
- ☐ (c) (4) - I am the dependent of an officer or employee of an international organization (G-1 or G-4). I have attached certification from the Department of State recommending employment. **NO FEE.**
- ☐ (c) (5) - I am the dependent of an exchange visitor and I have J-2 nonimmigrant status **FEE REQUIRED.**
- ☐ (c) (6) - I am a vocational foreign student (M-1). I have attached certification from the designated school official recommending employment for practical training. I have also attached my INS Form I-20ID Copy **FEE REQUIRED.**
- ☐ (c) (7) - I am the dependent of an individual classified as NATO-1 through NATO-7 **FEE REQUIRED**
- ☐ (c) (8) - I have filed a non-frivolous application for asylum in the United States and the application is pending **FEE REQUIRED FOR REPLACEMENT ONLY.**
- ☐ (c) (9) - I have filed an application for adjustment of status to lawful permanent resident status and the application is pending **FEE REQUIRED**
- ☐ (c) (10) - I have filed an application for suspension of deportation and the application is still pending **FEE REQUIRED.**
- ☐ (c) (11) - I have been paroled into the United States for emergent reasons or for reasons in the public interest **FEE REQUIRED**
- ☐ (c) (12) - I am a deportable alien and I have been granted voluntary departure either prior to or after my hearing before the immigration judge **FEE REQUIRED.**
- ☐ (c) (13) - I have been placed in exclusion or deportation proceedings. I have not received a final order of deportation or exclusion and I have not been detained. **I understand that I must show economic necessity and I will refer to the instructions concerning "Basic Criteria to Establish Economic Necessity." FEE REQUIRED.**
- ☐ (c) (14) - I have been granted deferred action by INS as an act of administrative convenience to the government. **I understand that I must show economic necessity and I will refer to the instructions concerning "Basic Criteria to Establish Economic Necessity." FEE REQUIRED.**
- ☐ (c) (16) - I entered the United States prior to January 1, 1972 and have been here since January 1, 1972. I have applied for registry as a lawful permanent resident alien and my application is pending **FEE REQUIRED**
- ☐ (c) (17) (i) - I am a (B-1) visitor for business. I am and have been (before coming to the United States) the domestic or personal servant for my employer who is temporarily in the United States **FEE REQUIRED**
- ☐ (c) (17) (ii) - I am a visitor for business (B-1) and am the employee of a foreign airline. I have B-1 nonimmigrant classification because I am unable to obtain visa classification as a treaty trader (E-1) **FEE REQUIRED.**
- ☐ (c) (18) - I am a deportable alien who has been placed under an order of supervision (OS). **I Understand that I must show economic necessity and I will refer to the instructions concerning "Basic Criteria to Establish Economic Necessity." FEE REQUIRED.**
- ☐ (c) (19) - I am an alien who is prima facie eligible for Temporary Protected Status (TPS) and (1) INS has not given me a reasonable chance to register during the first 30 days of the registration period **[FEE REQUIRED]**, or (2) INS has not made a final decison as to my eligibility for TPS **FEE REQUIRED**

U.S. Department of Justice
Immigration and Naturalization Service

For sale by the Superintendent of Documents
U S Government Printing Office
Washington, DC 20402

OMB #1115-0168
Petition for a Nonimmigrant Worker

START HERE - Please Type or Print

Part 1. Information about the employer filing this petition.
If the employer is an individual, use the top name line. Organizations should use the second line.

Family Name	Given Name	Middle Initial

Company or Organization Name

Address - Attn

Street Number and Name		Apt #

City	State or Province

Country	ZIP/Postal Code

IRS Tax #

Part 2. Information about this Petition.
(See instructions to determine the fee)

1. **Requested Nonimmigrant Classification:**
   (write classification symbol at right) _____

2. **Basis for Classification** (check one)
   a. ☐ New employment
   b. ☐ Continuation of previously approved employment without change
   c. ☐ Change in previously approved employment
   d. ☐ New concurrent employment

3. **Prior petition.** If you checked other than "New Employment" in item 2 (above) give the most recent prior petition number for the worker(s):

4. **Requested Action:** (check one)
   a. ☐ Notify the office in Part 4 so the person(s) can obtain a visa or be admitted (NOTE: a petition is not required for an E-1, E-2, or R visa)
   b. ☐ Change the person(s) status and extend their stay since they are all now in the U.S in another status (see instructions for limitations). This is available only where you check "New Employment" in item 2, above
   c. ☐ Extend or amend the stay of the person(s) since they now hold this status.

5. **Total number of workers in petition:** _____
   (See instructions for where more than one worker can be included.)

Part 3. Information about the person(s) you are filing for.
Complete the blocks below. Use the continuation sheet to name each person included in this petition

If an entertainment group, give their group name.

Family Name	Given Name	Middle Initial

Date of Birth (Month/Day/Year)	Country of Birth

Social Security #	A #

If in the United States, complete the following.

Date of Arrival (Month/Day/Year)	I-94 #

Current Nonimmigrant Status	Expires (Month/Day/Year)

FOR INS USE ONLY

Returned	Receipt

Resubmitted

Reloc Sent

Reloc Rec'd

Interviewed
☐ Petitioner
☐ Beneficiary

Class _____
# of Workers _____
Priority Number. _____
Validity Dates. From _____
To _____

☐ **Classification Approved**
   ☐ Consulate/POE/PFI Notified
   At. _____
   ☐ Extension Granted
   ☐ COS/Extension Granted

Partial Approval (explain)

Action Block

To Be Completed by Attorney or Representative, If any
☐ Fill in box if G-28 is attached to represent the applicant

VOLAG#

ATTY State License #

Form I-129 (Rev. 12/11/91) N

Continued on back.

Part 4. Processing Information.

a. If the person named in Part 3 is outside the U.S. or a requested extension of stay or change of status cannot be granted, give the U.S consulate or inspection facility you want notified if this petition is approved.

Type of Office (check one): ☐ Consulate ☐ Pre-flight inspection ☐ Port of Entry
Office Address (City) U.S. State or Foreign Country

Person's Foreign Address

b. Does each person in this petition have a valid passport?
☐ Not required to have passport ☐ No - explain on separate paper ☐ Yes
c. Are you filing any other petitions with this one? ☐ No ☐ Yes - How many? _____
d. Are applications for replacement/Initial I-94's being filed with this petition? ☐ No ☐ Yes - How many? _____
e. Are applications by dependents being filed with this petition? ☐ No ☐ Yes - How many? _____
f. Is any person in this petition in exclusion or deportation proceedings? ☐ No ☐ Yes - explain on separate paper
g. Have you ever filed an immigrant petition for any person in this petition? ☐ No ☐ Yes - explain on separate paper
h. If you indicated you were filing a new petition in Part 2, within the past 7 years has any person in this petition:
1) ever been given the classification you are now requesting? ☐ No ☐ Yes - explain on separate paper
2) ever been denied the classification you are now requesting? ☐ No ☐ Yes - explain on separate paper
i. If you are filing for an entertainment group, has any person in this petition not been with the group for at least 1 year?
☐ No ☐ Yes - explain on separate paper

Part 5. Basic Information about the proposed employment and employer.

Attach the supplement relating to the classification you are requesting

Job Title | Nontechnical Description of Job

Address where the person(s) will work if different from the address in Part 1.

Is this a full-time position? ☐ No - Hours per week ☐ Yes | Wages per week or per year

Other Compensation (Explain) | Value per week or per year | Dates of Intended employment From: To:

Type of Petitioner - check one: ☐ U.S. citizen or permanent resident ☐ Organization ☐ Other - explain on separate paper

Type of business: | Year established:

Current Number of Employees | Gross Annual Income | Net Annual Income

Part 6. Signature.

Read the information on penalties in the instructions before completing this section.

I certify, under penalty of perjury under the laws of the United States of America, that this petition, and the evidence submitted with it, is all true and correct. If filing this on behalf of an organization, I certify that I am empowered to do so by that organization If this petition is to extend a prior petition, I certify that the proposed employment is under the same terms and conditions as in the prior approved petition. I authorize the release of any information from my records, or from the petitioning organization's records, which the Immigration and Naturalization Service needs to determine eligibility for the benefit being sought.

Signature and title | Print Name | Date

Please Note: If you do not completely fill out this form and the required supplement, or fail to submit required documents listed in the instructions, then the person(s) filed for may not be found eligible for the requested benefit, and this petition may be denied

Part 7. Signature of person preparing form if other than above.

I declare that I prepared this petition at the request of the above person and it is based on all information of which I have any knowledge

Signature | Print Name | Date

Firm Name and Address

U.S. Department of Justice
Immigration and Naturalization Service

OMB #1115-0168
H Classification
Supplement to Form I-129

Name of person or organization filing petition.   Name of person or total number of workers or trainees you are filing for

List the alien's and any dependent family members, prior periods of stay in H classification in the U S for the last six years Be sure to list only those periods in which the alien and/or family members were actually in the U.S in an H classification If more space is needed, attach an additional sheet

Classification sought (check one).
- [ ] H-1A   Registered Professional nurse
- [ ] H-1B1 Specialty occupation
- [ ] H-1B2 Exceptional services relating to a cooperative research and development project administered by the U.S. Department of Defense
- [ ] H-1B3 Artist, entertainer or fashion model of national or international acclaim
- [ ] H-1B4 Artist or entertainer in unique or traditional art form
- [ ] H-1B5 Athlete
- [ ] H-1BS Essential Support Personnel for H-1B entertainer or athlete
- [ ] H-2A   Agricultural worker
- [ ] H-2B   Nonagricultural worker
- [ ] H-3   Trainee
- [ ] H-3   Special education exchange visitor program

Section 1. Complete this section if filing for H-1A or H-1B classification.

Describe the proposed duties

Alien's present occupation and summary of prior work experience

Statement for H-1B speciality occupations only:
By filing this petition, I agree to the terms of the labor condition application for the duration of the alien's authorized period of stay for H-1B employment.
Petitioner's Signature   Date

Statement for H-1B specialty occupations and DOD projects:
As an authorized official of the employer, I certify that the employer will be liable for the reasonable costs of return transportation of the alien abroad if the alien is dismissed from employment by the employer before the end of the period of authorized stay
Signature of authorized official of employer   Date

Statement for H-1B DOD projects only:
I certify that the alien will be working on a cooperative research and development project or a coproduction project under a reciprocal Government-to-Government agreement administered by the Department of Defense
DOD project manager's signature   Date

Section 2. Complete this section if filing for H-2A or H-2B classification.

Employment is.   [ ] Seasonal   Temporary need is.   [ ] Unpredictable
(check one)   [ ] Peakload   (check one)   [ ] Periodic
                    [ ] Intermittent   [ ] Recurrent annually
                    [ ] One-time occurrence

Explain your temporary need for the alien's services (attach a separate paper if additional space is needed).

Form I-129 Supplement H (12/11/91) N   **Continued on back.**

Section 3. Complete this section if filing for H-2A classification.

The petitioner and each employer consent to allow government access to the site where the labor is being performed for the purpose of determining compliance with H-2A requirements. The petitioner further agrees to notify the Service in the manner and within the time frame specified if an H-2A worker absconds or if the authorized employment ends more than five days before the relating certification document expires, and pay liquidated damages of ten dollars for each instance where it cannot demonstrate compliance with this notification requirement. The petitioner also agrees to pay liquidated damages of two hundred dollars for each instance where it cannot be demonstrated that the H-2A worker either departed the United States or obtained authorized status during the period of admission or within five days of early termination, whichever comes first.

The petitioner must execute Part A. If the petitioner is the employer's agent, the employer must execute Part B. If there are joint employers, they must each execute Part C.

Part A. Petitioner:

By filing this petition, I agree to the conditions of H-2A employment, and agree to the notice requirements and limited liabilities defined in 8 CFR 214.2 (h) (3) (vi).

Petitioner's signature Date

Part B. Employer who is not petitioner:

I certify that I have authorized the party filing this petition to act as my agent in this regard. I assume full responsibility for all representations made by this agent on my behalf, and agree to the conditions of H-2A eligibility.

Employer's signature Date

Part C. Joint Employers:

I agree to the conditions of H-2A eligibility.

Joint employer's signature(s) Date

Joint employer's signature(s) Date

Joint employer's signature(s) Date

Joint employer's signature(s) Date

Joint employer's signature(s) Date

Section 4. Complete this section if filing for H-3 classification.

If you answer "yes" to any of the following questions, attach a full explanation.

		No	Yes
a	Is the training you intend to provide, or similar training, available in the alien's country?	☐	☐
b	Will the training benefit the alien in pursuing a career abroad?	☐	☐
c	Does the training involve productive employment incidental to training?	☐	☐
d	Does the alien already have skills related to the training?	☐	☐
e.	Is this training an effort to overcome a labor shortage?	☐	☐
f	Do you intend to employ the alien abroad at the end of this training?	☐	☐

If you do not intend to employ this person abroad at the end of this training, explain why you wish to incur the cost of providing this training, and your expected return from this training

U.S. Department of Justice
Immigration and Naturalization Service

OMB#1115-0168
O and P Classifications
Supplement to Form I-129

Name of person or organization filing petition:

Name of person or group or total number of workers you are filing for

Classification sought (check one):

☐ O-1 Alien of extraordinary ability in sciences, art, education, or business.
☐ P-2 Artist or entertainer for reciprocal exchange program
☐ P-2S Essential Support Personnel for P-2

Explain the nature of the event

Describe the duties to be performed

If filing for O-2 or P support alien, dates of the alien's prior experience with the O-1 or P alien.

Have you obtained the required written consultations(s)?   ☐ Yes - attached   ☐ No - Copy of request attached
If not, give the following information about the organizations(s) to which you have sent a duplicate of this petition

O-1 Extraordinary ability

| Name of recognized peer group | Phone # |
| Address | Date sent |

O-1 Extraordinary achievement in motion pictures or television

Name of labor organization	Phone #
Address	Date sent
Name of management organization	Phone #
Address	Date sent

O-2 or P alien

| Name of labor organization | Phone # |
| Address | Date sent |

Form I-129 Supplement O/P/Q/R (12/11/91) N

U.S. Department of Justice
Immigration and Naturalization Service

OMB #1115-0168
Q & R Classifications
Supplement to Form I-129

Name of person or organization filing petition:

Name of person you are filing for:

Section 1. Complete this section if you are filing for a Q international cultural exchange alien.

I hereby certify that the participant(s) in this international cultural exchange program.
- is at least 18 years of age,
- has the ability to communicate effectively about the cultural attributes of his or her country of nationality to the American public, and
- has not previously been in the United States as a Q nonimmigrant unless he/she has resided and been physically present outside the U.S for the immediate prior year.

I also certify that the same wages and working conditions are accorded the participants as are provided to similarly employed U.S. workers.

Petitioner's signature   Date

Section 2. Complete this section if you are filing for an R religious worker.

List the alien's, and any dependent family members, prior periods of stay in R classification in the U.S. for the last six years. Be sure to list only those periods in which the alien and/or family members were actually in the U.S. in an R classification.

Describe the alien's proposed duties in the U.S.

Describe the alien's qualifications for the vocation or occupation

Description of the relationship between the U.S. religious organization and the organization abroad of which the alien was a member.

Form I-129 Supplement O/P/Q/R (12/11/91) N

U.S. Department of Justice
Immigration and Naturalization Service

OMB #1115-0168
E Classification
Supplement to Form I-129

Name of person or organization filing petition

Name of person you are filing for.

Classification sought (check one).
- [ ] E-1 Treaty trader
- [ ] E-2 Treaty investor

Name of country signatory to treaty with U.S

Section 1. Information about the Employer Outside the U.S. (If any)

Name

Address

Alien's Position - Title, duties and number of years employed

Principal Product, merchandise or service

Total Number of Employees

Section 2. Additional Information about the U.S. Employer.

The U.S. company is, to the company outside the U.S. (check one).
- [ ] Parent
- [ ] Branch
- [ ] Subsidiary
- [ ] Affiliate
- [ ] Joint Venture

Date and Place of Incorporation or establishment in the U.S.

Nationality of Ownership (Individual or Corporate)

Name	Nationality	Immigration Status	% Ownership

Assets   Net Worth   Total Annual Income

Staff in the U.S.   Executive/Manager   Specialized Qualifications or Knowledge

Nationals of Treaty Country in E or L Status

Total number of employees in the U.S

Total number of employees the alien would supervise, or describe the nature of the specialized skills essential to the U S company

Section 3. Complete if filing for an E-1 Treaty Trader

Total Annual Gross Trade/Business of the U.S. company   For Year Ending
$

Percent of total gross trade which is between the U S and the country of which the treaty trader organization is a national

Section 4. Complete if filing for an E-2 Treaty Investor

Total Investment.	Cash	Equipment	Other
	$	$	$
	Inventory	Premises	Total
	$	$	$

Form I-129 Supplement E/L (12/11/91) N

U.S. Department of Justice
Immigration and Naturalization Service

OMB #1115-0168
L Classification
Supplement to Form I-129

Name of person or organization filing petition:

Name of person you are filing for

This petition is (check one) ☐ An individual petition ☐ A blanket petition

Section 1. Complete this section if filing an individual petition.

Classification sought (check one) ☐ L-1A manager or executive ☐ L-1B specialized knowledge

List the alien's, and any dependent family members' prior periods of stay in an L classification in the U S for the last seven years. Be sure to list only those periods in which the alien and/or family members were actually in the U S in an L classification

Name and address of employer abroad

Dates of alien's employment with this employer. Explain any interruptions in employment

Description of the alien's duties for the past 3 years.

Description of alien's proposed duties in the U S

Summarize the alien's education and work experience

The U S company is, to the company abroad (check one)
☐ Parent ☐ Branch ☐ Subsidiary ☐ Affiliate ☐ Joint Venture
Describe the stock ownership and managerial control of each company

Do the companies currently have the same qualifying relationship as they did during the one-year period of the alien's employment with the company abroad? ☐ Yes ☐ No (attach explanation)

Is the alien coming to the U.S to open a new office?
☐ Yes (explain in detail on separate paper) ☐ No

Section 2. Complete this section if filing a Blanket Petition.

List all U S and foreign parent, branches, subsidiaries and affiliates included in this petition. (Attach a separate paper if additional space is needed.)
Name and Address   Relationship

Explain in detail on separate paper

Form I-129 Supplement E/L (12/11/91) N

Continued on back

Supplement-1

Attach to Form I-129 when more than one person is included in the petition. *(List each person separately. Do not include the person you named on the form).*

Family Name		Given Name	Middle Initial	Date of Birth (month/day/year)
Country of Birth		Social Security No.		A#
IF IN THE U.S.	Date of Arrival *(month/day/year)*		I-94#	
	Current Nonimmigrant Status:		Expires on *(month/day/year)*	
Country where passport issued		Expiration Date (month/day/year)	Date Started with group	
Family Name		Given Name	Middle Initial	Date of Birth (month/day/year)
Country of Birth		Social Security No		A#
IF IN THE U.S.	Date of Arrival *(month/day/year)*		I-94#	
	Current Nonimmigrant Status:		Expires on *(month/day/year)*	
Country where passport issued		Expiration Date (month/day/year)	Date Started with group	
Family Name		Given Name	Middle Initial	Date of Birth (month/day/year)
Country of Birth		Social Security No		A#
IF IN THE U.S.	Date of Arrival *(month/day/year)*		I-94#	
	Current Nonimmigrant Status		Expires on *(month/day/year)*	
Country where passport issued		Expiration Date (month/day/year)	Date Started with group	
Family Name		Given Name	Middle Initial	Date of Birth (month/day/year)
Country of Birth		Social Security No.		A#
IF IN THE U.S.	Date of Arrival *(month/day/year)*		I-94#	
	Current Nonimmigrant Status.		Expires on *(month/day/year)*	
Country where passport issued		Expiration Date (month/day/year)	Date Started with group	
Family Name		Given Name	Middle Initial	Date of Birth (month/day/year)
Country of Birth		Social Security No		A#
IF IN THE U.S.	Date of Arrival *(month/day/year)*		I-94#	
	Current Nonimmigrant Status:		Expires on *(month/day/year)*	
Country where passport issued		Expiration Date (month/day/year)	Date Started with group	

Supplement-1

Attach to Form I-129 when more than one person is included in the petition. *(List each person separately. Do not include the person you named on the form).*

Family Name	Given Name	Middle Initial	Date of Birth (month/day/year)
Country of Birth	Social Security No.		A#

IF IN THE U.S.	Date of Arrival (month/day/year)		I-94#
	Current Nonimmigrant Status:		Expires on (month/day/year)

Country where passport issued	Expiration Date (month/day/year)	Date Started with group

Family Name	Given Name	Middle Initial	Date of Birth (month/day/year)
Country of Birth	Social Security No.		A#

IF IN THE U.S.	Date of Arrival (month/day/year)		I-94#
	Current Nonimmigrant Status:		Expires on (month/day/year)

Country where passport issued	Expiration Date (month/day/year)	Date Started with group

Family Name	Given Name	Middle Initial	Date of Birth (month/day/year)
Country of Birth	Social Security No.		A#

IF IN THE U.S.	Date of Arrival (month/day/year)		I-94#
	Current Nonimmigrant Status:		Expires on (month/day/year)

Country where passport issued	Expiration Date (month/day/year)	Date Started with group

Family Name	Given Name	Middle Initial	Date of Birth (month/day/year)
Country of Birth	Social Security No.		A#

IF IN THE U.S.	Date of Arrival (month/day/year)		I-94#
	Current Nonimmigrant Status:		Expires on (month/day/year)

Country where passport issued	Expiration Date (month/day/year)	Date Started with group

Family Name	Given Name	Middle initial	Date of Birth (month/day/year)
Country of Birth	Social Security No.		A#

IF IN THE U.S.	Date of Arrival (month/day/year)		I-94#
	Current Nonimmigrant Status:		Expires on (month/day/year)

Country where passport issued	Expiration Date (month/day/year)	Date Started with group

U. S. Department of Justice
Immigration and Naturalization Service

OMB No 1115-0062

Affidavit of Support

(ANSWER ALL ITEMS: FILL IN WITH TYPEWRITER OR PRINT IN BLOCK LETTERS IN INK.)

I, _____, residing at _____
        (Name)   (Street and Number)

_____
(City)   (State)   (ZIP Code if in U S)   (Country)

BEING DULY SWORN DEPOSE AND SAY:

1. I was born on _____ at _____
              (Date)   (City)   (Country)

   If you are *not* a native born United States citizen, answer the following as appropriate.
   a. If a United States citizen through naturalization, give certificate of naturalization number _____
   b. If a United States citizen through parent(s) or marriage, give citizenship certificate number _____
   c. If United States citizenship was derived by some other method, attach a statement of explanation.
   d. If a lawfully admitted permanent resident of the United States, give "A" number _____

2. That I am _____ years of age and have resided in the United States since (date) _____
3. That this affidavit is executed in behalf of the following person:

Name				Sex	Age
Citizen of--(Country)		Marital Status	Relationship to Deponent		
Presently resides at--(Street and Number)	(City)		(State)		(Country)

Name of spouse and children accompanying or following to join person:

Spouse	Sex	Age	Child	Sex	Age
Child	Sex	Age	Child	Sex	Age
Child	Sex	Age	Child	Sex	Age

4. That this affidavit is made by me for the purpose of assuring the United States Government that the person(s) named in item 3 will not become a public charge in the United States.

5. That I am willing and able to receive, maintain and support the person(s) named in item 3. That I am ready and willing to deposit a bond, if necessary, to guarantee that such person(s) will not become a public charge during his or her stay in the United States, or to guarantee that the above named will maintain his or her nonimmigrant status if admitted temporarily and will depart prior to the expiration of his or her authorized stay in the United States

6. That I understand this affidavit will be binding upon me for a period of three (3) years after entry of the person(s) named in item 3 and that the information and documentation provided by me may be made available to the Secretary of Health and Human Services and the Secretary of Agriculture, who may make it available to a public assistance agency

7. That I am employed as, or engaged in the business of _____ with _____
                                                (Type of Business)   (Name of concern)

   at _____
       (Street and Number)   (City)   (State)   (Zip Code)

I derive an annual income of *(if self-employed, I have attached a copy of my last income tax return or report of commercial rating concern which I certify to be true and correct to the best of my knowledge and belief. See instruction for nature of evidence of net worth to be submitted.)* $_____

I have on deposit in savings banks in the United States $_____
I have other personal property, the reasonable value of which is $_____

Form I-134 (Rev. 12-1-84) Y   OVER

I have stocks and bonds with the following market value, as indicated on the attached list
which I certify to be true and correct to the best of my knowledge and belief. $ _____
I have life insurance in the sum of $ _____
With a cash surrender value of $ _____
I own real estate valued at $ _____
With mortgages or other encumbrances thereon amounting to $ _____

Which is located at _____
(Street and Number) (City) (State) (Zip Code)

8. That the following persons are dependent upon me for support: *(Place an "X" in the appropriate column to indicate whether the person named is **wholly or partially** dependent upon you for support.)*

Name of Person	Wholly Dependent	Partially Dependent	Age	Relationship to Me

9. That I have previously submitted affidavit(s) of support for the following person(s). If none, state *"None"*

Name   Date submitted

_____

_____

_____

10. That I have submitted visa petition(s) to the Immigration and Naturalization Service on behalf of the following person(s). If none, state none.

Name   Relationship   Date submitted

_____

_____

_____

11 *(Complete this block only if the person named in item 3 will be in the United States temporarily.)*
That I ☐ do intend ☐ do not intend, to make specific contributions to the support of the person named in item 3. *(If you check "do intend", indicate the exact nature and duration of the contributions. For example, if you intend to furnish room and board, state for how long and, if money, state the amount in United States dollars and state whether it is to be given in a lump sum, weekly, or monthly, or for how long)*

_____

_____

_____

OATH OR AFFIRMATION OF DEPONENT

I acknowledge at that I have read Part III of the Instructions, Sponsor and Alien Liability, and am aware of my responsibilities as an immigrant sponsor under the Social Security Act, as amended, and the Food Stamp Act, as amended.

I swear (affirm) that I know the contents of this affidavit signed by me and the statements are true and correct.

Signature of deponent _____

Subscribed and sworn to (affirmed) before me this _____ *day of* _____, 19_____

at _____ *My commission expires on* _____

Signature of Officer Administering Oath _____ *Title* _____

If affidavit prepared by other than deponent, please complete the following: I declare that this document was prepared by me at the request of the deponent and is based on all information of which I have knowledge.

(Signature)   (Address)   (Date)

(Please tear off this sheet before submitting Affidavit)

U. S. Department of Justice
Immigration and Naturalization Service

Affidavit of Support

INSTRUCTIONS

I. EXECUTION OF AFFIDAVIT. A separate affidavit must be submitted for each person. You must sign the affidavit in your full, true and correct name and affirm or make it under oath. If you are **in the United States** the affidavit may be sworn or affirmed before an immigration officer without the payment of fee, or before a notary public or other officer authorized to administer oaths for general purposes, in which case the official seal or certificate of authority to administer oaths must be affixed. If you are **outside the United States** the affidavit must be sworn to or affirmed before a United States consular or immigration officer.

II. SUPPORTING EVIDENCE. The deponent must submit in duplicate evidence of income and resources, as appropriate

    A. Statement from an officer of the bank or other financial institution in which you have deposits giving the following details regarding your account:
       1. Date account opened.
       2. Total amount deposited for the past year.
       3. Present balance.

    B. Statement of your employer on business stationery, showing:
       1. Date and nature of employment.
       2. Salary paid.
       3 Whether position is temporary or permanent

    C If self-employed.
       1. Copy of last income tax return filed or,
       2 Report of commercial rating concern.

    D. List containing serial numbers and denominations of bonds and name of record owner(s).

III. SPONSOR AND ALIEN LIABILITY. Effective October 1, 1980, amendments to section 1614(f) of the Social Security Act and Part A of Title XVI of the Social Security Act establish certain requirements for determining the eligibility of aliens who apply for the first time for Supplemental Security Income (SSI) benefits Effective October 1, 1981, amendments to section 415 of the Social Security Act establish similar requirements for determining the eligibility of aliens who apply for the first time for Aid to Families with Dependent Children (AFDC) benefits Effective December 22, 1981, amendments to the Food Stamp Act of 1977 affect the eligibility of alien participation in the Food Stamp Program These amendments require that the income and resources of any person who, as the sponsor of an alien's entry into the United States, executes an affidavit of support or similar agreement on behalf of the alien, and the income and resources of the sponsor's spouse (*if living with the sponsor*) shall be deemed to be the income and resources of the alien under formulas for determining eligibility for SSI, AFDC, and Food Stamp benefits during the three years following the alien's entry into the United States.

An alien applying for SSI must make available to the Social Security Administration documentation concerning his or her income and resources and those of the sponsor including information which was provided in support of the application for an immigrant visa or adjustment of status An alien applying for AFDC or Food Stamps must make similar information available to the State public assistance agency The Secretary of Health and Human Services and the Secretary of Agriculture are authorized to obtain copies of any such documentation submitted to INS or the Department of State and to release such documentation to a State public assistance agency

Sections 1621(e) and 415(d) of the Social Security Act and subsection 5(i) of the Food Stamp Act also provide that an alien and his or her sponsor shall be jointly and severally liable to repay any SSI, AFDC, or Food Stamp benefits which are incorrectly paid because of misinformation provided by a sponsor or because of a sponsor's failure to provide information. Incorrect payments which are not repaid will be withheld from any subsequent payments for which the alien or sponsor are otherwise eligible under the Social Security Act or Food Stamp Act, except that the sponsor was without fault or where good cause existed

These provisions do not apply to the SSI, AFDC or Food Stamp eligibility of aliens admitted as refugees, granted political asylum by the Attorney General, or Cuban/Haitian entrants as defined in section 501(e) of P L 96-422 and of dependent children of the sponsor or sponsor's spouse They also do not apply to the SSI or Food Stamp eligibility of an alien who becomes blind or disabled after admission into the United States for permanent residency

IV. AUTHORITY/USE/PENALTIES. Authority for the collection of the information requested on this form is contained in 8 U S C. 1182(a)(15), 1184(a), and 1258 The information will be used principally by the Service, or by any consular officer to whom it may be furnished, to support an alien's application for benefits under the Immigration and Nationality Act and specifically the assertion that he or she has adequate means of financial support and will not become a public charge Submission of the information is voluntary It may also, as a matter of routine use, be disclosed to other federal, state, local and foreign law enforcement and regulatory agencies including the Department of Health and Human Services, the Department of Agriculture, the Department of State, the Department of Defense and any component thereof (if the deponent has served or is serving in the armed forces of the United States), the Central Intelligence Agency, and individuals and organizations during the course of any investigation to elicit further information required to carry out Service functions Failure to provide the information may result in the denial of the alien's application for a visa, or his or her exclusion from the United States

Form I-134 (Rev. 12-1-84) Y

U.S. Department of Justice
Immigration and Naturalization Service (INS)

Petition for Alien Fiancé(e)

Instructions

Read the Instructions carefully. If you need extra space to answer, attach a continuation sheet, indicate the item number, and date and sign the sheet.

1. Who can file?

A. You are a United States citizen, and

B. You and your fiancé(e) are both free to marry, and have met in person within two years before filing this petition unless:

   (1) The requirement to meet your fiancé(e) in person would violate strict and long-established customs of your or your fiancé(e)'s foreign culture or social practice; or

   (2) It is established that the requirement to personally meet your fiancé(e) would result in extreme hardship to you; and

C. You and your fiancé(e) intend to marry within 90 days of your fiancé(e) entering the United States.

NOTE: Unmarried children of your fiancé(e) who are under 21 years old and are listed on this form will be eligible to apply to accompany your fiancé(e).

2. What documents do you need?

You must give INS certain documents with this form to show you are eligible to file.

A. For each document needed, give INS the original and one copy. However, because it is against the law to copy a Certificate of Naturalization or a Certificate of Citizenship, give INS the original only. **Originals will be returned to you.**

B. If you do not wish to give the original document, you may give INS a copy. The copy must be certified by:

   (1) an INS or U.S. consular officer, or

   (2) an attorney admitted to practice law in the United States, or

   (3) an INS accredited representative (INS still may require originals).

C. Documents in a foreign language must be accompanied by a complete English translation. The translator must certify that the translation is accurate and that he or she is competent to translate.

3. What documents do you need to show you are a United States citizen?

A. If you were born in the United States, give INS your birth certificate.

B. If you were naturalized, give INS your original Certificate of Naturalization.

C. If you were born outside the United States, and you are a U.S. citizen through your parents, give INS:

   (1) your original Certificate of Citizenship, or

   (2) your Form FS-240 (Report of Birth Abroad of a United States Citizen).

D. In place of any of the above, you may give INS your valid unexpired U.S. passport that was initially issued for at least 5 years.

E. If you do not have any of the above and were born in the United States, see the instructions under item 6, *"What if a document is not available?"*

4. What documents do you need to prove you can legally marry?

You must prove that you can legally marry your fiancé(e).

A. If either of you is of an age that requires special consent or permission for you to marry in the jurisdiction in which your marriage will occur, give proof of that consent or permission.

B. If either of you has been previously married, give INS documents to show that all previous marriages were legally ended. In cases where the names shown on the supporting documents have changed, give INS legal documents to show how the name change occurred (for example, a marriage certificate, adoption decree, court order, etc.)

5. What other documents do you need?

A. Give INS a color photo of you and one of your fiancé(e), taken within 30 days of the date of this petition. These photos must have a white background. They must be glossy, un-retouched, and not mounted. The dimension of the facial image should be about 1 inch from chin to top of hair in 3/4 frontal view, showing the right side of the face with the right ear visible. Using pencil or felt pen, lightly print name (and Alien Registration Number, if known) on the back of each photograph.

B. Give a completed and signed Form G-325A (Biographic Information) for you and one for your fiancé(e). Except for name and signature, you do not have to repeat on the Biographic Information forms the information given on your I-129F petition.

6. What if a document is not available?

If the documents needed above are not available, you can give INS the following instead. (INS may require a statement from the appropriate civil authority certifying that the needed document is not available.)

A. Church record: A certificate under the seal of the church where the baptism, dedication, or comparable rite occurred within two months after birth, showing the date and place of child's birth, the date of the religious ceremony, and the names of the child's parents.

B. School record: A letter from the authorities of the school attended (preferably the first school), showing the date of admission to the school, child's date and place of birth, and the names and places of birth of parents, if shown in the school records.

C. Census record: State or federal census record showing the name, place of birth, and date of birth or the age of the person listed.

Form I-129F (REV. 10-7-87)N

D. Affidavits: Written statements sworn to or affirmed by two persons who were living at the time, and who have personal knowledge of the event you are trying to prove; for example, the date and place of birth, marriage, or death. The persons making the affidavits need not be citizens of the United States. Each affidavit should contain the following information regarding the person making the affidavit: his or her full name, address, date and place of birth, and his or her relationship to you, if any; full information concerning the event; and complete details concerning how the person acquired knowledge of the event.

7. How should you prepare this form?

A. Type or print legibly in ink.

B. If extra space is needed to complete any item, attach a continuation sheet, indicate the item number, and date and sign each sheet.

C. Answer all questions fully and accurately. If any item does not apply, please write "N/A".

8. Where should you file this form?

A. If you live in the United States, send or take the form to the INS office that has jurisdiction over where you live.

B. If you live outside the United States, contact the nearest American Consulate to find out where to send or take the completed form.

9. What is the fee?

You must pay $75.00 to file this form. **The fee will not be refunded, whether the petition is approved or not.** DO NOT MAIL CASH. All checks or money orders, whether U.S. or foreign, must be payable in U.S. currency at a financial institution in the United States. When a check is drawn on the account of a person other than yourself, write your name on the face of the check. If the check is not honored, INS will charge you $5.00.

Pay by check or money order in the exact amount. Make the check or money order payable to "Immigration and Naturalization Service." However,

A. If you live in Guam: Make the check or money order payable to "Treasurer, Guam", or

B. If you live in the U.S. Virgin Islands: Make the check or money order payable to "Commissioner of Finance of the Virgin Islands".

10. How does your alien fiancé(e) get his or her permanent resident status?

Your alien fiancé(e) may apply for conditional permanent resident status after you have entered into a valid marriage to each other performed within ninety days of your fiancé's entry into the United States. Your new spouse should apply promptly to the Immigration and Naturalization Service for adjustment of status to conditional permanent residence using Form I-485. He or she will be a conditional permanent resident for a two-year period which begins on the date that he or she adjusts to conditional status.

The rights, privileges, responsibilities and duties which apply to all other permanent residents apply equally to a conditional permanent resident. For example, a conditional permanent resident has the right to apply for naturalization, to file petitions in behalf of qualifying relatives, or to reside permanently in the United States as an immigrant in accordance with the immigration laws.

11. How does your conditional permanent resident spouse become a lawful permanent resident without conditions?

Both you and your conditional permanent resident spouse are required to file a petition, Form I-751, Joint Petition to Remove the Conditional Basis of Alien's Permanent Resident Status, during the ninety day period immediately before the second anniversary of the date your alien spouse was granted conditional permanent residence. Children who have been admitted as conditional permanent residents may be included in the joint petition to remove conditions.

> FAILURE TO FILE FORM I-751, JOINT PETITION TO REMOVE THE CONDITIONAL BASIS OF ALIEN'S PERMANENT RESIDENCE STATUS, WILL RESULT IN TERMINATION OF PERMANENT RESIDENCE STATUS AND INITIATION OF DEPORTATION PROCEEDINGS.

12. What are the penalties for committing marriage fraud or submitting false information or both?

Title 18, United States Code, Section 1001 states that whoever willfully and knowingly falsifies a material fact, makes a false statement, or makes use of a false document will be fined up to $10,000 or imprisoned up to five years, or both.

Title 8 United States Code, Section 1325 states that any individual who knowingly enters into a marriage contract for the purpose of evading any provision of the immigration laws shall be imprisoned for not more than five years, or fined not more than $250,000.00, or both.

13. What is our authority for collecting this information?

We request the information on this form to carry out the immigration laws contained in Title 8, United States Code 1184(d). We need this information to determine whether a person is eligible for immigration benefits. The information you provide may also be disclosed to other federal, state, local, and foreign law enforcement and regulatory agencies during the course of the investigation required by this Service. You do not have to give this information. However, if you refuse to give some or all of it, your petition may be denied.

It is not possible to cover all the conditions for eligibility or to give instructions for every situation. If you have carefully read all the information and still have questions, please contact your nearest INS office.

U.S. Department of Justice
Immigration and Naturalization Service (INS)

Petition for Alien Fiancé(e)

OMB No. 1115-0054

DO NOT WRITE IN THIS BLOCK

Case ID#	Action Stamp	Fee Stamp
A#		
G-28 or Volag#		

The petition is approved for status under Section 101(a)(15)(k) It is valid for four months from date of action

AMCON _____
☐ Personal Interview
☐ Document Check
☐ Field Investigations

☐ Previously Forwarded

REMARKS

A. Information about you

1. **Name** (Family name in CAPS) (First) (Middle)

2. **Address** (Number and Street) (Apartment Number)
   (Town or City) (State/Country) (ZIP/Postal Code)

3. **Place of Birth** (Town or City) (State/Country)

4. **Date of Birth** (Mo/Day/Yr)
5. **Sex** ☐ Male ☐ Female
6. **Marital Status** ☐ Married ☐ Single ☐ Widowed ☐ Divorced

7. **Other Names Used** (including maiden name)

8. **Social Security Number**
9. **Alien Registration Number** (if any)

10. **Names of Prior Husbands/Wives**   11. **Date(s) Marriages(s) Ended**

12. **If you are a U.S. citizen, complete the following:**
    My citizenship was acquired through (check one)
    ☐ Birth in the U S
    ☐ Naturalization
       Give number of certificate, date and place it was issued
    ☐ Parents
       Have you obtained a certificate of citizenship in your own name?
       ☐ Yes ☐ No
       If "Yes", give number of certificate, date and place it was issued

13. **Have you ever filed for this or any other alien fiancé(e) or husband/wife before?** ☐ Yes ☐ No
    If you checked "yes," give name of alien, place and date of filing, and result

---

B. Information about your alien fiancé(e)

1. **Name** (Family name in CAPS) (First) (Middle)

2. **Address** (Number and Street) (Apartment Number)
   (Town or City) (State/Country) (ZIP/Postal Code)

3. **Place of Birth** (Town or City) (State/Country)

4. **Date of Birth** (Mo/Day/Yr)
5. **Sex** ☐ Male ☐ Female
6. **Marital Status** ☐ Married ☐ Single ☐ Widowed ☐ Divorced

7. **Other Names Used** (including maiden name)

8. **Social Security Number**
9. **Alien Registration Number** (if any)

10. **Names of Prior Husbands/Wives**   11. **Date(s) Marriage(s) Ended**

12. **Has your fiancé(e) ever been in the U.S.?** ☐ Yes ☐ No

13. **If your fiancé(e) is currently in the U.S., complete the following:**
    He or she last arrived as a (visitor, student, exchange alien, crewman, stowaway, temporary worker, without inspection, etc)

    Arrival/Departure Record (I-94) Number   Date arrived (Month/Day/Year)

    Date authorized stay expired, or will expire, as shown on Form I-94 or I-95

I-129F

	INITIAL RECEIPT	RESUBMITTED	RELOCATED		COMPLETED		
			Rec'd	Sent	Approved	Denied	Returned

Form I-129F (REV. 10-7-87)N

B. (Continued) Information about your alien fiancé(e)

14. List all children of your alien fiancé(e) (if any)

(Name) (Date of Birth) (Country of Birth) (Present Address)

15. Address in the United States where your fiancé(e) intends to live

(Number and Street) (Town or City) (State)

16. Your fiancé(e)'s address abroad

(Number and Street) (Town or City) (Province) (Country) (Phone Number)

17. If your fiancé(e)'s native alphabet is other than Roman letters, write his or her name and address abroad in the native alphabet:

(Name) (Number and Street) (Town or City) (Province) (Country)

18. Your fiancé(e) is related to you. ☐ Yes ☐ No

If you are related, state the nature and degree of relationship, e.g., third cousin or maternal uncle, etc.

19. Your fiancé(e) has met and seen you. ☐ Yes ☐ No

Describe the circumstances under which you met. If you have not personally met each other, explain how the relationship was established, and explain in detail any reasons you may have for requesting that the requirement that you and your fiancé(e) must have met should not apply to you.

20. Your fiancé(e) will apply for a visa abroad at the American Consulate in _____

(City) (Country)

(Designation of a consulate outside the country of your fiancé(e)'s last residence does not guarantee acceptance for processing by that consulate. Acceptance is at the discretion of the designated consulate.)

C. Other Information

If you are serving overseas in the armed forces of the United States, please answer the following:

I presently reside or am stationed overseas and my current mailing address is _____

I plan to return to the United States on or about _____

PENALTIES: You may, by law be imprisoned for not more than five years, or fined $250,000, or both, for entering into a marriage contract for the purpose of evading any provision of the immigration laws and you may be fined up to $10,000 or imprisoned up to five years or both, for knowingly and willfully falsifying or concealing a material fact or using any false document in submitting this petition.

Your Certification

I am legally able to and intend to marry my alien fiancé(e) within 90 days of his or her arrival in the United States. I certify, under penalty of perjury under the laws of the United States of America, that the foregoing is true and correct. Furthermore, I authorize the release of any information from my records which the Immigration and Naturalization Service needs to determine eligibility for the benefit that I am seeking.

Signature _____ Date _____ Phone Number _____

Signature of Person Preparing Form if Other than Above

I declare that I prepared this document at the request of the person above and that it is based on all information of which I have any knowledge.

(Print Name) (Address) (Signature) (Date)

G-28 ID Number _____

Volag Number _____

U.S. Department of Justice
Immigration and Naturalization Service

FORM G-325A
BIOGRAPHIC INFORMATION

OMB No 1115-0066

(Family name)	(First name)	(Middle name)	☐ MALE ☐ FEMALE	BIRTHDATE (Mo-Day-Yr)	NATIONALITY	FILE NUMBER A
ALL OTHER NAMES USED (including names by previous marriages)			CITY AND COUNTRY OF BIRTH			SOCIAL SECURITY NO (If any)

	FAMILY NAME	FIRST NAME	DATE, CITY AND COUNTRY OF BIRTH (If known)	CITY AND COUNTRY OF RESIDENCE
FATHER				
MOTHER (Maiden name)				

HUSBAND (If none, so state) OR WIFE	FAMILY NAME (For wife, give maiden name)	FIRST NAME	BIRTHDATE	CITY & COUNTRY OF BIRTH	DATE OF MARRIAGE	PLACE OF MARRIAGE

FORMER HUSBANDS OR WIVES (if none, so state)

FAMILY NAME (For wife, give maiden name)	FIRST NAME	BIRTHDATE	DATE & PLACE OF MARRIAGE	DATE AND PLACE OF TERMINATION OF MARRIAGE

APPLICANT'S RESIDENCE LAST FIVE YEARS LIST PRESENT ADDRESS FIRST

STREET AND NUMBER	CITY	PROVINCE OR STATE	COUNTRY	FROM MONTH	FROM YEAR	TO MONTH	TO YEAR
						PRESENT TIME	

APPLICANT'S LAST ADDRESS OUTSIDE THE UNITED STATES OF MORE THAN ONE YEAR

STREET AND NUMBER	CITY	PROVINCE OR STATE	COUNTRY	FROM MONTH	FROM YEAR	TO MONTH	TO YEAR

APPLICANT'S EMPLOYMENT LAST FIVE YEARS (IF NONE, SO STATE) LIST PRESENT EMPLOYMENT FIRST

FULL NAME AND ADDRESS OF EMPLOYER	OCCUPATION (SPECIFY)	FROM MONTH	FROM YEAR	TO MONTH	TO YEAR
				PRESENT TIME	

Show below last occupation abroad if not shown above (Include all information requested above)

THIS FORM IS SUBMITTED IN CONNECTION WITH APPLICATION FOR ☐ NATURALIZATION ☐ STATUS AS PERMANENT RESIDENT ☐ OTHER (SPECIFY):	SIGNATURE OF APPLICANT	DATE
Are all copies legible? ☐ Yes	IF YOUR NATIVE ALPHABET IS IN OTHER THAN ROMAN LETTERS, WRITE YOUR NAME IN YOUR NATIVE ALPHABET IN THIS SPACE	

PENALTIES SEVERE PENALTIES ARE PROVIDED BY LAW FOR KNOWINGLY AND WILLFULLY FALSIFYING OR CONCEALING A MATERIAL FACT

APPLICANT: BE SURE TO PUT YOUR NAME AND ALIEN REGISTRATION NUMBER IN THE BOX OUTLINED BY HEAVY BORDER BELOW.

COMPLETE THIS BOX (Family name) (Given name) (Middle name) (Alien registration number)

Form G-325 A (Rev. 10-1-82)   (1) Ident.

U.S. Department of Justice
Immigration and Naturalization Service

OMB No 1115-0127
Petition to Employ Intracompany Transferee

DO NOT WRITE IN THIS BLOCK

Case ID #	Action Stamp	Fee Stamp
A #		
G-28 or Volage #		
Petition Validity Period		AMCON/POE _____ Remarks

A Information about this petition

1 This petition is being filed for (check one)
- ☐ Managerial Capacity
- ☐ Executive Capacity
- ☐ Specialized Knowledge Capacity

2 This petition is a (check appropriate boxes)
- ☐ New Petition   ☐ Individual
- ☐ Amended Petition ☐ Blanket

B Information about employer

1 Company Name

2 Address (Number and Street)

(Town or City)   (State/Country)   ZIP/Postal Code

3 Address where employee will work (if different)

4 IRS Employer ID Number

5 Date established and number of employees

6 Gross and Net annual income

7 Number of transfers to U S in past 12 months
Managers ____ Executives ____ Specialized Knowledge ____

8 Description of business (nature)

9 Have you filed an immigrant visa petition or application for permanent labor certification in the alien's behalf?
☐ No   ☐ Yes (if Yes, explain)

10 Have you filed any other nonimmigrant visa petition(s) on behalf of the beneficiary?
☐ No   ☐ Yes (if Yes, explain)

C Information about employee

1 Name (Family Name in CAPS)   (First)   (Middle)

2 Address (Number and Street)   (Apartment Number)

(Town or City)   (State/Country)   ZIP/Postal Code

3 Place of Birth (Town or City)   (State/Country)

4 Date of Birth (Month/Day/Year)   5 Country of Citizenship

6 Profession or occupation and years of experience

7 Social Security Number

8 Alien Registration Number

9 Address to which prospective employee will return

10 Sex   11 Marital Status
☐ Male   ☐ Married   ☐ Divorced
☐ Female   ☐ Widowed   ☐ Single

12 Dates of prior periods of stay in the U S for the past 6 years and type(s) of visa

D Information about the position offered

1 Job Title   Wages per week   Hours per week   Overtime rate

2 Other compensation (explain)   Valued at (dollars per week)   Dates of intended employment (Month/Day/Year)
From   To

3 Give a nontechnical description of the services the prospective employee is to perform

Initial Receipt	Resubmitted	Relocated		Completed		
		Received	Sent	Approved	Denied	Returned

Form I-129 L (01/14/87)

E. Information about the alien's employment

1. Name and address of alien's employer abroad

2. Dates of employment with this employer. Explain any interruptions in employment

3. Describe alien's job duties for the immediate prior year

4. Summarize alien's education and other work experience

F. Relationship between entities

1. The U.S. entity is, to the company abroad (check one),
   - ☐ The parent
   - ☐ A branch
   - ☐ A subsidiary
   - ☐ An affiliate
   - ☐ A 50/50 joint venture

2. Describe stock ownership and managerial control of each entity

3. Describe the entity abroad (nature of business, date established, product or service, number of employees, and gross annual income)

G. Employee's present status (Check the appropriate box below and give the information required for the box you checked.)

☐ 1. Prospective employee is outside the United States and will apply for a visa abroad at the following American Consulate.
(Name City and Country)

☐ 2. Prospective employee is exempt from the nonimmigrant visa requirement and will apply for admission at the following U.S. port of entry.
(Provide City and State)

☐ 3. Prospective employee is in the United States and is applying for change of nonimmigrant status. Form I-506 is attached

☐ 4. Employee is in the United States and is applying for an extension. Form I-539 is attached for each employee

Penalties. You may, by law, be fined up to $10,000 or imprisoned up to five year, or both, for knowingly and willfully falsifying or concealing a material fact or using any false document in submitting this petition.

Your Certification I certify, under penalty of perjury under the laws of the United States of America, that the foregoing is true and correct. Furthermore, I authorize the release of any informaiton from my records which the Immigration Service needs to determine eligibility for the benefit that I am seeking

Name (Type or print) | Title

Signature | Date | Phone Number

Certification of Person Preparing Form if Other than Above

I declare that I prepared this document at the request of the person above and that is is based on all information of which I have any knowledge

Name (Type or print) | Address

Signature | Date

G-28 ID Number

Volag Number

Petition to Employ Intracompany Transferee

Instructions

Please read these instructions carefully
If you do not follow the instructions, we may have to return your petition which may delay final action

General Information

As a United States or foreign employer, you may use this form (I-129L petition) to apply for L-1 nonimmigrant classification for a foreign employee to come temporarily to the United States as an intracompany transferee to continue employment with your organization or with a parent, branch, subsidiary, or affiliate of your organization if

- There is a qualifying relationship between your organization and the organization which employs the prospective employee,
- the employee has been employed abroad continuously for the immediate prior year by your organization or a parent, branch, or subsidiary of your organization,
- the employee s employment for the previous year was and intended employment in the U S will be in a managerial, executive, or specialized knowledge capacity, and
- the L classification is not being requested for the principal purpose of enabling the employee to enter the United States permanently in advance of a visa number

What are the types of L petitions?

A Individual - A petition to classify a foreign employee as an intracompany transferee to transfer temporarily to a qualifying organization in the United States from a qualifying organization abroad

B Blanket - A single petition to request advance approval of an organization, its parent, branches, subsidiaries and affiliates as qualifying organizations under section 101 (a) (15) (L) and, later, classification as intracompany transferees of multiple numbers of aliens employed by these entities as managers, executives, or specialized knowledge professionals

What requirements apply to documents?

A You must give INS certain documents with this form about the relationship between the organizations and about the prospective employee's employment Submit an original and one copy of this form and each document *Originals will be returned to you*

B If you do not wish to give INS the original document, you may give INS a copy The copy must be certified by

1) an INS or U S consular officer, or
2) an attorney admitted to practice law in the United States, or
3) an INS accredited representative (INS may still require originals)

C Documents in a foreign language must be accompanied by a complete English translation The translator must certify that the translation is accurate and that he or she is competent to translate

What documents do you need with an individual petition?

A Evidence of the qualifying relationship between the U S and foreign employer based on ownership and control, such as annual report, statement from organization's president or corporate secretary, articles of incorporation, and financial statements

B Letter from the prospective employee's employer abroad detailing his/her dates of employment, job duties, qualifications, and salary for at least the previous year

C If the petition indicates that the beneficiary is coming to open a new office in the United States, evidence that

1) sufficient physical premises to house the new office have been secured,
2) the beneficiary's prior year abroad was in an executive or managerial capacity and the proposed employment involves executive or managerial authority over the new operation,
3) the intended United States operation, within one year of approval of the petition, will support an executive or managerial position as defined in subparagraph (1)(ii)(A) or (B), supported by information regarding,

   - the proposed number of employees and the types of positions they will hold
   - the size of the United States investment and the financial ability of the foreign entity to remunerate the beneficiary and to commence doing business in the United States, and
   - the size and staffing levels of the foreign entity

D If the prospective employee is an owner or major stockholder of the company, evidence that the employee's services are to be used for a temporary period and evidence that the employee will be transferrred to an assignment abroad upon the completion of authorized services in the United States

E If a permanent labor certification has been approved or a preference petition has been filed for the prospective employee, evidence that you intend to use the employee's classification is not being requested to circumvent the normal wait for a visa number, such as

1) your prior history of use of foreign employees in temporary and permanent positions,
2) description of your established program for rotation of international personnel, and
3) description of operations and an appropriate position abroad to which the employee could be transferred at the end of the authorized stay

167

What documents do you need for a blanket petition?

A. Evidence that you meet the requirements to file a blanket petition by documenting that

   1) You and your parent, branches, subsidiaries, and affiliates are engaged in commercial trade or services, and
   2) you have an office in the United States that has been doing business for one year or more, and
   3) you have three or more domestic and foreign branches, subsidiaries, or affiliates, and
   4) you and the other qualifying organizations have obtained approved petitions for at least 10 "L" managers, executives, or specialized knowledge professionals during the previous 12 months, or have U S subsidiaries or affiliates with combined annual sales of at least 25 million dollars; or have a United States workforce of at least 1,000 employees.

B. Evidence of the qualifying relationship between you and the parent, branches, subsidiaries, and affiliates listed in the petition based on ownership and control, such as, annual report, audit statements, or statement from the president or corporate secretary of the parent corporation

How should you prepare this form?

A. Type or print legibly in ink

B. If you need extra space to complete any item, attach a continuation sheet, indicate the item number, and date and sign each sheet

C. Answer all questions fully and accurately If any item does not apply, please write "N/A"

Where should you file this form?

A. Individual petition - You should file this form with the INS office which has jurisdiction over the area of intended employment

B. Blanket petition - You should file this form with the INS office which has jurisdiction over the area where the organization's petitioner office in the United States is located

What is the fee?

You must pay $80 to file this form. *The fee will not be refunded, whether the petition is approved or not.* Do not mail cash All checks or money orders, whether U S or foreign, must be payable in U S currency at a financial institution in the United States. When a check is drawn on the account of a person other than yourself, write your name on the face of the check If the check is not honored, INS will charge you $5

Pay by check or money order in the exact amount Make the check or money order payable to "Immigration and Naturalization Service" However,

A. if you live in Guam Make the check or money order payable to "Treasurer, Guam", or

B. if you live in the U S Virgin Islands Make the check or money order payable to "Commissioner of Finance of the Virgin Islands"

What are the penalties for submitting false information?

Title 18, United States Code, Section 1001 states that whoever willfully and knowingly falsifies a material fact, makes a false statement, or makes use of a false document will be fined up to $10,000 or imprisoned up to five years, or both

What is our authority for collecting this information?

We request the information on this form to carry out the immigration laws contained in Title 8, United States Code, Section 1154 (a) We need this information to determine whether a person is eligible for immigration benefits The information you provide may also be disclosed to other federal, state, local, and foreign law enforcement and regulatory agencies during the course of the investigation required by this Service You do not have to give this information However, if you refuse to give some or all of it, your petition may be denied

It is not possible to cover all the conditions for eligibility or to give instructions for every situation. If you have carefully read all the instructions and still have questions, please contact your nearest INS office.

For sale by the Superintendent of Documents, U S Government Printing Office
Washington, DC 20402

U.S. Department of Justice
Immigration and Naturalization Service

Certificate of Eligibility for Nonimmigrant (M-1) Student Status - For Vocational Students *(OMB No 1115-0051)*

This page must be completed and signed in the U.S. by a designated school official.

1. Family name *(surname)*

   First *(given) name (do not enter middle name)*

   Country of birth:

   Date of birth (mo./day/year):

   Country of citizenship:

   Admission number *(complete if known)*

For Immigration Only Use

Visa issuing post | Date visa issued

Reinstated, extension granted to:

2. School *(school district)* name:

   School official *to be notified of student's arrival in U.S. (Name and Title)*

   School address *(include zip code)*:

   School code *(include 3-digit suffix, if any)* and approval date:

   _____ 214F _____ Approved on _____

3. This certificate is issued to the student named above for *(check and fill out as appropriate)*
   a. ☐ Initial attendance at this school.
   b. ☐ Continued attendance at this school.
   c. ☐ School transfer.
      Transferred from _____.
   d. ☐ Use by dependents for entering the United States.
   e. ☐ Other _____.

4. Level of education the student is pursuing or will pursue in the United States: *(Check only one)*
   a. ☐ High school   b. ☐ Other vocational school

5. The student named above has been accepted for a full course of study at this school, majoring in _____.
   The student is expected to report to the school not later than (date) _____ and complete studies not later than (date) _____ the normal length of study is

6. ☐ English proficiency is required:
   ☐ The student has the required English proficiency
   ☐ The student is not yet proficient, English instructions will be given at the school.
   ☐ English proficiency is not required because _____

7. This school estimates the student's average costs for an academic term of _____ (up to 12) months to be:
   a. Tuition and fees $ _____
   b. Living expenses $ _____
   c. Expenses of dependents $ _____
   d. Other (specify): $ _____
                      Total $ _____

8. This school has information showing the following as the student's means of support, estimated for an academic term of _____ months (Use the same number of months given in item 7).
   a. Students personal funds $ _____
   b. Funds from this school
      (specify type) $ _____
   c. Funds from another source
      (specify type and source) $ _____
                      Total $ _____

9. Remarks: _____
   _____
   _____

I-20M-N (SCHOOL) COPY

10. School Certification I certify under penalty of perjury that all information provided above in items 1 through 8 was completed before I signed this form and is true and correct, I executed this form in the United States after review and evaluation in the United States by me or other officials of the school of the student's application, transcripts or other records of courses taken and proof of financial responsibility which were received at the school prior to the execution of this form, the school has determined that the above named student's qualifications meet all standards for admission to the school, the student will be required to pursue a full course of study as defined by 8 CFR 214.2(f)(6), I am a designated official of the above named school and I am authorized to issue this form.

Signature of designated school official: | Name of designated school official & title *(print or type)* | Date and place issued *(city and state)*

11. Student Certification I have read and agreed to comply with the terms and conditions of my admission and those of any extension of stay as specified on page 2. I certify that all information provided on this form refers to me and is true and correct to the best of my knowledge I certify that I seek to enter or remain in the United States temporarily, and solely for the purpose of pursuing a full course of study at the school named on item 2 of this form I also authorized the named school to release any information from my records which is needed by the INS pursuant to 8 CFR 214 3(g).

Signature of student: | Name of student *(print or type)* | Date

Signature of parent or guardian *(if student is under 18)* | Name of parent or guardian *(print or type)* | Date

Address of parent or guardian: | *(street)* | *(city)* | *(state or province)* | *(county)*

Form I-20M-N/I-20ID Copy (Rev. 5-3-90)N

For official use only
Microfilm Index Number

INSTRUCTIONS TO STUDENTS

FORM I-20M-N/I20ID COPY The first time you enter the United States, you must present a Form I-20M-N/I-20ID Copy It will be returned to you endorsed with admission number You must have your Form I-20-ID Copy (pages 3 and 4 of Form I-20M-N) with you at all times You must not surrender it when you leave the United States Failure to have it with you when you apply to reenter the United States will delay your entry into the United States (If you lose your Form I-20ID Copy, you must request a new one, on Form I-102, from the Immigration and Naturalization Service office having jurisdiction over the school you were last authorized to attend.

ADMISSION. You must give this Form (I-20 M-N) to the American consular officer at the time you apply for a visa (unless you are exempt from visa requirements), and to immigration officer with evidence of ability to support yourself while pursuing a full course of study when you arrive in the United States If you are exempt from visa requirements, and you are applying for admission to the United States as an M-1 student, you must give the immigration officer this form and evidence of your ability to support yourself while pursuing a full course of study

SCHOOL If you are applying for entry to the United States for the first time after being issued an M-M-1 visa, you will not be admitted unless you plan to attend the school specified in that visa If, before you enter the United States, you decide to attend another school, you will present an I-20M-N from the new school to an American consular officer to have that school specified in your visa

EMPLOYMENT. You are not permitted to work except for practical training or to engage in business You may apply for permission to work for practical training only after completing the educational program Your alien spouse or child (M 2 classification) may not work in the United States

PERIOD OF STAY You are permitted to remain in the United States only while maintaining nonimmigrant student status You must also maintain a valid passport You may not stay longer than authorized on your Form I-20ID Copy unless you apply to the Immigration and Naturalization Service (on Form I-538 accompanied by my Form I-20ID Copy) for an extension, between 15 and 60 days before the date that your authorized stay expires You may stay while the application is being processed and if it is approved, until the expiration of the extension

SCHOOL TRANSFER You will not be granted permission to transfer to another school within six months of the date you first become an M-1 student, unless you are unable to remain at the school to which you are first admitted due to circumstances beyond your control. If you want to transfer to another school, you must apply on Form I-538 accompanied by your Form I-20ID Copy. The application must be submitted to the Immigration and Naturalization Service office having jurisdiction over the school from which you wish to transfer Sixty days after filing your application, you may attend the new school subject to approval or denial of your application Your application will be denied, however, if you have not been taking a full course of study at the school you were last authorized to attend

EDUCATIONAL OBJECTIVE You are not permitted to change your educational objective

REENTRY If you want to reenter the United States as a nonimmigrant student after a temporary absence, you must be in possession of the following (1) a valid student visa, (2) a valid passport and either a new Form I-20 M-N or your I-20ID Copy (pages 3 & 4 of the Form I-20 M-N) properly endorsed for reentry if the information on the I-20 ID Copy form is current

NOTICE OF ADDRESS. If you move, you must submit a notice within 10 days of your change of address to the Immigration and Naturalization Service on Form AR-11 (available at any INS office).

ARRIVAL/DEPARTURE When you depart from the United States, you must give your "Arrival Departure Record" (Form I-94) to a representative of the steamship or airline if you leave via a seaport or airport, to a Canadian immigration officer if you leave across the Canadian border, or to a United States immigration officer if you leave across the Mexican border However, you may keep your I-94 for reentering United States from Mexico or Canada, if you return to the U.S within 30 days.

PENALTY. If you do not register at the school named in your Form I-20M-N or If you stop attending school, or take less than a full course of study, or accept unauthorized employment, you fail to maintain your status and may be deported from the United States

INSTRUCTIONS TO THE SCHOOL

Failure to comply the law provides severe criminal penalties for you and your school for failure to comply with the regulations and instructions governing issuance of this form Failure to comply with 8CFR 214 3(K) may subject you and your school to criminal prosecution If you issue this form improperly, provide false information, or fail to submit required reports, the Immigration and Naturalization Service may withdraw its approval of your school for attendance by nonimmigrant students

It Is Your Responsibility

A   To complete Page 1 for any alien you have accepted for a full course of study in your school, if that person
- (1) Intends to apply for admission to the United States as a nonimmigrant under Section 101(a)(15)(M)(i) of the Immigration and Nationality Act (M-1 classification),
- (2) Is in the United States as a M-1 nonimmigrant and has applied for transfer to your school, or
- (3) Is in the United States and will apply to change his/her nonimmigrant classification to M-1

B   To endorse Page 4 of this form for any alien you have accepted for a full course of study in your school if that person
- (1) Is in the United States in M-1 classification and is departing temporarily from the United States, and there has been no change in the information in items 3, 4, 7, and/or 8 on Page 1 If there has been a change in items 3, 4, 7, and/or 8 on Page 1, a new Form I-20M-N/I-20 ID Copy must be issued for reentry after a temporary absence
- (2) Has a spouse or children who wish to join the student in the United States and acquire nonimmigrant (M-2) classification, and there has been no change in the information in items 7 and/or 8 on Page 1 If there has been a change in items 7 and/or 8 on Page 1, a new Form I-20 M-N/I-20 ID Copy must be issued

C   To establish that any student to whom you issue this form
- (1) Is able to pay all expenses incurred (and those of any dependents with the student) while in the United States
- (2) Meets all requirements for admission to your school If you want assistance in determining the student's proficiency in English, contact the Cultural Affairs Officer at the Embassy of the student's country

D   To be sure each Form I-20M-N/I-20 ID Copy is signed and issued in the United States by a designated school official of your school as defined in 8CFR 214 3(i)(1) A designated school official who may be authorized by the school to issue this form must be a regularly employed member of the school administration, whose office is located at the school and whose compensation does not come from commissions for recruitment of foreign students Individuals whose principal obligation to the school is to recruit foreign students for compensation may not be authorized to issue this form

E.   To endorse Page 4 of this form at least every six months when the student leaves the United States for a temporary absence, if the student will be enrolled in your school immediately after reentry

F   To retain all evidence which shows the scholastic ability and financial status on which admission was based, as long as the student is attending your school.

G   To comply with request from the Immigration and Naturalization Service for information concerning the student's immigration status

IF YOU NEED MORE INFORMATION CONCERNING YOUR M-1 NONIMMIGRANT STUDENT STATUS AND THE RELATING IMMIGRATION PROCEDURES, PLEASE CONTACT EITHER YOUR FOREIGN STUDENT ADVISOR ON CAMPUS OR A NEARBY IMMIGRATION AND NATURALIZATION SERVICE OFFICE.

This page, when properly endorsed, may be used for entry of the spouse and children of an M-1 Student following to join the student in the United States, or reentry of the student to attend the same school after a temporary absence from the United States

For reentry of the student and/or the M2 dependents *(Each Certification Signature is valid for six months)*

Signature of Designated School Official	Name School Official & Title *(Print or Type)*	Date
Signature of Designated School Official	Name School Official & Title *(Print or Type)*	Date
Signature of Designated School Official	Name School Official & Title *(Print or Type)*	Date
Signature of Designated School Official	Name School Official & Title *(Print or Type)*	Date
Signature of Designated School Official	Name School Official & Title *(Print or Type)*	Date
Signature of Designated School Official	Name School Official & Title *(Print or Type)*	Date

Dependent spouse and children of the M-1 student who are seeking entry/reentry to the U.S.

Name Family *(Caps)* First:	Date of Birth.	Country of birth.	Relationship to the M-1 Student:

Other Student Records:

Authority for collecting: Authority for collecting the information on this and related student forms is contained in 8 U S C 1101 and 1184. The information solicited will be used by the Department of State and the Immigration and Naturalization Service to determine eligibility for the benefits requested The law provides severe penalties for knowingly and willfully falsifying or concealing a material fact, or using any false document in the submission of this form

Reporting Burden: Public reporting burden for this collection of information is estimated to average 30 minutes per response, including the time for reviewing instructions, searching existing data sources, gathering and maintaining the data needed, and completing and reviewing the collection of information Send comments regarding this burden estimated or any other aspect of this collection of information, including suggestions for reducing this burden, to U S Department of Justice, Immigration and Naturalization Service (Room 2011), Washington, D C 20536, and to the Office of Management and Budget, Paperwork Reduction Project, OMB No 1115-0051, Washington, D C 20503

U.S DEPARTMENT OF LABOR
Employment and Training Administration

APPLICATION
FOR
ALIEN EMPLOYMENT CERTIFICATION

IMPORTANT READ CAREFULLY BEFORE COMPLETING THIS FORM
PRINT legibly in ink or use a typewriter. If you need more space to answer questions on this form, use a separate sheet. Identify each answer with the number of the corresponding question. SIGN AND DATE each sheet in original signature.

To knowingly furnish any false information in the preparation of this form and any supplement thereto or to aid, abet, or counsel another to do so is a felony punishable by $10,000 fine or 5 years in the penitentiary, or both (18 U.S.C. 1001).

PART A. OFFER OF EMPLOYMENT

1. Name of Alien *(Family name in capital letter, First, Middle, Maiden)*

2. Present Address of Alien *(Number, Street, City and Town, State ZIP Code or Province, Country)*

3. Type of Visa *(If in US)*

The following information is submitted as evidence of an offer of employment

4. Name of Employer *(Full name of organization)*

5. Telephone *(Area Code and Number)*

6. Address *(Number, Street, City or Town, Country, State, ZIP Code)*

7. Address Where Alien Will Work *(if different from item 6)*

8. Nature of Employer's Business Activity

9. Name of Job Title

10. Total Hours Per Week
    a. Basic | b. Overtime

11. Work Schedule (Hourly)
    a m
    p m

12. Rate of Pay
    a. Basic $ per ....
    b. Overtime $ per hour

13. Describe Fully the Job to be Performed *(Duties)*

14. State in detail the MINIMUM education, training, and experience for a worker to perform satisfactorily the job duties described in Item 13 above

15. Other Special Requirements

EDU-CATION *(Enter number of years)*	Grade School	High School	College	College Degree Required *(specify)*
				Major Field of Study

TRAIN-ING	No Yrs	No Mos.	Type of Training

EXPERI-ENCE	Job Offered Yrs	Mos	Related Occupation Yrs	Mos.	Related Occupation *(specify)*

16. Occupational Title of Person Who Will Be Alien's Immediate Supervisor

17. Number of Employees Alien will Supervise

ENDORSEMENTS *(Make no entry in section - for government use only)*

Date Forms Received	
L O	S O
R O	N O
Ind Code	Occ Code
Occ. Title	

Replaces MA 7-50A B and C (Apr 1970 edition) which is obsolete.

ETA 750 (Oct 1979)

18 COMPLETE ITEMS ONLY IF JOB IS TEMPORARY			19 IF JOB IS UNIONIZED (Complete)	
a No. of Openings To Be Filled By Aliens Under Job Offer	b. Exact Dates You Expect To Employ Alien		a. Number of Local	b Name of Local
	From	To		
				c. City and State

20 STATEMENT FOR LIVE-AT-WORK JOB OFFERS (Complete for Private Household Job ONLY)

a Description of Residence		b No Persons Residing at Place of Employment				c. Will free board and private room not shared with anyone be provided?	("X" one)
("X" one)	Number of Rooms	Adults	Children		Ages		
☐ House			BOYS				☐ YES ☐ NO
☐ Apartment			GIRLS				

21. DESCRIBE EFFORTS TO RECRUIT U.S. WORKERS AND THE RESULTS (Specify Sources of Recruitment by Name)

22. Applications require various types of documentation. Please read PART II of the instructions to assure that appropriate supporting documentation is included with your application.

23. EMPLOYER CERTIFICATIONS

By virtue of my signature below, I HEREBY CERTIFY the following conditions of employment.

a. I have enough funds available to pay the wage or salary offered the alien.

b. The wage offered equals or exceeds the prevailing wage and I guarantee that, if a labor certification is granted, the wage paid to the alien when the alien begins work will equal or exceed the prevailing wage which is applicable at the time the alien begins work

c. The wage offered is not based on commissions, bonuses, or other incentives, unless I guarantee a wage paid on a weekly, bi-weekly or monthly basis.

d. I will be able to place the alien on the payroll on or before the date of the alien's proposed entrance into the United States.

e. The job opportunity does not involve unlawful discrimination by race, creed, color, national origin, age, sex, religion, handicap, or citizenship.

f. The job opportunity is not:

(1) Vacant because the former occupant is on strike or is being locked out in the course of a labor dispute involving a work stoppage.

(2) At issue in a labor dispute involving a work stoppage.

g. The job opportunity's terms, conditions and occupational environment are not contrary to Federal, State or local law.

h. The job opportunity has been and is clearly open to any qualified U.S. worker.

24. DECLARATIONS

DECLARATION OF EMPLOYER ➤ *Pursuant to 28 U S C 1746, I declare under penalty of perjury the foregoing is true and correct*

SIGNATURE	DATE

NAME (Type or Print)	TITLE

AUTHORIZATION OF AGENT OF EMPLOYER ➤ *I HEREBY DESIGNATE the agent below to represent me for the purposes of labor certification and I TAKE FULL RESPONSIBILITY for accuracy of any representations made by my agent*

SIGNATURE OF EMPLOYER	DATE

NAME OF AGENT (Type or Print)	ADDRESS OF AGENT (Number, Street, City, State, ZIP Code)

PART B. STATEMENT OF QUALIFICATIONS OF ALIEN

FOR ADVICE CONCERNING REQUIREMENTS FOR ALIEN EMPLOYMENT CERTIFICATION: *If alien is in the U.S., contact nearest office of Immigration and Naturalization Service. If alien is outside U.S., contact nearest U.S. Consulate.*

IMPORTANT: READ ATTACHED INSTRUCTIONS BEFORE COMPLETING THIS FORM.

Print legibly in ink or use a typewriter. If you need more space to fully answer any questions on this form, use a separate sheet. Identify each answer with the number of the corresponding question. Sign and date each sheet.

1. Name of Alien *(Family name in capital letters)*   First name   Middle name   Maiden name

2. Present Address *(No., Street, City or Town, State or Province and ZIP Code)*   Country   3. Type of Visa *(If in US)*

4. Alien's Birthdate *(Month, Day, Year)*   5. Birthplace *(City or Town, State or Province)*   Country   6. Present Nationality or Citizenship *(Country)*

7. Address in United States Where Alien Will Reside

8. Name and Address of Prospective Employer If Alien has Job offer in U.S.   9. Occupation in which Alien is Seeking Work

10. "X" the appropriate box below and furnish the information required for the box marked

    a. ☐ Alien will apply for a visa abroad at the American Consulate in ——→   City in Foreign Country   Foreign Country

    b. ☐ Alien is in the United States and will apply for adjustment of status to that of a lawful permanent resident in the office of the Immigration and Naturalization Service at ——→   City   State

11. Names and Addresses of Schools, Colleges and Universities Attended *(Include trade or vocational training facilities)* | Field of Study | FROM Month Year | TO Month Year | Degrees or Certificates Received |
|---|---|---|---|
| | | | |
| | | | |
| | | | |
| | | | |

SPECIAL QUALIFICATIONS AND SKILLS

12. Additional Qualifications and Skills Alien Possesses and Proficiency in the use of Tools, Machines or Equipment Which Would Help Establish If Alien Meets Requirements for Occupation in Item 9.

13. List Licenses *(Professional, journeyman, etc.)*

14. List Documents Attached Which are Submitted as Evidence that Alien Possesses the Education, Training, Experience, and Abilities Represented

Endorsements   DATE REC. DOL

    O.T. & C.

(Make no entry in this section — FOR Government Agency USE ONLY)

(Items continued on next page)

15. WORK EXPERIENCE.
List all jobs held during past three (3) years. Also, list any other jobs related to the occupation for which the alien is seeking certification as indicated in item 9

a. NAME AND ADDRESS OF EMPLOYER

NAME OF JOB	DATE STARTED Month Year	DATE LEFT Month Year	KIND OF BUSINESS

DESCRIBE IN DETAILS THE DUTIES PERFORMED, INCLUDING THE USE OF TOOLS, MACHINES, OR EQUIPMENT	NO OF HOURS PER WEEK

b. NAME AND ADDRESS OF EMPLOYER

NAME OF JOB	DATE STARTED Month Year	DATE LEFT Month Year	KIND OF BUSINESS

DESCRIBE IN DETAIL THE DUTIES PERFORMED, INCLUDING THE USE OF TOOLS, MACHINES, OR EQUIPMENT	NO OF HOURS PER WEEK

c. NAME AND ADDRESS OF EMPLOYER

NAME OF JOB	DATE STARTED Month Year	DATE LEFT Month Year	KIND OF BUSINESS

DESCRIBE IN DETAIL THE DUTIES PERFORMED, INCLUDING THE USE OF TOOLS, MACHINES, OR EQUIPMENT	NO OF HOURS PER WEEK

16. DECLARATIONS

DECLARATION OF ALIEN ▶▶ Pursuant to 28 U S C 1746 I declare under penalty of perjury the foregoing is true and correct

SIGNATURE OF ALIEN	DATE

AUTHORIZATION OF AGENT OF ALIEN ▶▶ I hereby designate the agent below to represent me for the purposes of labor certification and I take full responsibility for accuracy of any representations made by my agent

SIGNATURE OF ALIEN	DATE

NAME OF AGENT (Type or print)	ADDRESS OF AGENT (No, Street, City, State, ZIP Code)

ITEMIZED INSTRUCTIONS FOR COMPLETING FORM ETA 750

PART A. OFFER OF EMPLOYMENT *(To be completed by Employer)*.

Item 1. *Name of Alien.* Enter full name exactly as it appears on Part B, "Statement of Qualifications of Alien."

Item 2. *Present Address of Alien.* Enter whether in the United States or abroad.

Item 3. *Type of Visa.* If the alien is in the United States, enter the type of visa held, i.e., B-2 (visitor), F-1 (student), or current status as shown on INS Form I-94.

Item 4. *Name of Employer.* Enter full name of business, firm, or organization, or if an individual, enter name used for legal purposes on documents.

Item 5. *Telephone Number.* In job offers for private households, enter a business and home telephone number when all adults are employed.

Item 6. *Address of Employer.* Self explanatory.

Item 7. *Address Where Alien Will Work.* Enter the full address of site or location where the work will actually be performed, if different from the address in Item 6.

Item 8. *Nature of Employer's Business.* Enter a brief, non-technical description, i.e., retail store, household, university, financial institution.

Item 9. *Name of Job Title.* Enter the common name or payroll title of the job being offered.

Item 10. *Total Hours Per Week.* Enter the basic hours of work required per week and overtime hours per week in accordance with State or Federal law for the work and locality.

Item 11. *Work Schedule.* Show the daily work schedule for the job, i.e., 9 a.m. to 5 p.m., 7 a.m. to 11 a.m. and 4 p.m. to 8 p.m.

Item 12. *Rate of Pay.* Enter a guaranteed wage and the unit of pay, such as $5.00 per hour, $850 per month, or $12,500 per year. Wage offered cannot be based on commission, bonuses, or other incentives, unless the employer guarantees a wage paid on a weekly, bi-weekly, or monthly basis.

Item 13. *Job Duties.* Describe the job duties, in detail what would be performed by any worker filling the job. Specify equipment used and pertinent working conditions.

Item 14. *Minimum Education, Training, and Experience Required to Perform the Job Duties.* Do not duplicate the time requirements. For example, time required in training should not also be listed in education or experience. Indicate whether months or years are required. Do not include restrictive requirements which are not actual business necessities for performance of the job and which would limit consideration of otherwise qualified U.S. workers.

Item 15. *Other Special Requirements.* Enter the job-related requirements. Examples are shorthand and typing speeds, specific foreign language proficiency, test results. Document business necessity for a foreign language requirement.

Item 16. *Occupational Title of Person Who Will Supervise Alien.* Self explanatory.

Item 17. *Number of Employees Alien Will Supervise.* Self explanatory.

Item 18. *Complete Only if Job is Temporary.* Does not apply for offers of permanent employment.

Item 19. *If the Job is Unionized.* Enter the number of the local, the name of the union, and the City and State in which the local has its main office.

Item 20. *Statement of Live-At-Work Job Offers in Private Households. (Do not complete for other job offers).*

20(a). *Description of Residence.* Self explanatory.

20(b). *Number of Persons Residing at Place of Employment.* Enter the number of adults, children under 18 years old, their sex and specific ages of children.

20(c). *Room and Board.* Self explanatory.

Item 21. *Recruitment Efforts.* Describe in detail efforts to recruit U.S. workers for the job opportunity and the results. List sources of recruitment by name, i.e., Lane Technical School, the Daily Tribune Newspaper, Scientific Journal of America. Specify the number of applicants interviewed from each source and the lawful job-related reasons why they were not hired.

Item 22. Read the GENERAL INSTRUCTIONS for additional supporting documentation which must be submitted, in separate attachments, along with this application. General Instructions will provide information that may be required. Documentation for Schedule A may be found in Part II. Department of Labor regulations require that an employer submit documentation to clearly show that the job offer and the recruitment of U.S. workers are in compliance with regulations. In addition, special documentation is required for certain occupational groups.

Item 23. *Employer Certifications.* Read carefully. The employer certifies to these eight (8) conditions of employment by signing the form.

Item 24. *Employer Declaration.* All copies of this form must bear the original signature of the employer or the employer's duly authorized representative with hiring authority. False statements are subject to Federal perjury and fraud penalties. The authorization of agent is completed only when the employer designates an agent to represent the employer in applying for labor certification. It is recommended that the employer not sign a blank form, since the employer takes full responsibility for any representations of its agent.

PART B. STATEMENT OF QUALIFICATIONS OF ALIEN *(To be completed by the Alien)*

Item 1. *Name of Alien.* Self explanatory.

Item 2. *Present Address.* Enter the address where the alien currently resides, whether in the United States or abroad.

Item 3. *Type of Visa.* If alien is in the United States, specify the type of visa now held, i.e., B-2 (visitor), F-1 (student), etc., or the alien's current status as shown on INS Form I-94.

Item 4. *Alien's Birthdate.* Do not use number for the months. Write out, e.g., March 21, 1942.

Item 5. *Birthplace.* Self explanatory.

Item 6. *Present Nationality or Citizenship of Alien.* Enter the country of which alien is currently a national or citizen.

Item 7. *Address in U.S. Where Alien Will Reside.* Self explanatory.

Item 8. *Name and Address of Prospective Employer.* Enter the business name and address.

Item 9. *Occupation in Which Alien is Seeking Work.* Acceptable entries are physicist, bricklayer, registered nurse. Entries such as "construction work" or "scientific research" are not acceptable.

Item 10. *Self explanatory.*

Item 11. *Education Training.* Identify all educational facilities; including trade or vocational schools, attended by alien, which give evidence of the alien's education and training related to the occupation listed in Item 9.

Item 12. *Additional Qualifications and Skills.* Entries should relate to the occupation listed in Item 9 and should help establish the alien's qualifications for working in that occupation. Appropriate entries include any unusual occupational knowledge or abilities such as the ability to speak, read, and write languages other than the language of the alien's native country.

Item 13. *Licenses.* List licenses held by the alien which give evidence of proficiency in a profession, trade, or occupation.

Item 14. *Documentation.* List any documents submitted with this form as evidence of the alien's qualifications. These may include statements from past employers, diplomas, and educational or training certificates.

Item 15. *Work Experience.* Job descriptions should include specific details of the work performed, with emphasis on skills and knowledge required, services rendered, managerial or supervisory functions performed, materials or products handled, and machines, tools, and equipment used or operated.

Item 16. *Declarations.* All copies of this form must bear the alien's original signature. If an agent is involved, the alien must complete the authorization of agent and take full responsibility for any representations the agent makes on behalf of the alien. It is recommended that the alien not sign a blank form.

U S GOVERNMENT PRINTING OFFICE 1980 O—329-045

For sale by the Superintendent of Documents U S Government Printing Office
Washington D C 20402 (per 100)

U.S. Department of Justice
Immigration and Naturalization Service

OMB #1115-0081
Immigrant Petition by Alien Entrepreneur

INSTRUCTIONS

Purpose of This Form.
This form is for use by an entrepreneur to petition for status as an immigrant to the U.S.

Who May File.
You may file this petition for yourself if you have established a new commercial enterprise

- in which you will engage in a managerial or policy-making capacity, and
- in which you have invested or are actively in the process of investing the amount required for the area in which the enterprise is located, and
- which will benefit the U S economy, and
- which will create full-time employment in the U.S. for at least 10 U.S. citizens, permanent residents, or other immigrants authorized to be employed, other than yourself, your spouse, your sons or daughters, or any nonimmigrant aliens.

The establishment of a new commercial enterprise may include:
- creation of a new business;
- the purchase of an existing business with simultaneous or subsequent restructuring or reorganization resulting in a new commercial enterprise; or
- the expansion of an existing business through investment of the amount required, so that a substantial change (at least 40%) in either the net worth, number of employees, or both, results.

The amount of investment required in a particular area is set by regulation. Unless adjusted downward for targeted areas or upward for areas of high employment, the figure shall be $1,000,000. You may obtain this information from an INS office or American consulate.

General Filing Instructions.
Please answer all questions by typing or clearly printing in black ink Indicate that an item is not applicable with "N/A". If an answer to a question is "none," please so state. If you need extra space to answer any item, attach a sheet of paper with your name and your A#, if any, and indicate the number of the item. Your petition must be properly signed and filed with the correct fee

Initial Evidence Requirements.
The following evidence must be filed with your petition
- Evidence that you have established a lawful business entity under the laws of the jurisdiction in the U S in which it is located, or, if you have made an investment in an existing business, evidence that your investment has caused a substantial (at least 40%) increase in the net worth of the business, the number of employees, or both Such evidence shall consist of copies of articles of incorporation, certificate of merger or consolidation, partnership agreement, certificate of limited partnership, joint venture agreement, business trust agreement, or other similar organizational document, a certificate evidencing authority to do business in a state or municipality or if such is not required, a statement to that effect, or evidence that the required amount of capital has been transferred to an existing business resulting in a substantial increase in the net worth or number of employees, or both. This evidence must be in the form of stock purchase agreements, investment agreements, certified financial reports, payroll records or other similar instruments, agreements or documents evidencing the investment and the resulting substantial change.
- Evidence, if applicable, that your enterprise has been established in a targeted employment area. A targeted employment area is defined as a rural area or an area which has experienced high unemployment of at least 150% of the national average rate. A rural area is an area not within a metropolitan statistical area or not within the outer boundary of any city or town having a population of 20,000 or more.
- Evidence that you have invested or are actively in the process of investing the amount required for the area in which the business is located Such evidence may include, but not be limited to copies of bank statements, evidence of assets which have been purchased for use in the enterprise, evidence of property transferred from abroad for use in the enterprise, evidence of monies transferred or committed to be transferred to the new commercial enterprise in exchange for shares of stock, any loan or mortgage, promisory note, security agreement, or other evidence of borrowing which is secured by assets of the petitioner
- Evidence that capital is obtained through lawful means, the petition must be accompanied, as applicable, by: Foreign business registration records, tax returns of any kind filed within the last five years in or outside the United States, evidence of other sources of capital, or certified copies of any judgment, pending governmental civil or criminal actions, or private civil actions against the petitioner from any court in or outside the United States within the past fifteen years
- Evidence that the enterprise will create at least 10 full-time positions for U S citizens, permanent residents, or aliens lawfully authorized to be employed (except yourself, your spouse, sons, or daughters, and any nonimmigrant aliens). Such evidence may consist of copies of relevant tax records, Form I-9, or other similar documents, if the employees have already been hired, or a business plan showing when such employees will be hired within the next two years.
- Evidence that you are or will be engaged in the management of the enterprise, either through the exercise of day-to-day managerial control or through policy formulation Such evidence may include a statement of your position title and a complete description of your duties, evidence that you are a corporate officer or hold a seat on the board of directors, or if the new enterprise is a partnership, evidence that you are engaged in either direct management or policy-making activities.

Form I-526 (Rev 12-2-91)

Copies.
If these instructions state that a copy of a document may be filed with this application, and you choose to send us the original, we may keep that original for our records

Where to File.
The petition must be filed with the INS Service Center having jurisdiction over the area in which the new commercial enterprise will be principally doing business.

If the enterprise is in Alabama, Connecticut, Delaware, District of Columbia, Florida, Georgia, Maine, Maryland, Massachusetts, New Hampshire, New Jersey, New York, North Carolina, Pennsylvania, Puerto Rico, Rhode Island, South Carolina, Vermont, Virgin Islands, Virginia, or West Virginia, mail this petition to USINS, Eastern Service Center, 75 Lower Welden Street, St Albans, VT 05479-0001.

If the enterprise is in Arizona, California, Guam, Hawaii, or Nevada, mail this petition to USINS, Western Service Center, P.O. Box 30040, Laguna Nigel, CA 92607-0040.

If the enterprise is elsewhere in the U S., mail this petition to USINS, Northern Service Center, 100 Centennial Mall North, Room, B-26, Lincoln, NE 68508.

Fee.
The fee for this petition is $140.00 The fee must be submitted in the exact amount. It cannot be refunded DO NOT MAIL CASH All checks and money orders must be drawn on a bank or other institution located in the United States and must be payable in United States currency. The check or money order should be made payable to the Immigration and Naturalization Service, except that:
- If you live in Guam, and are filing this application in Guam, make your check or money order payable to the "Treasurer, Guam."
- If you live in the Virgin Islands, and are filing this application in the Virgin Islands, make your check or money order payable to the "Commissioner of Finance of the Virgin Islands."

Checks are accepted subject to collection An uncollected check will render the application and any document issued invalid. A charge of $5.00 will be imposed if a check in payment of a fee is not honored by the bank on which it is drawn.

Processing Information.
Acceptance. Any petition that is not signed or is not accompanied by the correct fee will be rejected with a notice that it is deficient. You may correct the deficiency and resubmit the petition. However, a petition is not considered properly filed until accepted by the Service. A priority date will not be assigned until the petition is properly filed.

Initial processing. Once the petition has been accepted, it will be checked for completeness, including submission of the required initial evidence. If you do not completely fill out the form, or file it without required initial evidence, you will not establish a basis for eligibility, and we may deny your petition.

Requests for more information or interview. We may request more information or evidence or we may request that you appear at an INS office for an interview We may also request that you submit the originals of any copy. We will return these originals when they are no longer required

Approval. If you have established that you qualify for investor status, the petition will be approved If you have requested that the petition be forwarded to an American consulate abroad, the petition will be sent there unless that consulate does not issue immigrant visas. If you are in the U.S and state that you will apply for adjustment of status, and the evidence indicates that you are not eligible for adjustment, the petition will be sent to an American consulate abroad You will be notified in writing of the approval of the petition and where it has been sent, and the reason for sending it to a place other than the one requested, if applicable

Meaning of petition approval. Approval of a petition shows only that you have established that you have made a qualifying investment. It does not guarantee that the American Consulate will issue the immigrant visa There are other requirements which must be met before a visa can be issued. The American Consulate will notify you of those requirements. Immigrant status granted based on this petition will be conditional. Two years after entry the conditional investor will have to apply for the removal of conditions based on the ongoing nature of the investment.

Denial. If you have not established that you qualify, the petition will be denied You will be notified in writing of the reasons for the denial.

Penalties.
If you knowingly and willfully falsify or conceal a material fact or submit a false document with this request, we will deny the benefit you are filing for, and may deny any other immigration benefit. In addition, you will face severe penalties provided by law, and may be subject to criminal prosecution.

Privacy Act Notice.
We ask for the information on this form, and associated evidence, to determine if you have established eligibility for the immigration benefit you are filing for. Our legal right to ask for this information is in 8 USC 1184, 1255 and 1258. We may provide this information to other government agencies. Failure to provide this information, and any requested evidence, may delay a final decision or result in denial of your request.

Paperwork Reduction Act Notice.
We try to create forms and instructions that are accurate, can be easily understood, and which impose the least possible burden on you to provide us with information. Often this is difficult because some immigration laws are very complex. Accordingly, the reporting burden for this collection of information is computed as follows: (1) learning about the law and form, 15 minutes; (2) completing the form, 25 minutes; and (3) assembling and filing the application, 35 minutes, for an estimated average of 1 hour and 15 minutes per response. If you have comments regarding the accuracy of this estimate, or suggestions for making this form simpler, you can write to both the Immigration and Naturalization Service, 425 I Street, N.W., Room 5304, Washington, D C. 20536, and the Office of Management and Budget, Paperwork Reduction Project, OMB No. 1115-0081, Washington, D.C. 20503.

Form I-526 (Rev 12-2-91)

U.S. Department of Justice
Immigration and Naturalization Service

OMB No. 1115-0081
Immigrant Petition by Alien Entrepreneur

START HERE - Please Type or Print

Part 1. Information about you.

Family Name	Given Name	Middle Initial

Address - In Care of:

Street # and Name	Apt #

City or town	State or Province

Country	Zip or Postal Code

Date of Birth (month/day/year)	Country of Birth

Social Security #	A#

If in the U.S.
Date of Arrival (month/day/year)	I-94#
Current Nonimmigrant Status	Expires on (month/day/year)

Part 2. Application Type (check one).

a. ☐ This petition is based on an investment in a commercial enterprise in a targeted employment area for which the required amount of capital invested has been adjusted downward.

b. ☐ This petition is based on an investment in a commercial enterprise in an area for which the required amount of capital invested has been adjusted upward

b. ☐ This petition is based on an investment in a commercial enterprise which is not in either a targeted area or in an upward adjustment area.

Part 3. Information about your investment.

Name of Commercial Enterprise Invested In

Street Address

Phone #	Business Organized as (Corporation, partnership, etc.)

Kind of Business
(Example Furniture Manufacturer)

Date established (month/day/year)	IRS Tax #

Date of your initial Investment(month/day/year)	Amount of your Initial Investment $

Your total Capital Investment in Enterprise to date $	% of Enterprise you own

If you are not the sole investor in the new commercial enterprise, list on separate paper the names of all other parties (natural and non-natural) who hold a percentage share of ownership of the new enterprise and indicate whether any of these parties is seeking classifications as an alien entrepreneur Include the name, percentage of ownership and whether or not the person is seeking classification under section 203(b)(5).

If you indicated in Part 2 that the enterprise was in a targeted employment area or in an upward adjustment area, give the location at right.   County   State

Form I-526 (Rev. 12-2-91)   *Continued on back.*

FOR INS USE ONLY

Returned	Receipt
Resubmitted	
Reloc Sent	
Reloc Rec'd	
☐ Applicant Interviewed	

Action Block

To Be Completed by Attorney or Representative, if any
☐ Fill in box if G-28 is attached to represent the applicant

VOLAG#

ATTY State License #

Part 4. Additional Information about the enterprise.

Type of enterprise (check one):
- ☐ new commercial enterprise resulting from the creation of a new business
- ☐ new commercial enterprise resulting from the reorganization of an existing business
- ☐ new commercial enterprise resulting from a capital investment in an existing business

Assets:
Total amount in U.S. bank account	$ _____
Total value of all assets purchased for use in the enterprise	$ _____
Total value of all property transferred from abroad to the new enterprise	$ _____
Total of all debt financing	$ _____
Total stock purchases	$ _____
Other (explain on separate paper)	$ _____
Total	$ _____

Income:
- When you made investment   Gross $ _____   Net $ _____
- Now   Gross $ _____   Net $ _____

Net worth
- When you made investment $ _____   Now $ _____

Part 5. Employment creation information.

# of full-time employees in Enterprise in U.S. (excluding you, spouse, sons & daughters)

When you made your initial investment _____   Now _____   Difference _____

How many of these new jobs were created by your investment? _____   How many additional new jobs will be created by your additional investment? _____

What is your position, office or title with the new commercial enterprise? _____

Briefly describe your duties, activities and responsibilities _____

Your Salary _____   Cost of Benefits _____

Part 6. Processing Information.

Below give the U S Consulate you want notified if this petition is approved and if any requested adjustment of status cannot be granted.

American Consulate.   City _____   Country _____

If you gave a U S address in Part 1, print your foreign address below. If your native alphabet does not use Roman letters, print your name and foreign address in the native alphabet

Name   **Foreign Address**

Is an application for adjustment of status attached to this petition?	☐ yes	☐ no
Are you in exclusion or deportation proceedings?	☐ yes (If yes, explain on separate paper)	☐ no
Have you ever worked in the U S without permission?	☐ yes (explain on separate paper)	☐ no

Part 7. Signature. *Read the information on penalties in the instructions before completing this section*

I certify under penalty of perjury under the laws of the United States of America that this petition, and the evidence submitted with it, is all true and correct. I authorize the release of any information from my records which the Immigration and Naturalization Service needs to determine eligibility for the benefit I am seeking

Signature _____   Date _____

Please Note: *If you do not completely fill out this form, or fail to submit required documents listed in the instructions, you may not be found eligible for the requested document and this application may be denied*

Part 8. Signature of person preparing form if other than above. *(Sign below)*

I declare that I prepared this application at the request of the above person and it is based on all information of which I have knowledge

Signature _____   Print Your Name _____   Date _____

Firm Name and Address _____

Form I-526 (Rev 12-2-91)

U.S. Department of Justice
Immigration and Naturalization Service

OMB No. 1115-0061
Immigrant Petition for Alien Worker

Purpose Of This Form.
This form is used to petition for an immigrant based on employment

Who May File.
Any person may file this petition in behalf of an alien who:
- has extraordinary ability in the sciences, arts, education, business, or athletics, demonstrated by sustained national or international acclaim, whose achievements have been recognized in the field, or
- is claiming exceptional ability in the sciences, arts, or business, and is seeking an exemption of the requirement of a job offer in the national interest

A U.S. employer may file this petition who wishes to employ:
- an outstanding professor or researcher, with at least 3 years of experience in teaching or research in the academic area, who is recognized internationally as outstanding,
  - in a tenured or tenure-track position at a university or institution of higher education to teach in the academic area,
  - in a comparable position at a university or institution of higher education to conduct research in the area, or
  - in a comparable position to conduct research for a private employer who employs at least 3 persons in full-time research activities and has achieved documented accomplishments in an academic field,
- an alien who, in the 3 years preceding the filing of this petition, has been employed for at least 1 year by a firm or corporation or other legal entity and who seeks to enter the U.S. to continue to render services to the same employer or to a subsidiary or affiliate in a capacity that is managerial or executive;
- a member of the professions holding an advanced degree or an alien with exceptional ability in the sciences, arts, or business who will substantially benefit the national economy, cultural or educational interests, or welfare of the U.S.;
- a skilled worker (requiring at least 2 years of specialized training or experience in the skill)- to perform labor for which qualified workers are not available in the U.S,
- a member of the professions with a baccalaureate degree, or
- an unskilled worker to perform labor for which qualified workers are not available in the U.S

General Filing Instructions.
Please answer all questions by typing or clearly printing in black ink. Indicate that an item is not applicable with "N/A". If an answer to a question is "none," write "none". If you need extra space to answer any item, attach a sheet of paper with your name and your A#, if any, and indicate the number of the item to which the answer refers. You must file your petition with the required Initial Evidence. Your petition must be properly signed and filed with the correct fee

Initial Evidence.
If you are filing for an alien of extraordinary ability in the sciences, arts, education, business, or athletics, you must file your petition with
- evidence of a one-time achievement (i.e., a major, internationally-recognized award), or
- at least three of the following:
  - receipt of lesser nationally or internationally recognized prizes or awards for excellence in the field of endeavor,
  - membership in associations in the field which require outstanding achievements as judged by recognized national or international experts,
  - published material about the alien in professional or major trade publications or other major media,
  - participation on a panel or individually as a judge of the work of others in the field or an allied field,
  - original scientific, scholarly, artistic, athletic, or business-related contributions of major significance in the field,
  - authorship of scholarly articles in the field, in professional or major trade publications or other major media,
  - display of the alien's work at artistic exhibitions or showcases,
  - evidence that the alien has performed in a leading or critical role for organizations or establishments that have a distinguished reputation,
  - evidence that the alien has commanded a high salary or other high remuneration for services, or
  - evidence of commercial successes in the performing arts, as shown by box office receipts or record, casette, compact disk, or video sales
- If the above standards do not readily apply to the alien's occupation, you may submit comparable evidence to establish the alien's eligibility.

A U.S. employer filing for an outstanding professor or researcher must file the petition with
- evidence of at least 2 of the following
  - receipt of major prizes or awards for outstanding achievement in the academic field,
  - membership in associations in the academic field, which require outstanding achievements of their members,
  - published material in professional publications written by others about the alien's work in the academic field,
  - participation on a panel or, individually, as the judge of the work of others in the same or an allied academic field,
  - original scientific or scholarly research contributions to the academic field,
  - authorship of scholarly books or articles, in scholarly journals with international circulation, in the academic field,
- evidence the beneficiary has at least 3 years of experience in teaching and/or research in the academic field, and
- if you are a university or other institution of higher education, a letter indicating that you intend to employ the beneficiary in a tenured or tenure-track position as a teacher or in a permanent position as a researcher in the academic field, or
- if you are a private employer, a letter indicating that you intend to employ the beneficiary in a permanent research position in the academic field, and evidence that you employ at least 3 full-time researchers and have achieved documented accomplishments in the field

A U.S. employer filing for a multinational executive or manager must file the petition with a statement which demonstrates that:
- if the alien is outside the U.S., he/she has been employed outside the U.S. for at least 1 year in the past 3 years in a managerial or executive capacity by a firm or corporation or other legal entity, or by its affiliate or subsidiary; or
- if the alien is already in the U.S. working for the same employer, or a subsidiary or affiliate of the firm or corporation or other legal entity, by which the alien was employed abroad, he/she was employed by the entity abroad in a managerial or executive capacity for at least one year in the 3 years preceding his/her entry as a nonimmigrant,
  - the prospective employer in the U.S. is the same employer or a subsidiary or affiliate of the firm or corporation or other legal entity by which the alien was employed abroad,
  - the prospective U.S. employer has been doing business for at least one year, and
  - the alien is to be employed in the U.S. in a managerial or executive capacity and describing the duties to be performed.

A U.S. employer filing for a member of the professions with an advanced degree or a person with exceptional ability in the sciences, arts, or business must file the petition with:
- a labor certification (see GENERAL EVIDENCE) and either
- an official academic record showing that the alien has a U.S. advanced degree or an equivalent foreign degree, or an official academic record showing that the alien has a U.S. baccalaureate degree or an equivalent foreign degree and letters from current or former employers showing that the alien has at least 5 years of progressive post-baccalaureate experience in the specialty, or
- at least 3 of the following:
  - an official academic record showing that the alien has a degree, diploma, certificate, or similar award from an institution of learning relating to the area of exceptional ability,
  - letters from current or former employers showing that the alien has at least 10 years of full-time experience in the occupation for which he/she is being sought,
  - a license to practice the profession or certification for a particular profession or occupation,
  - evidence that the alien has commanded a salary, or other remuneration for services, which demonstrates exceptional ability,
  - evidence of membership in professional associations; or
  - evidence of recognition for achievements and significant contributions to the industry or field by peers, governmental entities, or professional or business organizations
- If the above standards do not readily apply to the alien's occupation, you may submit comparable evidence to establish the alien's eligibility

A U.S. employer filing for a skilled worker must file the petition with
- a labor certification (see GENERAL EVIDENCE), and requirement is 2 years of training or experience)
- evidence that the alien meets the educational, training, or experience and any other requirements of the labor certification (the minimum requirement is 2 years of training or experience)

Form I 140 (Rev. 12 02 91)

A U.S. employer filing for a professional must file the petition with.
- a labor certification (see GENERAL EVIDENCE);
- evidence that the alien holds a U S baccalaureate degree or equivalent foreign degree, and
- evidence that a baccalaureate degree is required for entry into the occupation.

A U.S. employer filing for its employee in Hong Kong must file its petition with a statement that demonstrates that.
- the company is owned and organized in the United States
- the employee is a resident of Hong Kong;
- the company, or its subsidiary or affiliate, is employing the person in Hong Kong, and has been employing him or her there for the past 12 months, or the company, or its subsidiary or affiliate, is employing him or her outside of Hong Kong during a temporary absence (i e , of limited duration) and he or she had been employed in Hong Kong for 12 consecutive months prior to such absence(s), and that such employment is, and for that period has been, as an officer or supervisor, or in a capacity that is executive, managerial or involves specialized knowledge,
- the company employs at least 100 employees in the U.S. and at least 50 employees outside the U.S. and has a gross annual income of at least $50,000,000, and
- the company intends to employ the person in the United States as an officer or supervisor, or in a capacity that is executive, managerial or involves specialized knowledge, with salary and benefits comparable to others with similar responsibilities and experience within the company A specific job description is required for immediate immigration, a commitment to a qualifying job is required for deferred immigration.

A U.S. employer filing for an unskilled worker must file the petition with:
- a labor certification (see GENERAL EVIDENCE), and
- evidence that the beneficiary meets any education, training, or experience requirements required in the labor certification.

General Evidence.
Labor certification. Petitions for certain classifications must be filed with a certification from the Department of Labor or with documentation to establish that the alien qualifies for one of the shortage occupations in the Department of Labor's Labor Market Information Pilot Program or for an occupation in Group I or II of the Department of Labor's Schedule A. A certification establishes that there are not sufficient workers who are able, willing, qualified, and available at the time and place where the alien is to be employed and that employment of the alien if qualified, will not adversely affect the wages and working conditions of similarly employed U S workers. Application for certification is made on Form ETA-750 and is filed at the local office of the State Employment Service. If the alien is in a shortage occupation, or for a Schedule A/Group I or II occupation, you may file a fully completed, uncertified Form ETA-750 in duplicate with your petition for determination by INS that the alien belongs to the shortage occupation.

Translations. Any foreign language document must be accompanied by a full English translation which the translator has certified as complete and correct, and by the translator's certification that he or she is competent to translate from the foreign language into English.

Copies. If these instructions state that a copy of a document may be filed with this petition, and you choose to send us the original, we may keep that original for our records.

Where To File.
File this petition at the INS Service Center with jurisdiction over the place where the alien will be employed.

If the employment will be in Alabama, Connecticut, Delaware, District of Columbia, Florida, Georgia, Maine, Maryland, Massachusetts, New Hampshire, New Jersey, New York, North Carolina, Pennsylvania, Puerto Rico, Rhode Island, South Carolina, Vermont, the Virgin Islands, Virginia, or West Virginia, mail your petition to. USINS Eastern Service Center, 75 Lower Welden Street, St. Albans, VT 05479-0001.

If the employment will be in Arizona, California, Guam, Hawaii, or Nevada, mail your petition to USINS Western Service Center, P.O Box 30040, Laguna Niguel, CA 92607-0040.

If the employment will be elsewhere in the U S , mail your petition to. USINS Northern Service Center, 100 Centennial Mall North, Room, B-26, Lincoln, NE 68508

Fee.
The fee for this petition is $70.00. The fee must be submitted in the exact amount. It cannot be refunded DO NOT MAIL CASH All checks and money orders must be drawn on a bank or other institution located in the United States and must be payable in United States currency The check or money order should be made payable to the Immigration and Naturalization Service, except that:
- If you live in Guam, and are filing this application in Guam, make your check or money order payable to the "Treasurer, Guam."
- If you live in the Virgin Islands, and are filing this application in the Virgin Islands, make your check or money order payable to the "Commissioner of Finance of the Virgin Islands."

Checks are accepted subject to collection. An uncollected check will render the application and any document issued invalid. A charge of $5.00 will be imposed if a check in payment of a fee is not honored by the bank on which it is drawn.

Processing Information.
Acceptance. Any petition that is not signed or is not accompanied by the correct fee will be rejected with a notice that it is deficient. You may correct the deficiency and resubmit the petition. However, a petition is not considered properly filed until accepted by the Service. A priority date will not be assigned until the petition is properly filed.

Initial processing. Once the petition has been accepted, it will be checked for completeness, including submission of the required initial evidence If you do not completely fill out the form, or file it without required initial evidence, you will not establish a basis for eligibility, and we may deny your petition.

Requests for more information or interview. We may request more information or evidence or we may request that you appear at an INS office for an interview We may also request that you submit the originals of any copy. We will return these originals when they are no longer required.
Decision. If you have established eligibility for the benefit requested, your petition will be approved. If you have not established eligibility, your petition will be denied. You will be notified in writing of the decision on your petition.

Meaning of petition approval.
Approval of a petition means you have established that the person you are filing for is eligible for the requested classification. This is the first step towards permanent residence. However, this does not in itself grant permanent residence or employment authorization. You will be given information about the requirements for the person to receive an immigrant visa, or to adjust status, after your petition is approved.

Penalties.
If you knowingly and willfully falsify or conceal a material fact or submit a false document with this request, we will deny the benefit you are filing for, and may deny any other immigration benefit. In addition, you will face severe penalties provided by law, and may be subject to criminal prosecution.

Privacy Act Notice.
We ask for the information on this form, and associated evidence, to determine if you have established eligibility for the immigration benefit you are filing for Our legal right to ask for this information is in 8 USC 1185४. We may provide this information to other government agencies. Failure to provide this information, and any requested evidence, may delay a final decision or result in denial of your request

Paperwork Reduction Act Notice.
We try to create forms and instructions that are accurate, can be easily understood, and which impose the least possible burden on you to provide us with information Often this is difficult because some immigration laws are very complex. The estimated average time to complete and file this application is as follows. (1) 20 minutes to learn about the law and form, (2) 15 minutes to complete the form, and (3) 45 minutes to assemble and file the petition, for a total estimated average of 1 hour and 20 minutes per petition. If you have comments regarding the accuracy of this estimate, or suggestions for making this form simpler, you can write to both the Immigration and Naturalization Service, 425 I Street, N.W., Room 5304, Washington, D.C. 20536; and the Office of Management and Budget, Paperwork Reduction Project, OMB No. 1115-0061, Washington, D C. 20503.

U.S. Department of Justice
Immigration and Naturalization Service

OMB #1115-0061
Immigrant Petition for Alien Worker

START HERE - Please Type or Print

Part 1. Information about the person or organization filing this petition.

If an individual is filing, use the top Name line. Organizations should use the second line.

Family Name	Given Name	Middle Initial

Company or Organization:

Address - Attn

Street Number and Name		Room #
City	State or Province	
Country	ZIP/Postal Code	
IRS Tax #	Social Security #	

Part 2. Petition Type. This petition is being filed for: (check one)

a. ☐ An alien of extraordinary ability
b. ☐ An outstanding professor or researcher
c. ☐ A multinational executive or manager
d. ☐ A member of the professions holding an advanced degree or an alien of exceptional ability
e. ☐ A skilled worker (requiring at least two years of specialized training or experience) or professional
f. ☐ An employee of a U.S. business operating in Hong Kong
g. ☐ Any other worker (requiring less than two years training or experience)

Part 3. Information about the person you are filing for.

Family Name	Given Name	Middle Initial

Address - C/O

Street # and Name		Apt. #
City	State or Province	
Country	Zip or Postal Code	
Date of Birth (month/day/year)	Country of Birth	
Social Security # (if any)	A # (if any)	
If in the U.S.	Date of Arrival (month/day/year)	I-94#
	Current Nonimmigrant Status	Expires on (month/day/year)

Part 4. Processing Information.

Below give the U.S. Consulate you want notified if this petition is approved and if any requested adjustment of status cannot be granted.

U.S Consulate: City _____ Country _____

Form I-140 (Rev 12-2-91)   *Continued on back.*

FOR INS USE ONLY

Returned	Receipt
Resubmitted	
Reloc Sent	
Reloc Rec'd	

☐ Petitioner Interviewed
☐ Beneficiary Interviewed

Classification
☐ 203(b)(1)(A) Alien Of Extraordinary Ability
☐ 203(b)(1)(B) Outstanding Professor or Researcher
☐ 203(b)(1)(C) Multi-national executive or manager
☐ 203(b)(2) Member of professions w/adv degree or of exceptional ability
☐ 203(b)(3) (A) (i) Skilled worker
☐ 203(b)(3) (A) (ii) Professional
☐ 203(b)(3) (A) (iii) Other worker
☐ Sec 124 IMMACT-Employee of US business in Hong Kong

Priority Date	Consulate

Remarks

Action Block

To Be Completed by Attorney or Representative, if any
☐ Fill in box if G-28 is attached to represent the petitioner

VOLAG#

ATTY State License #

Part 4. Processing Information. *(continued)*

If you gave a U S. address in Part 3, print the person's foreign address below. If his/her native alphabet does not use Roman letters, print his/her name and foreign address in the native alphabet.

Name Address

Are you filing any other petitions or applications with this one?	☐ No	☐ yes attach an explanation
Is the person you are filing for in exclusion or deportation proceedings?	☐ No	☐ yes attach an explanation
Has an immigrant visa petition ever been filed by or in behalf of this person?	☐ No	☐ yes attach an explanation

Part 5. Additional Information about the employer.

Type of petitioner (check one) ☐ Self ☐ Individual U S Citizen ☐ Company or organization
 ☐ Permanent Resident ☐ Other explain _____

If a company, give the following.
Type of business

Date Established	Current # of employees	Gross Annual Income	Net Annual Income

If an individual, give the following:
Occupation Annual Income

Part 6. Basic Information about the proposed employment.

Job Title	Nontechnical description of job

Address where the person will work if different from address in Part 1.

Is this a full-time position?	☐ yes	☐ No (hours per week _____)	Wages per week

Is this a permanent position?	☐ yes ☐ No	Is this a new position? ☐ yes ☐ No

Part 7. Information on spouse and all children of the person you are filing for.

Provide an attachment listing the family members of the person you are filing for. Be sure to include their full name, relationship, date and country of birth, and present address.

Part 8. Signature. *Read the information on penalties in the instructions before completing this section*

I certify under penalty of perjury under the laws of the United States of America that this petition, and the evidence submitted with it, is all true and correct. I authorize the release of any information from my records which the Immigration and Naturalization Service needs to determine eligibility for the benefit I am seeking.

Signature Date

Please Note: If you do not completely fill out this form, or fail to submit required documents listed in the instructions, you cannot be found eligible for the requested document and this application may to be denied.

Part 9. Signature of person preparing form if other than above. *(Sign below)*

I declare that I prepared this application at the request of the above person and it is based on all information of which I have knowledge

Signature Print Your Name Date

Firm Name and Address

*U S GPO 1992-312-328/51143

Form I-140 (Rev. 12-2-91)

U.S. Department of Justice
Immigration and Naturalization Service INS

Petition for Alien Relative

Instructions

Read the instructions carefully. If you do not follow the instructions, we may have to return your petition, which may delay final action. If more space is needed to complete an answer continue on separate sheet of paper.

1. Who can file?

A citizen or lawful permanent resident of the United States can file this form to establish the relationship of certain alien relatives who may wish to immigrate to the United States. You must file a separate form for each eligible relative.

2. For whom can you file?

A. If you are a citizen, you may file this form for
   1) your husband, wife, or unmarried child under 21 years old
   2) your unmarried child over 21, or married child of any age
   3) your brother or sister if you are at least 21 years old
   4) your parent if you are at least 21 years old

B. If you are a lawful permanent resident you may file this form for
   1) your husband or wife
   2) your unmarried child

NOTE If your relative qualifies under instruction A(2) or A(3) above, separate petitions are not required for his or her husband or wife or unmarried children under 21 years old. If your relative qualifies under instruction B(2) above, separate petitions are not required for his or her unmarried children under 21 years old. These persons will be able to apply for the same type of immigrant visa as your relative.

3. For whom can you *not* file?.

You cannot file for people in the following categories

A. An adoptive parent or adopted child if the adoption took place after the child became 16 years old or if the child has not been in the legal custody and living with the parent(s) for at least two years

B. A natural parent if the United States citizen son or daughter gained permanent residence through adoption

C. A stepparent or stepchild, if the marriage that created this relationship took place after the child became 18 years old

D. A husband or wife, you were not both physically present at the marriage ceremony, and the marriage was not consummated

E. A husband or wife if you gained lawful permanent resident status by virtue of a prior marriage to a United States citizen or lawful permanent resident unless
   1) a period of five years has elapsed since you became a lawful permanent resident, OR
   2) you can establish by clear and convincing evidence that the prior marriage (through which you gained your immigrant status) was not entered into for the purpose of evading any provision of the immigration laws, OR
   3) your prior marriage (through which you gained your immigrant status) was terminated by the death of your former spouse

F. A husband or wife if he or she was in exclusion, deportation, rescission, or judicial proceedings regarding his or her right to remain in the United States when the marriage took place, unless such spouse has resided outside the United States for a two-year period after the date of the marriage

G. A husband or wife if the Attorney General has determined that such alien has attempted or conspired to enter into a marriage for the purpose of evading the immigration laws

H. A grandparent, grandchild, nephew, niece, uncle, aunt, cousin, or in-law

4. What documents do you need?

You must give INS certain documents with this form to show you are eligible to file. You must also give the INS certain documents to prove the family relationship between you and your relative

A. For each document needed, give INS the original and one copy. However, because it is against the law to copy a Certificate of Naturalization, a Certificate of Citizenship or an Alien Registration Receipt Card (Form I-151 or I-551), give INS the original only. **Originals will be returned to you.**

B. If you do not wish to give INS the original document, you may give INS a copy. The copy must be certified by
   1) an INS or U S consular officer, or
   2) an attorney admitted to practice law in the United States, or
   3) an INS accredited representative
   (INS may still require originals)

C) Documents in a foreign language must be accompanied by a complete English translation. The translator must certify that the translation is accurate and that he or she is competent to translate

5. What documents do you need to show you are a United States citizen?

A. If you were born in the United States, give INS your birth certificate

B. If you were naturalized, give INS your original Certificate of Naturalization

C. If you were born outside the United States, and you are a U S citizen through your parents, give INS
   1) your original Certificate of Citizenship, or
   2) your Form FS-240 (Report of Birth Abroad of a United States Citizen)

D. In place of any of the above, you may give INS your valid unexpired U S passport that was initially issued for at least 5 years

E. If you do not have any of the above and were born in the United States, see the instructions under 8, below "What if a document is not available?"

6. What documents do you need to show you are a permanent resident?

You must give INS your alien registration receipt card (Form I-151 or Form I-551). Do not give INS a photocopy of the card

7. What documents do you need to prove family relationship?

You have to prove that there is a family relationship between your relative and yourself

In any case where a marriage certificate is required, if either the husband or wife was married before, you must give INS documents to show that all previous marriages were legally ended. In cases where the names shown on the supporting documents have changed, give INS legal documents to show how the name change occurred (for example a marriage certificate, adoption decree, court order, etc.)

Find the paragraph in the following list that applies to the relative you are filing for

Form I-130 (Rev 5-4-89)Y

If you are filing for your

A **husband or wife,** give INS
1) your marriage certificate
2) a color photo of you and one of your husband or wife, taken within 30 days of the date of this petition. These photos must have a white background. They must be glossy, un-retouched, and not mounted. The dimension of the facial image should be about 1 inch from chin to top of hair in 3/4 frontal view, showing the right side of the face with the right ear visible. Using pencil or felt pen, lightly print name (and Alien Registration Number, if known) on the back of each photograph
3) a completed and signed Form G-325A (Biographic Information) for you and one for your husband or wife. Except for name and signature, you do not have to repeat on the G-325A the information given on your I-130 petition

B **child** and you are the **mother,** give the child's birth certificate showing your name and the name of your child

C **child** and you are the **father or stepparent,** give the child's birth certificate showing both parents' names and your marriage certificate. **Child** born out of wedlock and you are the **father,** give proof that a parent/child relationship exists or existed. For example, the child's birth certificate showing your name and evidence that you have financially supported the child. (A blood test may be necessary)

D **brother or sister,** your birth certificate and the birth certificate of your brother or sister showing both parents' names. If you do not have the same mother, you must also give the marriage certificates of your father to both mothers

E **mother,** give your birth certificate showing your name and the name of your mother

F **father,** give your birth certificate showing the names of both parents and your parents' marriage certificate

G **stepparent,** give your birth certificate showing the names of both natural parents and the marriage certificate of your parent to your stepparent

H **adoptive parent or adopted child,** give a certified copy of the adoption decree, the legal custody decree if you obtained custody of the child before adoption and a statement showing the dates and places you have lived together with the child

8. What if a document is not available?

If the documents needed above are not available, you can give INS the following instead. (INS may require a statement from the appropriate civil authority certifying that the needed document is not available.)

A Church record. A certificate under the seal of the church where the baptism, dedication, or comparable rite occurred within two months after birth, showing the date and place of child's birth, date of the religious ceremony, and the names of the child's parents

B School record. A letter from the authorities of the school attended (preferably the first school), showing the date of admission to the school, child's date and place of birth, and the names and places of birth of parents, if shown in the school records

C Census record. State or federal census record showing the name, place of birth, and date of birth or the age of the person listed

D Affidavits. Written statements sworn to or affirmed by two persons who were living at the time and who have personal knowledge of the event you are trying to prove, for example, the date and place of birth, marriage, or death. The persons making the affidavits need not be citizens of the United States. Each affidavit should contain the following information regarding the person making the affidavit: his or her full name, address, date and place of birth, and his or her relationship to you, if any, full information concerning the event, and complete details concerning how the person acquired knowledge of the event

9. How should you prepare this form?

A Type or print legibly in ink
B If you need extra space to complete any item, attach a continuation sheet, indicate the item number, and date and sign each sheet
C Answer all questions fully and accurately. If any item does not apply, please write "N/A"

10. Where should you file this form?

A If you live in the United States, send or take the form to the INS office that has jurisdiction over where you live
B If you live outside the United States, contact the nearest American Consulate to find out where to send or take the completed form

11. What is the fee?

You must pay $75.00 file this form. **The fee will not be refunded, whether the petition is approved or not.** DO NOT MAIL CASH. All checks or money orders, whether U.S. or foreign, must be payable in U.S. currency at a financial institution in the United States. When a check is drawn on the account of a person other than yourself, write your name on the face of the check. If the check is not honored, INS will charge you $5.00

Pay by check or money order in the exact amount. Make the check or money order payable to "Immigration and Naturalization Service". However,

A if you live in Guam. Make the check or money order payable to "Treasurer, Guam", or
B if you live in the U.S. Virgin Islands. Make the check or money order payable to "Commissioner of Finance of the Virgin Islands"

12. When will a visa become available?

When a petition is approved for the husband, wife, parent, or unmarried minor child of a United States citizen, these relatives do not have to wait for a visa number, as they are not subject to the immigrant visa limit. However, for a child to qualify for this category, all processing must be completed and the child must enter the United States before his or her 21st birthday

For all other alien relatives there are only a limited number of immigrant visas each year. The visas are given out in the order in which INS receives properly filed petitions. To be considered properly filed, a petition must be completed accurately and signed, the required documents must be attached, and the fee must be paid

For a monthly update on dates for which immigrant visas are available, you may call (202) 663-1514

13. What are the penalties for committing marriage fraud or submitting false information or both?

Title 8, United States Code, Section 1325 states that any individual who knowingly enters into a marriage contract for the purpose of evading any provision of the immigration laws shall be imprisoned for not more than five years, or fined not more than $250,000.00 or both

Title 18, United States Code, Section 1001 states that whoever willfully and knowingly falsifies a material fact, makes a false statement, or makes use of a false document will be fined up to $10,000 or imprisoned up to five years, or both

14. What is our authority for collecting this information?

We request the information on the form to carry out the immigration laws contained in Title 8, United States Code, Section 1154(a). We need this information to determine whether a person is eligible for immigration benefits. The information you provide may also be disclosed to other federal, state, local, and foreign law enforcement and regulatory agencies during the course of the investigation required by this Service. You do not have to give this information. However, if you refuse to give some or all of it, your petition may be denied

It is not possible to cover all the conditions for eligibility or to give instructions for every situation. If you have carefully read all the instructions and still have questions, please contact your nearest INS office.

U.S. Department of Justice (INS)   **Petition for Alien Relative**   OMB No 1115-0054

DO NOT WRITE IN THIS BLOCK — FOR EXAMINING OFFICE ONLY

Case ID#	Action Stamp	Fee Stamp
A#		
G-28 or Volag #		

Section of Law
- ☐ 201 (b) spouse   ☐ 203 (a)(1)
- ☐ 201 (b) child   ☐ 203 (a)(2)
- ☐ 201 (b) parent   ☐ 203 (a)(4)
- ☐ 203 (a)(5)

AM CON _____

REMARKS

Petition was filed on _____ (priority date)
- ☐ Personal Interview   ☐ Previously Forwarded
- ☐ Pet ☐ Ben "A" File Reviewed   ☐ Stateside Criteria
- ☐ Field Investigations   ☐ I-485 Simultaneously
- ☐ 204 (a)(2)(A) Resolved ☐ 204 (h) Resolved

A. Relationship

1. The alien relative is my:
   ☐ Husband/Wife ☐ Parent ☐ Brother/Sister ☐ Child
2. Are you related by adoption?   ☐ Yes   ☐ No
3. Did you gain permanent residence through adoption?   ☐ Yes   ☐ No

B. Information about you

1. Name (Family name in CAPS)   (First)   (Middle)
2. Address (Number and Street)   (Apartment Number)

   (Town or City)   (State/Country)   (ZIP/Postal Code)
3. Place of Birth (Town or City)   (State/Country)
4. Date of Birth (Mo/Day/Year)   5. Sex ☐ Male ☐ Female   6. Marital Status ☐ Married ☐ Widowed ☐ Single ☐ Divorced
7. Other Names Used (including maiden name)
8. Date and Place of Present Marriage (if married)
9. Social Security number   10. Alien Registration Number (if any)
11. Names of Prior Husbands/Wives   12. Date(s) Marriage(s) Ended

13. If you are a U.S. citizen, complete the following:
    My citizenship was acquired through (check one)
    ☐ Birth in the U S
    ☐ Naturalization
    Give number of certificate, date and place it was issued

    ☐ Parents
    Have you obtained a certificate of citizenship in your own name?
    ☐ Yes ☐ No
    If "Yes," give number of certificate, date and place it was issued

14a. If you are a lawful permanent resident alien, complete the following:
     Date and place of admission for, or adjustment to, lawful permanent residence, and class of admission

14b. Did you gain permanent resident status through marriage to a United States citizen or lawful permanent resident?   ☐ Yes   ☐ No

C. Information about your alien relative

1. Name (Family name in CAPS)   (First)   (Middle)
2. Address (Number and Street)   (Apartment Number)

   (Town or City)   (State/Country)   (ZIP/Postal Code)
3. Place of Birth (Town or City)   (State/Country)
4. Date of Birth (Mo/Day/Year)   5. Sex ☐ Male ☐ Female   6. Marital Status ☐ Married ☐ Widowed ☐ Single ☐ Divorced
7. Other Names Used (including maiden name)
8. Date and Place of Present Marriage (if married)
9. Social Security number   10. Alien Registration Number (if any)
11. Names of Prior Husbands/Wives   12. Date(s) Marriage(s) Ended

13. Has your relative ever been in the U.S.?   ☐ Yes   ☐ No
14. If your relative is currently in the U.S., complete the following:
    He or she last arrived as a (visitor, student, stowaway, without inspection, etc)

    Arrival/Departure Record (I-94) Number   Date arrived (Month/Day/Year)

    Date authorized stay expired, or will expire as shown on Form I-94 or I-95

15. Name and address of present employer (if any)

    Date this employment began (Month/Day/Year)

16. Has your relative ever been under immigration proceedings?
    ☐ Yes ☐ No   Where _____ When _____
    ☐ Exclusion ☐ Deportation ☐ Rescission ☐ Judicial Proceedings

INITIAL RECEIPT	RESUBMITTED	RELOCATED		COMPLETED		
		Rec'd	Sent	Approved	Denied	Returned

Form I-130 (Rev 5-4-89)Y

C. (Continued) Information about your alien relative

16. List husband/wife and all children of your relative (if your relative is your husband/wife, list only his or her children)

Name	Relationship	Date of Birth	Country of Birth

17. Address in the United States where your relative intends to reside

(Number and Street)   (Town or City)   (State)

18. Your relative's address abroad

(Number and Street)   (Town or City)   (Province)   (Country)

19. If your relative's native alphabet is other than Roman letters, write his/her name and address abroad in the native alphabet:

(Name)   (Number and Street)   (Town or City)   (Province)   (Country)

20. If filing for your husband/wife, give last address at which you both lived together: From   To

(Name)   (Apt No)   (Town or City)   (State or Province)   (Country)   (Month)   (Year)   (Month)   (Year)

21. Check the appropriate box below and give the information required for the box you checked:

☐ Your relative will apply for a visa abroad at the American Consulate in _____
                                                                                        (City)   (Country)

☐ Your relative is in the United States and will apply for adjustment of status to that of a lawful permanent resident in the office of the Immigration and Naturalization Service at _____ . If your relative is not eligible for adjustment of status, he or she will
                                  (City)   (State)
apply for a visa abroad at the American Consulate in _____
                                                                     (City)   (Country)

(Designation of a consulate outside the country of your relative's last residence does not guarantee acceptance for processing by that consulate. Acceptance is at the discretion of the designated consulate.)

D. Other Information

1. If separate petitions are also being submitted for other relatives, give names of each and relationship.

2. Have you ever filed a petition for this or any other alien before?   ☐ Yes   ☐ No
If "Yes," give name, place and date of filing, and result

Warning: The INS Investigates claimed relationships and verifies the validity of documents. The INS seeks criminal prosecutions when family relationships are falsified to obtain visas.

Penalites: You may, by law be imprisoned for not more than five years, or fined $250,000, or both, for entering into a marriage contract for the purpose of evading any provision of the immigration laws and you may be fined up to $10,000 or imprisoned up to five years or both, for knowingly and willfully falsifying or concealing a material fact or using any false document in submitting this petition.

Your Certification

I certify, under penalty of perjury under the laws of the United States of America, that the foregoing is true and correct. Furthermore, I authorize the release of any information from my records which the Immigration and Naturalization Service needs to determine eligibility for the benefit that I am seeking.

Signature _____ Date _____ Phone Number _____

Signature of Person Preparing Form if Other than Above

I declare that I prepared this document at the request of the person above and that it is based on all information of which I have any knowledge

(Print Name)   (Address)   (Signature)   (Date)

Volag Number _____   G-28 ID Number _____

NOTICE TO PERSONS FILING FOR SPOUSES IF MARRIED LESS THAN TWO YEARS

Pursuant to section 216 of the Immigration and Nationality Act, your alien spouse may be granted conditional permanent resident status in the United States as of the date he or she is admitted or adjusted to conditional status by an officer of the Immigration and Naturalization Service. Both you and your conditional permanent resident spouse are required to file a petition, Form I-751, Joint Petition to Remove Conditional Basis of Alien's Permanent Resident Status, during the ninety day period immediately before the second anniversary of the date your alien spouse was granted conditional permanent residence.

Otherwise, the rights, privileges, responsibilities and duties which apply to all other permanent residents apply equally to a conditional permanent resident. A conditional permanent resident is not limited to the right to apply for naturalization, to file petitions in behalf of qualifying relatives, or to reside permanently in the United States as an immigrant in accordance with the immigration laws.

Failure to file Form I-751, Joint Petition to Remove the Conditional Basis of Alien's Permanent Resident Status, will result in termination of permanent residence status and initiation of deportation proceedings.

NOTE: You must complete Items 1 through 6 to assure that petition approval is recorded. Do not write in the section below item 6.

1. Name of relative (Family name in CAPS)   (First)   (Middle)
2. Other names used by relative (Including maiden name)
3. Country of relative's birth
4. Date of relative's birth (Month/Day/Year)
5. Your name (Last name in CAPS)   (First)   (Middle)
6. Your phone number

Action Stamp

SECTION
- ☐ 201 (b)(spouse)
- ☐ 201 (b)(child)
- ☐ 201 (b)(parent)
- ☐ 203 (a)(1)
- ☐ 203 (a)(2)
- ☐ 203 (a)(4)
- ☐ 203 (a)(5)

DATE PETITION FILED

☐ STATESIDE CRITERIA GRANTED

SENT TO CONSUL AT:

CHECKLIST

Have you answered each question?
Have you signed the petition?
Have you enclosed:

- ☐ The filing fee for each petition?
- ☐ Proof of your citizenship or lawful permanent residence?
- ☐ All required supporting documents for each petition?

If you are filing for your husband or wife have you included:

- ☐ Your picture?
- ☐ His or her picture?
- ☐ Your G-325A?
- ☐ His or her G-325A?

Relative Petition Card
Form I-130A (Rev 5-4-89)Y

U.S. Department of Justice
Immigration and Naturalization Service

OMB No 1115-0049
Petition to Classify Orphan as an Immidiate Relative [Section 101 (b)(1)(F) of the Immigration and Nationality Act, as amended]

Please do not write in this block.

TO THE SECRETARY OF STATE,
The petition was filed by
☐ Married petitioner   ☐ Unmarried petitioner

The petition is approved for orphan
☐ Adopted abroad   ☐ Coming to U S for adoption Preadoption requirements have been met

Remarks

Fee Stamp

File number

DATE OF ACTION

DD

DISTRICT

Please type or print legibly in ink. Use a separate petition for each child.
Petition is being made to classify the named orphan as an immediate relative.

BLOCK I - Information About Prospective Petitioner	8. If you are now married, give the following information
1. My name is (Last) (First) (Middle)	Date and place of present marriage
2. Other names used (including maiden name if appropriate).	Name of present spouse (include maiden name of wife)
3. I reside in the U S at (C/O if appropriate) (Apt No)	Date of birth of spouse Place of birth of spouse
(Number and street) (Town or city) (State) (ZIP Code)	Number of prior marriages of spouse
4. Address abroad (if any) (Number and street) (Apt No)	My spouse resides ☐ With me ☐ Apart from me (provide address below)
(Town or city) (Province) (Country)	(Apt No) (No and street) (City) (State) (Country)
5. I was born on (Month) (Day) (Year)	9. I am a citizen of the United States through ☐ Birth ☐ Parents ☐ Naturalization ☐ Marriage
In (Town or City) (State or Province) (Country)	If acquired through naturalization, give name under which naturalized, number of naturalization certificate, and date and place of naturalization
6. My phone number is. (Include Area Code)	

7. My marital status is
☐ Married
☐ Widowed
☐ Divorced
☐ Single
   ☐ I have never been married
   ☐ I have been previously married _____ time(s)
	If not, submit evidence of citizenship See Instruction 2 a(2)
	If acquired through parentage or marriage, have you obtained a certificate in your own name based on that acquisition?
	☐ No ☐ Yes
	Have you or any person through whom you claimed citizenship ever lost United States citizenship?
	☐ No ☐ Yes (If yes, attach detailed explanation)

Continue on reverse.

Received	Trans. In	Ret'd Trans Out	Completed

Form I-600 (Rev. 4/11/91) Y

BLOCK II - Information About Orphan Beneficiary

10. Name at birth　　(First)　　(Middle)　　(Last)

11. Name at present　(First)　　(Middle)　　(Last)

12. Any other names by which orphan is or was known

13. Sex　☐ Male　　14. Date of birth (Month/Day/Year)
　　　　☐ Female

15. Place of birth　(City)　(State or Province)　(Country)

16. The beneficiary is an orphan because (check one)
　　☐ He/she has no parents
　　☐ He/she has only one parent who is the sole or surviving parent

17. If the orphan has only one parent, answer the following:
　a State what has become of the other parent

　b Is the remaining parent capable of providing for the orphan's support?　☐ Yes　☐ No
　c Has the remaining parent, in writing, irrevocably released the orphan for emigration and adoption?　☐ Yes　☐ No

18. Has the orphan been adopted abroad by the petitioner and spouse jointly or the unmarried petitioner?　☐ Yes　☐ No
　　If yes, did the petitioner and spouse or unmarried petitioner personally see and observe the child prior to or during the adoption proceedings?　☐ Yes　☐ No
　　Date of adoption

　　Place of adoption

19. If either answer in question 18 is "No", answer the following:
　a Do petitioner and spouse jointly or does the unmarried petitioner intend to adopt the orphan in the United States?　☐ Yes　☐ No
　b Have the preadoption requirements, if any, of the orphan's proposed state of residence been met?　☐ Yes　☐ No
　c If b is answered "No", will they be met later?　☐ Yes　☐ No

20. To petitioner's knowledge, does the orphan have any physical or mental affliction?　☐ Yes　☐ No
　　If "Yes", name the affliction

21. Who has legal custody of the child?

22. Name of child welfare agency, if any, assisting in this case

23. Name of attorney abroad, if any, representing petitioner in this case
　　Address of above

24. Address in the United States where orphan will reside

25. Present address of orphan

25. If orphan is residing in an institution, give full name of institution

26. If orphan is not residing in an institution, give full name of person with whom orphan is residing

27. Give any additional information necessary to locate orphan such as name of district, section, zone or locality in which orphan resides

28. Location of American Consulate where application for visa will be made
　　(City in Foreign Country)　(Foreign Country)

Certification of Prospective Petitioner
I certify under penalty of perjury under the laws of the United States of America that the foregoing is true and correct and that I will care for an orphan/orphans properly if admitted to the United States

(Signature of Prospective Petitioner)

Executed on (Date)

Certification of Married Prospective Petitioner's Spouse
I certify under penalty of perjury under the laws of the United States of America that the foregoing is true and correct and that my spouse and I will care for an orphan/orphans properly if admitted to the United States

(Signature of Prospective Petitioner)

Executed on (Date)

Signature of Person Preparing Form if Other Than Petitioner
I declare that this document was prepared by me at the request of the prospective petitioner and is based on all information of which I have any knowledge

(Signature)

Address

Executed on (Date)

U.S. Department of Justice
Immigration and Naturalization Service
Petition to Classify Orphan as an Immediate Relative

1. **Eligibility.**

   a. *Child* Under immigration law, an orphan is an alien child who has no parents because of the death or disappearance of, abandonment or desertion by, or separation or loss from both parents. An orphan is also a child who has only one parent who is not capable of taking care of the orphan and has, in writing, irrevocably released the orphan for emigration and adoption. A petition to classify an alien as an orphan may not be filed in behalf of a child in the United States unless that child is in parole status and has not been adopted in the United States. The petition must be filed before the child's sixteenth birthday.

   b. *Parent(s)* The petition may be filed by a married United States citizen and spouse or unmarried United States citizen at least twenty-five years of age. The spouse does not need to be a United States citizen.

   c. *Adoption abroad* If the orphan was adopted abroad, it must be established that both the married petitioner and spouse or the unmarried petitioner personally saw and observed the child prior to or during the adoption proceedings. The adoption decree must show that a married petitioner and spouse adopted the child jointly or that an unmarried petitioner was at least twenty-five years of age at the time of the adoption.

   d. *Proxy adoption abroad.* If both the petitioner and spouse or the unmarried petitioner did not personally see and observe the child prior to or during the adoption proceedings abroad, the petitioner (and spouse, if married) must submit a statement indicating the petitioner's (and, if married, the spouse's) willingness and intent to readopt the child in the United States. If requested, the petitioner must submit a statement by an official of the state in which the child will reside that readoption is permissible in that state. In addition, evidence of compliance with the preadoption requirements, if any, of that state must be submitted.

   e. *Preadoption requirements.* If the orphan has not been adopted abroad, the petitioner and spouse or the unmarried petitioner must establish that the child will be adopted in the United States by the petitioner and spouse jointly or by the unmarried petitioner and that the preadoption requirement, if any, of the state of the orphan's proposed residence have been met.

2. **Filing petition for known child.** An orphan petition for a child who has been identified must be submitted on a completed Form I-600 with the certification of petitioner executed and the required fee. If the petitioner is married, the Form I-600 must also be signed by the petitioner's spouse. The petition must be accompanied by the following:

   a. Proof of United States citizenship of the petitioner

   (1) If the petitioner is a citizen by reason of birth in the United States, submit the petitioner's birth certificate, or if birth certificate is unobtainable, a copy of petitioner's baptismal certificate under seal of the church, showing place of birth, (baptism must have occurred within 2 months after birth), or if birth or baptismal certificate cannot be obtained, affidavits of two United States citizens who have personal knowledge of petitioner's birth in the United States.

   (2) If the petitioner was born outside the United States and became a citizen through the naturalization or citizenship of a parent or husband and has not been issued a certificate of citizenship in his/her own name, submit evidence of the citizenship and marriage of the parent or husband, as well as termination of any prior marriages. Also, if petitioner claims citizenship through a parent, submit petitioner's birth certificate and a separate statement showing the date, place, and means of all his/her arrivals and departures into and out of the United States.

   (3) If petitioner's naturalization occurred within 90 days immediately preceding the filing of this petition, or if it occurred prior to September 27, 1906, the naturalization certificate must accompany the petition.

   An unexpired U.S. passport valid for five years may also be submitted.

   b. Proof of marriage of petitioner and spouse
   The married petitioner should submit a certificate of the marriage and proof of termination of all prior marriages of himself/herself and spouse. In the case of an unmarried petitioner who was previously married, submit proof of termination of all prior marriages. NOTE: If any change occurs in the petitioner's marital status while the case is pending, the District Director should be notified immediately.

   c. Proof of age of orphan
   Petitioner should submit certificate of orphan's birth if obtainable, if not obtainable, submit an explanation together with the best available evidence of birth.

   d. Death certificate(s) of the child's parent(s), if applicable.

   e. A certified copy of adoption decree together with certified translation, if the orphan has been lawfully adopted abroad.

   f. Evidence that the sole or surviving parent is incapable of providing for the orphan's care and has in writing irrevocably released the orphan for emigration and adoption, if the orphan has only one parent.

   g. Evidence that the orphan has been unconditionally abandoned to an orphanage, if the orphan has been placed in an orphanage by his/her parent or parents.

   h. Evidence that the preadoption requirements, if any, of the state of the orphan's proposed residence have been met, if the child is to be adopted in the United States. If it is not possible to submit this evidence upon initial filing of the petition under the laws of the state of proposed residence, it may be submitted later. The petition, however, will not be approved without it.

   i. A home study with a statement or attachment recommending or approving of the adoption or proposed adoption signed by an official of the responsible state agency in the state of the child's proposed residence or of an agency authorized by that state, or, in the case of a child adopted abroad, of an appropriate public or private adoption agency which is licensed in the United States. Both individuals and organizations may qualify as agencies. If the recommending agency is a licensed agency, the recommendation must set forth that it is licensed, the state in which it is licensed, its license number, if any, and the period of validity of its license. The research, including interviewing, however, and the preparation of the home study may be done by an individual or group in the United States or abroad satisfactory to the recommending agency. A responsible state agency or licensed agency can accept a home study made by an unlicensed or foreign agency and use that home study as a basis for a favorable recommendation. The home study must contain, but is not limited to, the following elements.

Form I-600 (Rev. 4/11/91) Y

(1) The financial ability of the adoptive or prospective parent or parents to read and educate the child

(2) A detailed description of the living accommodations where the adoptive or prospective parent or parents currently reside

(3) A detailed description of the living accommodations where the child will reside

(4) A factual evaluation of the physical, mental, and moral capabilities of the adoptive or prospective parent or parents in relation to rearing and educating the child

j Fingerprints
Completed fingerprint cards (Forms FD-258) must be submitted by both the married petitioner and spouse or by the unmarried petitioner The cards are available at any office of the Immigration and Naturalization Service The fingerprints may be recorded on Form FD-258 by Service employees, other law enforcement officers, Service outreach centers, charitable and voluntary agencies, and any other reputable persons or organizations

3. **Filing petition for known child without full documentation on child or home study.** When a child has been identified but the documentary evidence relating to him/her or the home study is not yet available, an orphan petition may be filed without that evidence or home study The evidence outlined in Instructions 2a, 2b, and 2j, however, must be submitted If the necessary evidence relating to the child or the home study is not submitted within one year from the date of submission of the petition, the petition will be considered abandoned, and the fee will not be refunded. Any further proceeding will require the filing of a new petition

4. **Submitting an application for advance processing of an orphan petition in behalf of a child who has not been identified.** A prospective petitioner may request advance processing when the child has not been identified or when the prospective petitioner and/or spouse are/is going abroad to locate or adopt a child. If unmarried, the prospective petitioner must be at least twenty-four years of age provided that he/she will be at least twenty-five at the time of the adoption and the completed petition in behalf of a child is filed The request must be on Form I-600A, Application for Advance Processing of Orphan Petition, and must be accompanied by the evidence required by that form After a child or children are located and/or identified, a separate Form I-600, Petition to Classify Orphan as an Immediate Relative, must be filed for each child A new fee is not required if only one Form I-600 is filed, if it is filed within one year of completion of all advance processing in a case where there has been a favorable determination concerning the prospective petitioner's ability to care for a beneficiary orphan Normally, Form I-600 should be submitted to the office of this Service where the advance processing application was filed A prospective petitioner who is going abroad to adopt or locate a child in a country other than Austria, Germany, Greece, Italy, Korea, the Philippines, Hong Kong, Mexico, Singapore, Uruguay, or Thailand, however, should file Form I-600 at the American consulate or embassy having jurisdiction over the place where the child is residing or will be located unless the case is being retained at the stateside office A prospective petitioner who is going aboard to adopt or locate a child in Austria, Germany, Greece, Italy, Korea, the Philippines, Singapore, Hong Kong, Mexico, Uruguay, or Thailand should file Form I-600 at the Service office having jurisdiction over the place where the child is residing or will be located unless the case is being retained at the stateside office The case may be retained at the stateside office if the petitioner requests it and it appears that the case will be processed more quickly that way

5. **Documents in General.** All supporting documents must be originals or official copies of the original records issued by and bearing the seals of the official custodians of the records. If return of the originals is desired and if copies are by law permitted to be made, photostatic or typewritten copies may be submitted. A photostatic copy unaccompanied by the original may be accepted if the copy bears a certification by an immigration or consular office that the copy was compared with the original and found to be identical Any document in a foreign language must be accompanied by a translation in English The translator must certify that he/she is competent to translate and that the translation is accurate **Do not make a photostat of a certificate of naturalization or citizenship.**

Submission of petition. A petitioner residing in the United States should send the completed petition to the office of this Service having jurisdiction over his/her place of residence. A petitioner residing outside the United States should consult the nearest American consulate or embassy designated to act on the petition.

7. **Fee. Read instructions carefully.** A fee of one hundred forty dollars ($140) must be paid for filing this petition. It cannot be refunded regardless of the action taken on the petition. **Do not mail cash. All fees must be submitted in the exact amount.** Payment by check or money order must be drawn on a bank or other institution located in the United States and be payable in United States currency If petitioner resides in Guam, check or money order must be payable to the "Treasurer, Guam". If petitioner resides in the Virgin Islands, check or money order must be payable to the "Commissioner of Finance of the Virgin Islands". All other petitioners must make the check or money order payable to the "Immigration and Naturalization Service" When a check is drawn on the account of a person other than the petitioner, the name of the petitioner must be entered on the face of the check. If petition is submitted from outside the United States, remittance may be made by bank international money order or foreign draft drawn on a financial institution in the United States and payable to the Immigration and Naturalization Service in United States currency Personal checks are accepted subject to collectibility An uncollectible check will render the petition and any document issued pursuant to it invalid. A charge of $5 00 will be imposed if a check in payment of a fee is not honored by the bank on which it is drawn **When more than one petition is submitted by the same petitioner in behalf of orphans who are brothers and/or sisters, only one fee will be required.**

8. **Assistance.** Assistance may be obtained from a recognized social agency or from any public or private agency. The following recognized social agencies, which have offices in may of the principal cities of the United States, have agreed to furnish assistance:

   American Branch of International Social Services, Inc.
   345 East 46th Street
   New York, New York 10017

   Greek Archdiocese of North and South America
   10 East 79th Street
   New York, New York 10021

   United HIAS Service, Inc.
   200 Park Avenue South
   New York, New York 10003

   Catholic Committee for Refugees
   United States Catholic Conference
   201 Park Avenue South
   New York, New York 10003

   Church World Service, Inc.
   475 Riverside Drive
   New York, New York 10027

9. **Penalties.** Willful false statements on this form or supporting documents can be punished by fine or imprisonment. U S Code, Title 18, Sec. 1001 (Formerly Sec 80.)

10. **Authority.** 8 U.S C 1154(a). Routine uses for disclosure under the Privacy Act of 1974 have been published in the Federal Register and are available upon request The Immigration and Naturalization Service will use the information to determine immigrant eligibility Submission of the information is voluntary, but failure to provide any or all of the information may result in denial of the petition

11. **Reporting Burden.** Public reporting burden for this collection of information is estimated to average 30 minutes per response, including the time for reviewing instructions, searching existing data sources, gathering and maintaining the data needed, and completing and reviewing the collection of information. Send comments regarding this burden estimate or any other aspect of this collection of information, including suggestions for reducing this burden, to. U S Department of Justice, Immigration and Naturalization Service (Room 5304), Washington, D C 20536, and to the Office of Management and Budget, Paperwork Reduction Project, OMB No. 1115-0049, Washington, D.C 20503.

☆ US GPO 1992 -- 342-483 / 72375

For sale by the Superintendent of Documents, U S Government Printing Office
Washington, D C 20402

U.S. Department of Justice
Immigration and Naturalization Service

Application for Advance Processing
of Orphan Petition (8CFR 204.1(b)(3))

Advanced processing is a precedure for completing the part of an orphan petition relating to the petitioner before an orphan is located so that there will be no unnecessary delays in processing the petition after an orphan is located
USE THIS FORM ONLY IF YOU WISH TO ADOPT AN ORPHAN WHO HAS NOT YET BEEN LOCATED AND IDENTIFIED OR YOU AND OR YOUR SPOUSE, IF MARRIED, ARE/IS GOING ABROAD TO ADOPT OR LOCATE A CHILD.
This application is not a petition to classify orphan as an immediate relative (Form I-600)

1. **Eligibility**
   a. Eligibility for advance processing application (Form I-600A) An application for advance processing may be filed by a married United States citizen and spouse The spouse does not need to be a United States citizen It may also be filed by an unmarried United States citizen at least twenty-four years of age provided that he/she will be at least twenty-five at the time of the adoption and of filing an orphan petition in behalf of a child
   b. Eligibility for Orphan Petition (Form I-600) In addition to the requirements concerning the citizenship and age of the petitioner described in Instruction 1a, when a child is located and identified, the following eligibility requirements will apply
      (1) *Child* Under immigration law, an orphan is an alien child who has no parents because of the death or disappearance of, abandonment or desertion by, or separation or loss from both parents An orphan is also a child who has only one parent who is not capable of taking care of the orphan and has, in writing, irrevocably released the orphan for emigration and adoption A petition to classify an alien as an orphan may not be filed in behalf of a child in the United States unless that child is in parole status and has not been adopted in the Untied States The petition must be filed before the child's sixteenth birthday
      (2) *Adoption abroad.* If the orphan was adopted abroad, it must be established that both the married petitioner and spouse or the unmarried petitioner personally saw and observed the child prior to or during the adoption proceedings The adoption decree must show that a married petitioner and spouse adopted the child jointly or that an unmarried petitioner was at least twenty-five years of age at the time of the adoption
      (3) *Proxy adoption abroad.* If both the petitioner and spouse or the unmarried petitioner did not personally see and observe the child prior to or during the adoption proceedings abroad, the petitioner (and spouse, if married) must submit a statement indicating the petitioner's (and, if married, the spouse's) willingness and intent to readopt the child in the United States If requested, the petitioner must submit a statement by an official of the state in which the child will reside that readoption is permissible in that state In addition, evidence of compliance with the preadoption requirements, if any, of that state must be submitted
      (4) *Preadoption requirements.* If the orphan has not been adopted abroad, the petitioner and spouse or the unmarried petitioner must establish that the child will be adopted in the United States by the petitioner and spouse jointly or by the unmarried petitioner and that the preadoption requirement, if any, of the state of the orphan's proposed residence have been met
2. **Filing advance processing application.** An advance processing application must be submitted on Form I-600A with the certification of prospective petitioner executed and the required fee If the prospective petitioner is married, the Form I-600A must also be signed by the prospective petitioner's spouse The application must be accompanied by

   a. Proof of United States citizenship of the prospective petitioner
      (1) If the petitioner is a citizen by reason of birth in the United States, submit the petitioner's birth certificate, or if birth certificate is unobtainable, a copy of petitioner's baptismal certificate under seal of the church, showing place of birth, (baptism must have occurred within 2 months after birth), or if birth or baptismal certificate cannot be obtained, affidavits of two United States citizens who have personal knowledge of petitioner's birth in the United States
      (2) If the petitioner was born outside the United States and became a citizen through the naturalization or citizenship of a parent or husband and has not been issued a certificate of citizenship in his/her own name, submit evidence of the citizenship and marriage of the parent or husband, as well as termination of any prior marriages Also, if petitioner claims citizenship through a parent, submit petitioner's birth certificate and a separate statement showing the date, place, and means of all his/her arrivals and departures into and out of the United States
      (3) If petitioner's naturalization occurred within 90 days immediately preceding the filing of this petition, or if it occurred prior to September 27, 1906, the naturalization certificate must accompany the petition

      An unexpired U.S. passport valid for five years may also be submitted.

   b. Proof of marriage of petitioner and spouse
      The married petitioner should submit a certificate of the marriage and proof of termination of all prior marriages of himself/herself and spouse In the case of an unmarried petitioner who was previously married, submit proof of termination of all prior marriages NOTE If any change occurs in the petitioner's marital status while the case is pending, the District Director should be notified immediately

   c. A home study with a statement or attachment recommending or approving of the adoption or proposed adoption signed by an official of the responsible state agency in the state of the child's proposed residence or of an agency authorized by that state, or, in the case of a child adopted abroad, of an appropriate public or private adoption agency which is licensed in the United States Both individuals and organizations may qualify as agencies If the recommending agency is a licensed agency, the recommendation must set forth that it is licensed, the state in which it is licensed, its license number, if any, and the period of validity of its license The research, including interviewing, however, and the preparation of the home study may be done by an individual or group in the United States or abroad satisfactory to the recommending agency A responsible state agency or licensed agency can accept a home study made by an unlicensed or foreign agency and use that home study as a basis for a favorable recommendation The home study must contain, but is not limited to, the following elements

197

Form I-600A (Rev 4/11/91) Y

(1) The financial ability of the adoptive or prospective parent or parents to read and educate the child

(2) A detailed description of the living accommodations where the adoptive or prospective parent or parents currently reside.

(3) A detailed description of the living accommodations where the child will reside

(4) A factual evaluation of the physical, mental, and moral capabilities of the adoptive or prospective parent or parents in relation to rearing and educating the child

d Fingerprints
Completed fingerprint cards (Forms FD-258) must be submitted by both the married petitioner and spouse or by the unmarried petitioner The cards are available at any office of the Immigration and Naturalization Service The fingerprints may be recorded on Form FD-258 by Service employees, other law enforcement officers, Service outreach centers, charitable and voluntary agencies, and any other reputable persons or organizations

3. **Documents in General.** All supporting documents must be originals or official copies of the original records issued by and bearing the seals of the official custodians of the records If return of the originals is desired and if copies are by law permitted to be made, photostatic or typewritten copies may be submitted A photostatic copy unaccompanied by the original may be accepted if the copy bears a certification by an immigration or consular office that the copy was compared with the original and found to be identical Any document in a foreign language must be accompanied by a translation in English The translator must certify that he/she is competent to translate and that the translation is accurate **Do not make a photostat of a certificate of naturalization or citizenship.**

4. **Submission of application.** A prospective petitioner residing in the United States should send the completed application to the office of this Service having jurisdiction over his/her place of residence A prospective petitioner residing outside the United States should consult the nearest American consulate for the overseas or stateside office of this Service designated to act on the application.

5. **Fee. Read instructions carefully.** A fee of one hundred forty dollars ($140) must be paid for filing this petition It cannot be refunded regardless of the action taken on the petition **Do not mail cash. All fees must be submitted in the exact amount.** Payment by check or money order must be drawn on a bank or other institution located in the United States and be payable in United States currency If petitioner resides in Guam, check or money order must be payable to the "Treasurer, Guam". If petitioner resides in the Virgin Islands, check or money order must be payable to the "Commissioner of Finance of the Virgin Islands" All other petitioners must make the check or money order payable to the "Immigration and Naturalization Service" When a check is drawn on the account of a person other than the petitioner, the name of the petitioner must be entered on the face of the check If petition is submitted from outside the United States, remittance may be made by bank international money order or foreign draft drawn on a financial institution in the United States and payable to the Immigration and Naturalization Service in United States currency. Personal checks are accepted subject to collectibility An uncollectible check will render the petition and any document issued pursuant to it invalid. A charge of $5 00 will be imposed if a check in payment of a fee is not honored by the bank on which it is drawn. **When more than one petition is submitted by the same petitioner in behalf of orphans who are brothers and/or sisters, only one fee will be required.**

6. **When Child/children located and/or identified.** A separate Form I-600, Petition to Classify Orphan as an Immediate Relative, must be filed for each child A new fee is not required if only one Form I-600 is filed and it is filed within one year of completion of all advance processing in a case where there has been a favorable determination concerning the prospective petitioner's ability to care for a beneficiary orphan Normally, Form I-600 should be submitted to the office of this Service where the advance processing application was filed. A prospective petitioner who is going abroad to adopt or locate a child in a country other than Austria, Germany, Greece, Italy, Korea, the Philippines, Hong Kong, Mexico, Singapore, Uruguay, or Thailand, however, should file Form I-600 at the American consulate or embassy having jurisdiction over the place where the child is residing or will be located unless the case is being retained at the stateside office A prospective petitioner who is going abroad to adopt or locate a child in Austria, Germany, Greece, Italy, Korea, the Philippines, Hong Kong, Mexico, Singapore, Uruguay, or Thailand should file Form I-600 at the Service office having jurisdiction over the place where the child is residing or will be located unless the case is being retained at the stateside office The case may be retained at the stateside office if the petitioner requests it and it appears that the case will be processed more quickly that way Form I-600 must be accompanied by all the evidence required on the instruction sheet of that form except that the evidence required by and submitted with this form need not be furnished

7. **Assistance.** Assistance may be obtained from a recognized social agency or from any public or private agency The following recognized social agencies, which have offices in may of the principal cities of the United States, have agreed to furnish assistance

    American Branch of International Social Services, Inc.
    345 East 46th Street
    New York, New York 10017

    Greek Archdiocese of North and South America
    10 East 79th Street
    New York, New York 10021

    United HIAS Service, Inc.
    200 Park Avenue South
    New York, New York 10003

    Catholic Committee for Refugees
    United States Catholic Conference
    201 Park Avenue South
    New York, New York 10003

    Church World Service, Inc.
    475 Riverside Drive
    New York, New York 10027

8. **Penalties.** Willful false statements on this form or supporting documents can be punished by fine or imprisonment U S. Code, Title 18, Sec 1001 (Formerly Sec 80)

9. **Authority.** 8 U S C 1154(a) Routine uses for disclosure under the Privacy Act of 1974 have been published in the Federal Register and are available upon request The Immigration and Naturalization Service will use the information to determine immigrant eligibility Submission of the information is voluntary, but failure to provide any of all of the information may result in denial of the petition

10. **Reporting Burden.** Public reporting burden for this collection of information is estimated to average 30 minutes per response, including the time for reviewing instructions, searching existing data sources, gathering and maintaining the data needed, and completing and reviewing the collection of information. Send comments regarding this burden estimate or any other aspect of this collection of information, including suggestions for reducing this burden, to. U S Department of Justice, Immigration and Naturalization Service (Room 5304), Washington, D C 20536, and to the Office of Management and Budget, Paperwork Reduction Project, OMB No 1115-0049, Washington, D C 20503

★ U.S. GPO:1992-342-483/72376

U.S. Department of Justice
Immigration and Naturalization Service

OMB No 1115-0049
Application for Advance Processing of Orphan Petition [8CFR 204.1(b)(3)]

Please do not write in this block.

It has been determined that the
☐ Married   ☐ Unmarried
prospective petitioner will furnish proper care to a beneficiary orphan if admitted to the United Sates

There
☐ are   ☐ are not
preadoptive requirements in the state of the child's proposed residence

The following is a description of the preadoption requirements, if any, of the state of the child's proposed residence

_____
_____

The preadoption requirements, if any,
☐ have been met   ☐ have not been met

Fee Stamp

DATE OF FAVORABLE DETERMINATION

DD

DISTRICT

File number of petitioner, if applicable

Please type or print legibly in ink.

Application is made by the named prospective petitioner for advance processing of an orphan petition.

BLOCK I - Information About Prospective Petitioner

1. My name is (Last) (First) (Middle)

2. Other names used (including maiden name if appropriate)

3. I reside in the U S at (C/O if appropriate) (Apt No)
   (Number and street) (Town or city) (State) (ZIP Code)

4. Address abroad (if any) (Number and street) (Apt No)
   (Town or city) (Province) (Country)

5. I was born on (Month) (Day) (Year)
   In (Town or City) (State or Province) (Country)

6. My phone number is (Include Area Code)

7. My marital status is
   ☐ Married
   ☐ Widowed
   ☐ Divorced
   ☐ Single
      ☐ I have never been married
      ☐ I have been previously married _____ time(s)

8. If you are now married, give the following information
   Date and place of present marriage

   Name of present spouse (include maiden name of wife)

   Date of birth of spouse   Place of birth of spouse

   Number of prior marriages of spouse

   My spouse resides ☐ With me   ☐ Apart from me
   (provide address below)
   (Apt No) (No and street) (City) (State) (Country)

9. I am a citizen of the United States through
   ☐ Birth ☐ Parents ☐ Naturalization ☐ Marriage
   If acquired through naturalization, give name under which naturalized, number of naturalization certificate, and date and place of naturalization

   If not, submit evidence of citizenship See Instruction 2 a(2)
   If acquired through parentage or marriage, have you obtained a certificate in your own name based on that acquisition?
   ☐ No   ☐ Yes
   Have you or any person through whom you claimed citizenship ever lost United States citizenship?
   ☐ No   ☐ Yes (If yes, attach detailed explanation)

Continue on reverse.

Received	Trans. In	Ret'd Trans. Out	Completed

Form I-600A (Rev. 4/11/91) Y

BLOCK II - General Information

10. Name and address of organization or individual assisting you in locating or identifying an orphan

    (Name) _____

    (Address) _____

11. Do you plan to travel abroad to locate or adopt a child?
    ☐ Yes   ☐ No

12. Does your spouse, if any, plan to travel abroad to locate or adopt a child?
    ☐ Yes   ☐ No

13. If the answer to question 11 or 12 is "yes", give the following information
    a. Your date of intended departure _____
    b. Your spouse's date of intended departure _____
    c. City, province _____

14. Will the child come to the United States for adoption after compliance with the preadoption requirements, if any, of the state of proposed residence?
    ☐ Yes   ☐ No

15. If the answer to question 14 is "no", will the child be adopted abroad after having been personally seen and observed by you and your spouse, if married?
    ☐ Yes   ☐ No

16. Where do you wish to file your orphan petition?
    The service office located at _____
    The American Consulate or Embassy at _____

17. Do you plan to adopt more than one child?
    ☐ Yes   ☐ No
    If "Yes", how many children do you plan to adopt? _____

Certification of Prospective Petitioner

I certify under penalty of perjury under the laws of the United States of America that the foregoing is true and correct and that I will care for an orphan/orphans properly if admitted to the United States

(Signature of Prospective Petitioner) _____

Executed on (Date) _____

Certification of Married Prospective Petitioner's Spouse

I certify under penalty of perjury under the laws of the United States of America that the foregoing is true and correct and that my spouse and I will care for an orphan/orphans properly if admitted to the United States

(Signature of Prospective Petitioner) _____

Executed on (Date) _____

Signature of Person Preparing Form if Other Than Petitioner

I declare that this document was prepared by me at the request of the prospective petitioner and is based on all information of which I have any knowledge

(Signature) _____

Address _____

Executed on (Date) _____

For sale by the Superintendent of Documents, U S Government Printing Office, Washington, D C. 20402

U.S. Department of Justice
Immigration and Naturalization Service

OMB No. 1115-0093
Application to Extend/Change Nonimmigrant Status

Purpose Of This Form.
This form is for a nonimmigrant to apply for an extension of stay or change to another nonimmigrant status. However, an employer should file Form I-129 to request an extension/change to E, H, L, O, P, Q or R status for an employee or prospective employee. Dependents of such employees should file for an extension/change of status on this form, not on Form I-129. This form is also for a nonimmigrant F-1 or M-1 student to apply for reinstatement.

This form consists of a basic application and a supplement to list co-applicants.

Who May File.
For extension of stay or change of status.
If you are a nonimmigrant in the U.S., you may apply for an extension of stay or a change of status on this form except as noted above. However, you may not be granted an extension or change of status if you were admitted under the Visa Waiver Program or if your current or proposed status is as
- an alien in transit (C) or in transit without a visa (TWOV),
- a crewman (D), or
- a fiance(e) or dependent of a fiance(e) (K)

There are additional limits on change of status
- A J-1 exchange visitor whose status was for the purpose of receiving graduate medical training is ineligible for change of status
- A J-1 exchange visitor subject to the foreign residence requirement who has not received a waiver of that requirement, is only eligible for a change of status to A or G
- An M-1 student is not eligible for a change to F-1 status, and is not eligible for a change to any H status if training received as an M-1 student helped him/her qualify for the H status
- You may not be granted a change to M-1 status for training to qualify for H status

For F-1 or M-1 student reinstatement. You will only be considered for reinstatement if you establish when filing this application
- that the violation of status was solely due to circumstances beyond your control or that failure to reinstate you would result in extreme hardship,
- you are pursuing, or will pursue, a full course of study;
- you have not been employed off campus without authorization or, if an F-1 student, that your only unauthorized off-campus employment was pursuant to a scholarship, fellowship, or assistantship, or did not displace a U.S. resident, and
- you are not in deportation proceedings

Multiple Applicants.
You may include your spouse and your unmarried children under age 21 as co-applicants in your application for the same extension or change of status if you are all in the same status now or they are all in derivative status.

General Filing Instructions.
Please answer all questions by typing or clearly printing in black ink. Indicate that an item is not applicable with "N/A". If the answer is "none," please so state. If you need extra space to answer any item, attach a sheet of paper with your name and your alien registration number (A#), if any, and indicate the number of the item to which the answer refers. Your application must be filed with the required Initial Evidence. Your application must be properly signed and filed with the correct fee. If you are under 14 years of age, your parent or guardian may sign your application.

Copies. If these instructions state that a copy of a document may be filed with this application and you choose to send us the original, we may keep that original for our records.

Translations. Any foreign language document must be accompanied by a full English translation which the translator has certified as complete and correct, and by the translator's certification that he or she is competent to translate from the foreign language into English.

Initial Evidence.
Form I-94, Nonimmigrant Arrival-Departure Record. You must file your application with the original Form I-94, Nonimmigrant Arrival/Departure Record, of each person included in the application, if you are filing for

- an extension as a B-1 or B-2, or change to such status,
- reinstatement as an F-1 or M-1 or filing for change to F or M status, or
- an extension as a J, or change to such status

In all other instances, file this application with a copy of the Form I-94 of each person included in the application

If the required Form I-94 or required copy cannot be submitted, you must file Form I-102, Application for Replacement/Initial Nonimmigrant Arrival/Departure Document, with this application

Valid Passport. A nonimmigrant who is required to have a passport to be admitted must keep that passport valid during his/her entire nonimmigrant stay. If a required passport is not valid when you file this application, submit an explanation with your application

Additional Initial Evidence. An application must also be filed with the following evidence
- If you are filing for an extension/change of status as the dependent of an employee who is an E, H, L, O, P, Q or R nonimmigrant, this application must be filed with
  - the petition filed for that employee or evidence it is pending with the Service; or
  - a copy of the employee's Form I-94 or approval notice showing that he/she has already been granted status to the period requested in your application
- If you are requesting an extension/change to A-3 or G-5 status, this application must be filed with
  - a copy of your employer's Form I-94 or approval notice demonstrating A or G status,
  - an original letter from your employer describing your duties and stating that he/she intends to personally employ you, and
  - an original Form I-566, certified by the Department of State, indicating your employer's continuing accredited diplomatic status
- If you are filing for an extension/change to other A or G status, you must submit Form I-566, certified by the Department of State to indicate your accredited diplomatic status
- If you are filing for an extension/change to B-1 or B-2 status, this application must be filed with a statement explaining in detail
  - the reasons for your request,
  - why your extended stay would be temporary including what arrangement you have made to depart the U.S., and
  - any effect of the extended stay on your foreign employment and residency
- If you are requesting an extension/change to F-1 or M-1 student status, this application must be filed with an original Form I-20 issued by the school which has accepted you. If you are requesting reinstatement to F-1 or M-1 status, you must also submit evidence establishing that you are eligible for reinstatement
- If you are filing for an extension/change to I status, this application must be filed with a letter describing the employment and establishing that it is as the representative of qualifying foreign media
- If you are filing for an extension/change to J-1 exchange visitor status, this application must be filed with an original Form IAP-66 issued by your program sponsor
- If you are filing for an extension/change to N-1 or N-2 status as the parent or child of an alien admitted as a special immigrant under section 101(a)(27)(I), this application must be filed with a copy of that person's alien registration card

When To File.
You must submit an application for extension of stay or change of status before your current authorized stay expires. We suggest you file at least 45 days before your stay expires, or as soon as you determine you need to change status. Failure to file before the expiration date may be excused if you demonstrate when you file the application
- the delay was due to extraordinary circumstances beyond your control,
- the length of the delay was reasonable,
- that you have not otherwise violated your status,
- that you are still a bona fide nonimmigrant, and
- that you are not in deportation proceedings

Form I-539 (Rev. 12-2-91)

Where To File.

File this application at your local INS office if you are filing
- for an extension as a B-1 or B-2, or change to such status,
- for reinstatement as an F-1 or M-1 or filing for change to F or M status, or
- for an extension as a J, or change to such status

In all other instances, file your application at an INS Service Center, as follows

If you live in Connecticut, Delaware, District of Columbia, Maine, Maryland, Massachusetts, New Hampshire, New Jersey, New York, Pennsylvania, Puerto Rico, Rhode Island, Vermont, Virgin Islands, Virginia, or West Virginia, mail your application to USINS Eastern Service Center, 75 Lower Welden Street, St Albans, VT 05479-0001

If you live in Alabama, Arkansas, Florida, Georgia, Kentucky, Louisiana, Mississippi, New Mexico, North Carolina, Oklahoma, South Carolina, Tennessee, or Texas, mail your application to USINS Southern Service Center, P O Box 152122, Dept A, Irving, TX 75015-2122

If you live in Arizona, California, Guam, Hawaii, or Nevada, mail your application to USINS Western Service Center, P O Box 30040, Laguna Niguel, CA 92607-0040

If you live elsewhere in the United States, mail your application to USINS Northern Service Center, 100 Centennial Mall North, Room, B-26, Lincoln, NE 68508

Fee.

The fee for this application is $70 00 for the first person included in the application, and $10 00 for each additional person. The fee must be submitted in the exact amount. It cannot be refunded. DO NOT MAIL CASH

All checks and money orders must be drawn on a bank or other institution located in the United States and must be payable in United States currency. The check or money order should be made payable to the Immigration and Naturalization Service, except that
- If you live in Guam, and are filing this application in Guam, make your check or money order payable to the "Treasurer, Guam"
- If you live in the Virgin Islands, and are filing this application in the Virgin Islands, make your check or money order payable to the "Commissioner of Finance of the Virgin Islands"

Checks are accepted subject to collection. An uncollected check will render the application and any document issued invalid. A charge of $5 00 will be imposed if a check in payment of a fee is not honored by the bank on which it is drawn

Processing Information.

Acceptance Any application that is not signed or is not accompanied by the correct fee will be rejected with a notice that the application is deficient. You may correct the deficiency and resubmit the application. An application is not considered properly filed until accepted by the Service

Initial processing Once the application has been accepted, it will be checked for completeness. If you do not completely fill out the form, or file it without required initial evidence, you will not establish a basis for eligibility, and we may deny your application

Requests for more information or interview. We may request more information or evidence or we may request that you appear at an INS office for an interview. We may also request that you submit the originals of any copy. We will return these originals when they are no longer required

Decision An application for extension of stay, change of status, or reinstatement may be approved in the discretion of the Service. You will be notified in writing of the decision on your application

Penalties.

If you knowingly and willfully falsify or conceal a material fact or submit a false document with this request, we will deny the benefit you are filing for, and may deny any other immigration benefit. In addition, you will face severe penalties provided by law, and may be subject to criminal prosecution

Privacy Act Notice

We ask for the information on this form, and associated evidence, to determine if you have established eligibility for the immigration benefit you are filing for. Our legal right to ask for this information is in 8 USC 1184, and 1258. We may provide this information to other government agencies. Failure to provide this information, and any requested evidence, may delay a final decision or result in denial of your request

Paperwork Reduction Act Notice.

We try to create forms and instructions that are accurate, can be easily understood, and which impose the least possible burden on you to provide us with information. Often this is difficult because some immigration laws are very complex. The estimated average time to complete and file this application is as follows (1) 10 minutes to learn about the law and form, (2) 10 minutes to complete the form, and (3) 25 minutes to assemble and file the application, for a total estimated average of 45 per application. If you have comments regarding the accuracy of this estimate, or suggestions for making this form simpler, you can write to both the Immigration and Naturalization Service, 425 I Street, N W, Room 5304, Washington, D C 20536; and the Office of Management and Budget, Paperwork Reduction Project, OMB No 1115-0093, Washington, D.C. 20503

Mailing Label--Complete the following mailing label and submit this page with your application if you are required to submit your original Form I-94.

Name and address of applicant

Name

Street

City, State, & Zip Code

Your I-94 Arrival-Departure Record is attached. It has been amended to show the extension of stay/change of status granted

Form I 539 (Rev 12 2 91)

U.S. Department of Justice
Immigration and Naturalization Service

OMB #1115-0093
Application to Extend/Change Nonimmigrant Status

START HERE - Please Type or Print

Part 1. Information about you.

Family Name	Given Name	Middle Initial

Address - In Care of:

Street # and Name	Apt. #

City	State

Zip Code

Date of Birth (month/day/year)	Country of Birth

Social Security # (if any)	A# (if any)

Date of Last Arrival Into the U.S.	I-94#

Current Nonimmigrant Status	Expires on (month/day/year)

Part 2. Application Type. (See instructions for fee.)

1. I am applying for: (check one)
   a. ☐ an extension of stay in my current status
   b. ☐ a change of status The new status I am requesting is: _____
2. Number of people included in this application: (check one)
   a. ☐ I am the only applicant
   b. ☐ Members of my family are filing this application with me. The Total number of people included in this application is _____ (complete the supplement for each co-applicant)

Part 3. Processing information.

1. I/We request that my/our current or requested status be extended until (month/day/year) _____
2. Is this application based on an extension or change of status already granted to your spouse, child or parent?
   ☐ No ☐ Yes (receipt # _____)
3. Is this application being filed based on a separate petition or application to give your spouse, child or parent an extension or change of status?
   ☐ No ☐ Yes, filed with this application ☐ Yes, filed previously and pending with INS
4. If you answered yes to question 3, give the petitioner or applicant name
   _____
   If the application is pending with INS, also give the following information
   Office filed at _____ Filed on _____ (date)

Part 4. Additional information.

1. For applicant #1, provide passport information
Country of issuance	Valid to: (month/day/year)

2. Foreign address
Street # and Name	Apt#
City or Town	State or Province
Country	Zip or Postal Code

Form I-539 (Rev 12-2-91)   *Continued on back.*

FOR INS USE ONLY

Returned
Date _____

Resubmitted
Date _____

Reloc Sent
Date _____

Reloc Rec'd
Date _____

Date _____
☐ Applicant Interviewed

☐ *Extension Granted*
   to (date) _____
☐ *Change of Status/Extension Granted*
   New Class _____ To (date) _____

If denied
☐ Still within period of stay
☐ V/D to _____
☐ S/D to _____
☐ Place under docket control

Remarks

Action Block

To Be Completed by *Attorney* or *Representative*, if any
☐ Fill in box if G-28 is attached to represent the applicant
VOLAG# _____
ATTY State License # _____

Part 4. Additional Information. (continued)

3 Answer the following questions. If you answer yes to any question, explain on separate paper.	Yes	No
a. Are you, or any other person included in this application, an applicant for an immigrant visa or adjustment of status to permanent residence?		
b. Has an immigrant petition ever been filed for you, or for any other person included in this application?		
c. Have you, or any other person included in this application ever been arrested or convicted of any criminal offense since last entering the U S ?		
d. Have you, or any other person included in this application done anything which violated the terms of the nonimmigrant status you now hold?		
e. Are you, or any other person included in this application, now in exclusion or deportation proceedings?		
f. Have you, or any other person included in this application, been employed in the U S since last admitted or granted an extension or change of status?		

If you answered YES to question 3f, give the following information on a separate paper Name of person, name of employer, address of employer, weekly income, and whether specifically authorized by INS

If you answered NO to question 3f, fully describe how you are supporting yourself on a separate paper Include the source and the amount and basis for any income

Part 5. Signature.
Read the information on penalties in the instructions before completing this section You must file this application while in the United States

I certify under penalty of perjury under the laws of the United States of America that this application, and the evidence submitted with it, is all true and correct I authorize the release of any information from my records which the Immigration and Naturalization Service needs to determine eligibility for the benefit I am seeking

Signature	Print your name	Date

Please Note: If you do not completely fill out this form, or fail to submit required documents listed in the instructions, you cannot be found eligible for the requested document and this application will have to be denied

Part 6. Signature of person preparing form if other than above. (Sign below)

I declare that I prepared this application at the request of the above person and it is based on all information of which I have knowledge.

Signature	Print Your Name	Date

Firm Name and Address

(Please remember to enclose the mailing label with your application)

Form I-539 (Rev. 12-2-91)

Supplement-1

Attach to Form I-539 when more than one person is included in the petition or application. *(List each person separately. Do not include the person you named on the form).*

Family Name		Given Name		Middle Initial	Date of Birth (month/day/year)
Country of Birth		Social Security No			A#
IF IN THE U.S.	Date of Arrival (month/day/year)			I-94#	
	Current Nonimmigrant Status			Expires on (month/day/year)	
Country where passport issued		Expiration Date (month/day/year)			

Family Name		Given Name		Middle Initial	Date of Birth (month/day/year)
Country of Birth		Social Security No			A#
IF IN THE U.S.	Date of Arrival (month/day/year)			I-94#	
	Current Nonimmigrant Status			Expires on (month/day/year)	
Country where passport issued		Expiration Date (month/day/year)			

Family Name		Given Name		Middle Initial	Date of Birth (month/day/year)
Country of Birth		Social Security No			A#
IF IN THE U.S.	Date of Arrival (month/day/year)			I-94#	
	Current Nonimmigrant Status			Expires on (month/day/year)	
Country where passport issued		Expiration Date (month/day/year)			

Family Name		Given Name		Middle Initial	Date of Birth (month/day/year)
Country of Birth		Social Security No			A#
IF IN THE U.S.	Date of Arrival (month/day/year)			I-94#	
	Current Nonimmigrant Status			Expires on (month/day/year)	
Country where passport issued		Expiration Date (month/day/year)			

Family Name		Given Name		Middle Initial	Date of Birth (month/day/year)
Country of Birth		Social Security No			A#
IF IN THE U.S.	Date of Arrival (month/day/year)			I-94#	
	Current Nonimmigrant Status			Expires on (month/day/year)	
Country where passport issued		Expiration Date (month/day/year)			

U.S. Department of Justice
Immigration and Naturalization Service

Medical Examination of Aliens Seeking Adjustment of Status

Instructions To Alien Applying for Adjustment of Status

A medical examination is necessary as part of your application for adjustment of status Please communicate immediately with one of the physicians on the attached list to arrange for your medical examination, which must be completed before your status can be adjusted The purpose of the medical examination is to determine if you have certain health conditions which may need further follow-up The information requested is required in order for a proper evaluation to be made of your health status The results of your examination will be provided to an Immigration officer and may be shared with health departments and other public health or cooperating medical authorities All expenses in connection with this examination must be paid by you

The examining physician may refer you to your personal physician or a local public health department and you must comply with some health follow-up or treatment recommendations for certain health conditions before your status will be adjusted

This form should be presented to the examining physician You must sign the form in the presence of the examining physician *The law provides severe penalties for knowingly and willfully falsifying or concealing a material fact or using any false documents in connection with this medical examination The medical examination must be completed in order for us to process your application*

Medical Examination and Health Information

A medical examination is necessary as part of your application for adjustment of status You should go for your medical examination as soon as possible You will have to choose a doctor from a list you will be given The list will have the names of doctors or clinics in your area that have been approved by the Immigration and Naturalization Service for this examination You must pay for the examination If you become a temporary legal resident and later apply to become a permanent resident, you may need to have another medical examination at that time

The purpose of the medical examination is to find out if you have certain health conditions which may need further follow-up The doctor will examine you for certain physical and mental health conditions You will have to take off your clothes If you need more tests because of a condition found during your medical examination, the doctor may send you to your own doctor or to the local public health department For some conditions, before you can become a temporary or permanent resident, you will have to show that you have followed the doctor's advice to get more tests or take treatment

If you have any records of immunizations (vaccinations), you should bring them to show to the doctor This is especially important for pre-school and school-age children The doctor will tell you if any more immunizations are needed, and where you can get them (usually at your local public health department) It is important for your health that you follow the doctor's advice and go to get any immunizations

One of the conditions you will be tested for is tuberculosis If you are 15 years of age or older, you will be required to have a chest X-ray examination *Exception:* If you are pregnant or applying for adjustment of status under the Immigration Reform and Control Act of 1986, you may choose to have either a chest X-ray or a tuberculin skin test If you choose the skin test you will have to return in 2 - 3 days to have it checked If you do not have any reaction to the skin test you will not need any more tests for tuberculosis If you do have any reaction to the skin test, you will also need to have a chest X-ray examination If the doctor thinks you are infected with tuberculosis, you may have to go to the local health department and more tests may have to be done The doctor will explain these to you

If you are 14 years of age or younger, you will not need to have a test for tuberculosis unless a member of your immediate family has chest X-ray findings that may be tuberculosis If you are in this age group and you do have to be tested for tuberculosis, you may choose either the chest X-ray or the skin test

You must also have a blood test for syphilis if you are 15 years of age or older

You will also be tested to see if you have the human immunodeficiency virus (HIV) infection This virus is the cause of AIDS If you have this virus, it may damage your body's ability to fight off other disease The blood test you will take will tell if you have been exposed to this virus

Instructions To Physician Performing the Examination

Please medically examine for adjustment of status the individual presenting this form The medical examination should be performed according to the U S Public Health Service "Guidelines for Medical Examination of Aliens in the United States" and Supplements, which have been provided to you separately

If the applicant is free of medical defects listed in Section 212(a) of the Immigration and Nationality Act, endorse the form in the space provided While in your presence, the applicant must also sign the form in the space provided You should retain one copy for your files and return all other copies in a sealed envelope to the applicant for presentation at the immigration interview

If the applicant has a health condition which requires follow-up as specified in the "Guidelines for Medical Examination of Aliens in the United States" and Supplements, complete the referral information on the pink copy of the medical examination form, and advise the applicant that appropriate follow-up must be obtained before medical clearance can be granted Retain the blue copy of the form for your files and return all other copies to the applicant in a sealed envelope The applicant should return to you when the necessary follow-up has been completed for your final verification and signature *Do not* sign the form until the applicant has met health follow-up requirements All medical documents, including chest X-ray films if a chest X ray examination was performed, should be returned to the applicant upon final medical clearance

Instructions To Physician Providing Health Follow-up

The individual presenting this form has been found to have a medical condition(s) requiring resolution before medical clearance for adjustment of status can be granted Please evaluate the applicant for the condition(s) identified

The requirements for clearance are outlined on the reverse of this page When the individual has completed clearance requirements, please sign the form in the space provided and return the medical examination form to the applicant

Form I-693 (Rev 09/01/87) N

U.S. Department of Justice
Immigration and Naturalization Service

OMB #1115-0134
Medical Examination of Aliens Seeking Adjustment of Status

(Please type or print clearly)
I certify that on the date shown I examined

1 Name (Last in CAPS) _____

(First) _____ (Middle Initial) _____

2 Address (Street number and name) _____ (Apt number) _____

(City) _____ (State) _____ (ZIP Code) _____

3 File number (A number) _____

4 Sex
☐ Male   ☐ Female

5 Date of birth (Month/Day/Year) _____

6 Country of birth _____

7 Date of examination (Month/Day/Year) _____

General Physical Examination
I examined specifically for evidence of the conditions listed below. My examination revealed,

☐ No apparent defect, disease, or disability
☐ The conditions listed below were found (check all boxes that apply)

Class A Conditions
☐ Chancroid
☐ Chronic alcoholism
☐ Gonorrhea
☐ Granuloma inguinale
☐ Hansen's disease, infectious
☐ HIV infection
☐ Insanity
☐ Lymphogranuloma venereum
☐ Mental defect
☐ Mental retardation
☐ Narcotic drug addiction
☐ Previous occurrence of one or more attacks of insanity
☐ Psychopathic personality
☐ Sexual deviation
☐ Syphilis, infectious
☐ Tuberculosis, active

☐ Other physical defect, disease or disability (specify below)

Class B Conditions
☐ Hansen's disease, not infectious   ☐ Tuberculosis, not active

Examination for Tuberculosis - Tuberculin Skin Test
☐ Reaction _____ mm   ☐ No reaction   ☐ Not done
Doctor's name (please print) _____ Date read _____

Examination for Tuberculosis - Chest X-Ray Report
☐ Abnormal   ☐ Normal   ☐ Not done
Doctor's name (please print) _____ Date read _____

Serologic Test for Syphilis
☐ Reactive Titer (confirmatory test performed)   ☐ Nonreactive
Test Type _____
Doctor's name (please print) _____ Date read _____

Serologic Test for HIV Antibody
☐ Positive (confirmed by Western blot)   ☐ Negative
Test Type _____
Doctor's name (please print) _____ Date read _____

Immunization Determination (DTP, OPV, MMR, Td-Refer to *PHS Guidelines* for recommendations.)
☐ Applicant is current for recommended age-specific immunizations
☐ Applicant is not current for recommended age-specific immunizations and I have encouraged that appropriate immunizations be obtained

REMARKS

Civil Surgeon Referral for Follow-up of Medical Condition
☐ The alien named above has applied for adjustment of status. A medical examination conducted by me identified the conditions above which require resolution before medical clearance is granted or for which the alien may seek medical advice. Please provide follow-up services or refer the alien to an appropriate health care provider. The actions necessary for medical clearance are detailed on the reverse of this form

Follow-up Information
The alien named above has complied with the recommended health follow-up
Doctor's name and address (please type or print clearly) _____ Doctor's signature _____ Date _____

Applicant Certification
I certify that I understand the purpose of the medical examination, I authorize the required tests to be completed, and the information on this form refers to me
Signature _____ Date _____

Civil Surgeon Certification
My examination showed the applicant to have met the medical examination and health follow-up requirements for adjustment of status
Doctor's name and address (please type or print clearly) _____ Doctor's signature _____ Date _____

The Immigration and Naturalization Service is authorized to collect this information under the provisions of the Immigration and Nationality Act and the Immigration Reform and Control Act of 1986, Public Law 99-603

Form I 693 (Rev 09/01/87) N

ORIGINAL INS A-FILE

Medical Clearance Requirements
for Aliens Seeking Adjustment of Status

Medical Condition	Estimated Time For Clearance	Action Required
*Suspected Mental Conditions	5 - 30 Days	The applicant must provide to a civil surgeon a psychological or psychiatric evaluation from a specialist or medical facility for final classification and clearance
Tuberculin Skin Test Reaction and Normal Chest X-Ray	Immediate	The applicant should be encouraged to seek further medical evaluation for possible preventive treatment
Tuberculin Skin Test Reaction and Abnormal Chest X-Ray or Abnormal Chest X-Ray (Inactive/Class B)	10 - 30 Days	The applicant should be referred to a physician or local health department for further evaluation. Medical clearance may not be granted until the applicant returns to the civil surgeon with documentation of medical evaluation for tuberculosis
Tuberculin Skin Test Reaction and Abnormal Chest X-Ray or Abnormal Chect X-Ray (Active or Suspected Active/Class A)	10 - 300 Days	The applicant should obtain an appointment with physician or local health department. If treatment for active disease is started, it must be completed (usually 9 months) before a medical clearance may be granted. At the completion of treatment, the applicant must present to the civil surgeon documentation of completion. If treatment is not started, the applicant must present to the civil surgeon documentation of medical evaluation for tuberculosis
Hansen's Disease	30 - 210 Days	Obtain an evaluation from a specialist or Hansen's disease clinic. If the disease is indeterminate or Tuberculoid, the applicant must present to the civil surgeon documentation of medical evaluation. If disease is Lepromotous or Borderline (dimorphous) and treatment is started, the applicant must complete at least 6 months and present documentation to the civil surgeon showing adequate supervision, treatment, and clinical response before a medical clearance is granted
**Venereal Diseases	1 - 30 Days	Obtain an appointment with a physician or local public health department. An applicant with a reactive serologic test for syphilis must provide to the civil surgeon documentation of evaluation for treatment. If any of the venereal diseases are infectious, the applicant must present to the civil surgeon documentation of completion of treatment
Immunizations Incomplete	Immediate	Immunizations are not required, but the applicant should be encouraged to go to physician or local health department for appropriate immunizations
HIV Infection	Immediate	Post-test counseling is not required, but the applicant should be encouraged to seek appropriate post-test counseling

* Mental retardation; insanity; previous attack of insanity; psychopathic personality, sexual deviation or mental defect; narcotic drug addition; and chronic alcoholism.

** Chancroid; gonorrhea; granuloma inguinale; lymphogranuloma venereum; and syphilis.

Form I-693 (Rev 09/01/87) N

U.S. Department of Justice
Immigration and Naturalization Service

OMB No 1115-0145
Petition to Remove the Conditions on Residence

Purpose Of This Form
This form is for a conditional resident who obtained such status through marriage to apply to remove the conditions on his or her residence

Who May File.
If you were granted conditional resident status through marriage to a U S citizen or permanent resident, use this form to petition for the removal of those conditions. Your petition should be filed jointly by you and the spouse through whom you obtained conditional status if you are still married. However, you can apply for a waiver of this joint filing requirement on this form if

- you entered into the marriage in good faith, but your spouse subsequently died,
- you entered into the marriage in good faith, but the marriage was later terminated due to divorce or annulment,
- you entered into the marriage in good faith, and remain married, but have been battered or subjected to extreme mental cruelty by your U S citizen or permanent resident spouse, or
- the termination of your status, and deportation, would result in extreme hardship

You may include your conditional resident children in your petition, or they can file separately

General Filing Instructions.
Please answer all questions by typing or clearly printing in black ink. Indicate that an item is not applicable with "N/A". If an answer is "none," write "none". If you need extra space to answer any item, attach a sheet of paper with your name and your alien registration number (A#), and indicate the number of the item to which the answer refers. You must file your petition with the required Initial Evidence. Your petition must be properly signed and accompanied by the correct fee. If you are under 14 years of age, your parent or guardian may sign the petition in your behalf

Translations Any foreign language document must be accompanied by a full English translation which the translator has certified as complete and correct, and by the translator's certification that he or she is competent to translate from the foreign language into English

Copies If these instructions state that a copy of a document may be filed with this petition, and you choose to send us the original, we may keep that original for our records

Initial Evidence.
Alien Registration Card You must file your petition with a copy of your alien registration card, and with a copy of the alien registration card of any of your conditional resident children you are including in your petition

Evidence of the relationship Submit copies of documents indicating that the marriage upon which you were granted conditional status was entered into in "good faith", and was not for the purpose of circumventing immigration laws You should submit copies of as many documents as you wish to establish this fact and to demonstrate the circumstances of the relationship from the date of the marriage to date, and to demonstrate any circumstances surrounding the end of the relationship, if it has ended. The documents should cover as much of the period since your marriage as possible. Examples of such documents are
- Birth certificate(s) of child(ren) born to the marriage
- Lease or mortgage contracts showing joint occupancy and/or ownership of your communal residence
- Financial records showing joint ownership of assets and joint responsibility for liabilities, such as joint savings and checking accounts, joint federal and state tax returns, insurance policies which show the other as the beneficiary, joint utility bills, joint installment or other loans
- Other documents you consider relevant to establish that your marriage was not entered into in order to evade the immigration laws of the United States

- Affidavits sworn to or affirmed by at least 2 people who have known both of you since your conditional residence was granted and have personal knowledge of your marriage and relationship (Such persons may be required to testify before an immigration officer as to the information contained in the affidavit) The original affidavit must be submitted, and it must also contain the following information regarding the person making the affidavit his or her full name and address, date and place of birth, relationship to you or your spouse, if any, and full information and complete details explaining how the person acquired his or her knowledge. Affidavits must be supported by other types of evidence listed above

If you are filing to waive the joint filing requirement due to the death of your spouse, also submit a copy of the death certificate with your petition

If you are filing to waive the joint filing requirement because your marriage has been terminated, also submit a copy of the divorce decree or other document terminating or annulling the marriage with your petition

If you are filing to waive the joint filing requirement because you and/or your conditional resident child were battered or subjected to extreme mental cruelty, also file your petition with the following
- Evidence of the physical abuse, such as copies of reports or official records issued by police, judges, medical personnel, school officials, and representatives of social service agencies, and original affidavits as described under *Evidence of the Relationship*, or
- Evidence of the extreme mental cruelty, and an original evaluation by a professional recognized by the Service as an expert in the field. These experts include clinical social workers, psychologists and psychiatrists. A clinical social worker who is not licensed only because the State in which he or she practices does not provide for licensing is considered a licensed professional recognized by the Service if he or she is included by the National Association of Social Workers or is certified by the American Board of Examiners in Clinical Social Work. Each evaluation must contain the professional's full name, professional address and license number. It must also identify the licensing, certifying or registering authority
- A copy of your divorce decree if your marriage was terminated by divorce on grounds of physical abuse or mental cruelty

If you are filing for a waiver of the joint filing requirement because the termination of your status, and deportation would result in "extreme hardship", you must also file your petition with evidence your deportation would result in hardship significantly greater than the hardship encountered by other aliens who are deported from this country after extended stays. The evidence must relate only to those factors which arose since you became a conditional resident

If you are a child filing separately from your parent, also file your petition with a full explanation as to why you are filing separately, along with copies of any supporting documentation

When To File.
Filing jointly If you are filing this petition jointly with your spouse, you must file it during the 90 days immediately before the second anniversary of the date you were accorded conditional resident status. This is the date your conditional residence expires. However, if you and your spouse are outside the United States on orders of the U S Government during the period in which the petition must be filed, you may file it within 90 days of your return to the U S

Form I-751 (Rev. 12-4-91)

Filing with a request that the joint filing requirement be waived
You may file this petition at any time after you are granted conditional resident status and before you are deported

Effect Of Not Filing If this petition is not filed, you will automatically lose your permanent resident status as of the second anniversary of the date on which you were granted this status. You will then become deportable from the United States. If your failure to file was through no fault of your own, you may file your petition late with a written explanation and request that INS excuse the late filing. Failure to file before the expiration date may be excused if you demonstrate when you file the application that the delay was due to extraordinary circumstances beyond your control and that the length of the delay was reasonable

Effect of Filing.
Filing this petition extends your conditional residence for six months. You will receive a filing receipt which you should carry with your alien registration card (Form I-551). If you travel outside the U.S. during this period, you may present your card and the filing receipt to be readmitted

Where To File.
If you live in Connecticut, Delaware, District of Columbia, Maine, Maryland, Massachusetts, New Hampshire, New Jersey, New York, Pennsylvania, Puerto Rico, Rhode Island, Vermont, Virgin Islands, Virginia, or West Virginia, mail your petition to USINS Eastern Service Center, 75 Lower Welden Street, St Albans, VT 05479-0001

If you live in Alabama, Arkansas, Florida, Georgia, Kentucky, Louisiana, Mississippi, New Mexico, North Carolina, Oklahoma, South Carolina, Tennessee, or Texas, mail your petition to USINS Southern Service Center, P O Box 152122, Dept A, Irving, TX 75015-2122

If you live in Arizona, California, Guam, Hawaii, or Nevada, mail your petition to USINS Western Service Center, P O Box 30111, Laguna Niguel, CA 92607-0111

If you live in elsewhere in the U S, mail your petition to USINS Northern Service Center, 100 Centennial Mall North, Room B-26, Lincoln, NE 68508

Fee.
The fee for this petition is $75.00. The fee must be submitted in the exact amount. It cannot be refunded. **DO NOT MAIL CASH**

All checks and money orders must be drawn on a bank or other institution located in the United States and must be payable in United States currency. The check or money order should be made payable to the Immigration and Naturalization Service, except that
- If you live in Guam, and are filing this petition in Guam, make your check or money order payable to the "Treasurer, Guam"
- If you are living in the Virgin Islands, and are filing this application in the Virgin Islands, make your check or money order payable to the "Commissioner of Finance of the Virgin Islands"

Checks are accepted subject to collection. An uncollected check will render the application and any document issued invalid. A charge of $5.00 will be imposed if a check in payment of a fee is not honored by the bank on which it is drawn

Processing Information.
Acceptance Any petition that is not signed, or is not accompanied by the correct fee, will be rejected with a notice that the petition is deficient. You may correct the deficiency and resubmit the petition. A petition is not considered properly filed until accepted by the Service

Initial processing Once a petition has been accepted, it will be checked for completeness, including submission of the required initial evidence. If you do not completely fill out the form, or file if without required initial evidence, you will not establish a basis for eligibility, and we may deny your petition

Requests for more information or interview We may request more information or evidence, or we may request that you appear at an INS office for an interview. We may also request that you submit the originals of any copy. We will return these originals when they are no longer required

Decision You will be advised in writing of the decision on your petition

Penalties.
If you knowingly and willfully falsify or conceal a material fact or submit a false document with this request, we will deny the benefit you are filing for, and may deny any other immigration benefit. In addition, you will face severe penalties provided by law, and may be subject to criminal prosecution

Privacy Act Notice
We ask for the information on this form, and associated evidence, to determine if you have established eligibility for the immigration benefit you are filing for. Our legal right to ask for this information is in 8 USC 1184, 1255 and 1258. Failure to provide this information, and any requested evidence, may delay a final decision or result in denial of your request

All the information provided on this form, including addresses, are protected by the Privacy Act and the Freedom of Information Act. This information will not be released in any form whatsoever to a third party, other than another government agency, who requests it without a court order, or without your written consent, or, in the case of a child, the written consent of the parent or legal guardian who filed the form on the child's behalf

Paperwork Reduction Act Notice.
We try to create forms and instructions that are accurate, can be easily understood, and which impose the least possible burden on you to provide us with information. Often this is difficult because some immigration laws are very complex. The estimated average time to complete and file this application is as follows (1) 15 minutes to learn about the law and form, (2) 15 minutes to complete the form, and (3) 50 minutes to assemble and file the petition, for a total estimated average of 1 hour and 20 minutes per petition. If you have comments regarding the accuracy of this estimate, or suggestions for making this form simpler, you can write to both the Immigration and Naturalization Service, 425 I Street, N W, Room 5304, Washington, D C 20536, and the Office of Management and Budget, Paperwork Reduction Project, OMB No 1115-0145 Washington, D C 20503

Form I 751 (Rev 12-4-91)

U.S. Department of Justice
Immigration and Naturalization Service

OMB No 1115-0145
Petition to Remove the Conditions on Residence

START HERE - Please Type or Print

Part 1. Information about you.

Family Name	Given Name	Middle Initial

Address - C/O

Street Number and Name	Apt #

City	State or Province

Country	ZIP/Postal Code

Date of Birth (month/day/year)	Country of Birth

Social Security #	A #

Conditional residence expires on (month/day/year)

Mailing address if different from residence in C/O

Street Number and Name	Apt #

City	State or Province

Country	ZIP/Postal Code

Part 2. Basis for petition (check one).

a ☐ My conditional residence is based on my marriage to a U S citizen or permanent resident, and we are filing this petition together

b ☐ I am a child who entered as a conditional permanent resident and I am unable to be included in a Joint Petition to Remove the Conditional Basis of Alien's Permanent Residence (Form I-751) filed by my parent(s)

My conditional residence is based on my marriage to a U S citizen or permanent resident, but I am unable to file a joint petition and I request a waiver because (check one)

c ☐ My spouse is deceased

d ☐ I entered into the marriage in good faith, but the marriage was terminated though divorce/annulment

e ☐ I am a conditional resident spouse who entered in to the marriage in good faith, or I am a conditional resident child, who has been battered or subjected to extreme mental cruelty by my citizen or permanent resident spouse or parent

f ☐ The termination of my status and deportation from the United States would result in an extreme hardship

Part 3. Additional information about you.

Other names used (including maiden name)	Telephone #

Date of Marriage	Place of Marriage

If your spouse is deceased, give the date of death (month/day/year)

Are you in deportation or exclusion proceedings? ☐ Yes ☐ No

Was a fee paid to anyone other than an attorney in connection with this petition? ☐ Yes ☐ No

Form I 751 (Rev 12-4-91)   Continued on back

FOR INS USE ONLY

Returned	Receipt

Resubmitted

Reloc Sent

Reloc Rec'd

☐ Applicant Interviewed

Remarks

Action

To Be Completed by Attorney or Representative, if any
☐ Fill in box if G-28 is attached to represent the applicant

VOLAG #

ATTY State License #

Part 3. Additional Information about you. (con't)

Since becoming a conditional resident, have you ever been arrested, cited, charged, indicted, convicted, fined or imprisoned for breaking or violating any law or ordinance (excluding traffic regulations), or committed any crime for which you were not arrested?   ☐ Yes ☐ No

If you are married, is this a different marriage than the one through which conditional residence status was obtained?   ☐ Yes ☐ No

Have you resided at any other address since you became a permanent resident?   ☐ Yes ☐ No *(If yes attach a list of all addresses and dates)*

Is your spouse currently serving employed by the U.S. government and serving outside the U.S.?   ☐ Yes ☐ No

Part 4. Information about the spouse or parent through whom you gained your conditional residence

Family Name	Given Name	Middle Initial	Phone Number ( )

Address

Date of Birth (month/day/year)	Social Security #	A#

Part 5. Information about your children. List *all* your children Attach another sheet if necessary

#	Name	Date of Birth (month/day/year)	If in U.S., give A#, current immigration status and U.S. Address	Living with you?
1				☐ Yes ☐ No
2				☐ Yes ☐ No
3				☐ Yes ☐ No
4				☐ Yes ☐ No

Part 6. Complete if you are requesting a waiver of the joint filing petition requirement based on extreme mental cruelty.

Evaluator's ID Number	State	Number	Expires on (month/day/year)	Occupation

Last Name	First Name	Address

Part 7. Signature. *Read the information on penalties in the instructions before completing this section. If you checked block "a" in Part 2 your spouse must also sign below.*

I certify, under penalty of perjury under the laws of the United States of America, that this petition, and the evidence submitted with it, is all true and correct. If conditional residence was based on a marriage, I further certify that the marriage was entered into in accordance with the laws of the place where the marriage took place, and was not for the purpose of procuring an immigration benefit. I also authorize the release of any information from my records which the Immigration and Naturalization Service needs to determine eligibility for the benefit being sought.

Signature	Print Name	Date
Signature of Spouse	Print Name	Date

Please note: If you do not completely fill out this form, or fail to submit any required documents listed in the instructions, then you cannot be found eligible for the requested benefit, and this petition may be denied.

Part 8. Signature of person preparing form if other than above.

I declare that I prepared this petition at the request of the above person and it is based on all information of which I have knowledge.

Signature	Print Name	Date

Firm Name and Address

Form I-751 (Rev 12-4-91)   * GPO : 1992 0 - 316-463

U.S. Department of Justice
Immigration and Naturalization Service

OMB NO. 1115-0086

Request for Asylum in the United States

INSTRUCTIONS
READ ALL INSTRUCTIONS CAREFULLY BEFORE COMPLETING THIS FORM

1. PREPARATION OF FORM. Type or print legibly in ink. **The form must be completed in English.** Do not leave any questions unanswered or blank. If any questions do not apply to you, write "none" or "not applicable." It is in your best interest to provide as much detail on the form and to be as complete as possible. Substantially incomplete applications will be returned for completion and may delay your request for asylum and for employment authorization. To the extent possible, questions should be answered directly on the form. However, if you need more space to complete your answers/questions fully, attach a continuation sheet(s) indicating the question number(s) being answered, date and sign each sheet.

After completing the form, you are strongly urged to attach any additional written statements which are important to your claim. To the extent possible, your written statements should follow some chronology and include experiences, events and dates in as much detail as possible. Your written statements should focus on your reason(s) for leaving your country, your fear of returning, if any, the reason(s) for any such fears, the consequences of your return, and the reasons for such consequences. If you need or would like assistance in completing this form and preparing your written statements, assistance from pro bono attorneys and/or voluntary agencies may be available. A list of accredited representatives is available from your local INS District Office or the Asylum Office covering your area.

2. NUMBER OF COPIES. One form may include your entire family (husband, wife and unmarried children under age 21) if they are in the U.S. The original and three (3) copies of your completed form plus continuation sheets and/or supplementary statements should be sent to the INS. An additional copy should be sent for each family member listed under question 17. Documentary evidence of relationship(s), such as birth records of your children, marriage certificate, or proof of termination of marriage, should be sent with the form. Children who are married or over 21 must file separate forms.

3. REQUIRED DOCUMENTS. Each applicant and dependents 14 years of age or older must complete the **Biographic Information Form G-325A and Fingerprint Card, FD-258.** Applicants may be fingerprinted by law enforcement officers, outreach centers, charitable and voluntary agencies, or other reputable persons or organizations.

The Fingerprint Card (FD-258) on which the prints are submitted, the ink used, and the quality of the prints must meet standards prescribed by the Federal Bureau of Investigation. The card must be signed by you in the presence of the person taking your fingerprints, who must then sign his/her name and enter the date in the spaces provided. **It is important to furnish all the information on the card.**

4. PHOTOGRAPHS. Two (2) ADIT photographs of every applicant and their dependents included in the application, must be submitted regardless of age. Photographs must be taken within 30 days of application date. These photographs should be about one inch from chin to top of hair. You should be shown in 3/4 frontal view showing right side of face with right ear visible.

5. SUPPORTING DOCUMENTS. Background materials such as newspaper articles, affidavits of witnesses or experts, periodicals, journals, books, photographs, official documents, your own statements, should include explanations from you on how they support your case. You should submit any documentation which helps verify your specific claim. Attach as many sheets and explanations as necessary to fully explain the basis of your claim.

6. TRANSLATION. Any document in a foreign language must be accompanied by a translation in English. The translator must certify that he or she is competent to translate and that the translation is accurate.

7. BURDEN OF PROOF. The burden of proof is on you to establish that you qualify as a refugee, and that you are unable or unwilling to return to your country. This may be based on actual past persecution, or a well-founded fear of future persecution on account of your race, religion, nationality, membership in a particular social group, or political opinion.

8. SUBMISSION OF FORM. Unless you are under deportation or exclusion proceedings, the correct number of copies should be sent to the Asylum Office having jurisdiction over your area. A list of these offices is available from your local INS office. One copy of the completed application should be retained by you. Although the INS Asylum Office will confirm in writing its receipt of your application, you may wish to send the completed forms by registered mail (return receipt requested.)

Form I 589 (Rev. 08-01-91)N

If you are under deportation or exclusion proceedings (that is, if you have been served with Form I-221, Order to Show Cause, or with Form I-122, Notice to Applicant for Admission Detained for Hearing), file four copies of your asylum application and all supporting documents with the Office of the Immigration Court having jurisdiction over your case. Your application should be filed only <u>after</u> your case has been set for a hearing.

9. **UNITED NATIONS.** You may, if you wish, forward a copy of your form and other supporting documents to: United Nations High Commissioner for Refugees, 1718 Connecticut Avenue, N.W., Suite 200; Washington, D C. 20009; (Telephone: (202) 387-8546) - (Fax: (202) 387-9038). UNHCR may be able to assist you in identifying resources to help you complete the form.

10. **IDENTITY AND TRAVEL DOCUMENTS.** You will be notified to appear for an interview with an Asylum Officer. If you have a passport, other travel or identification document, Form I-94, Arrival/Departure Record, you must bring it or them with you to the interview. If other members of your family are included in your application for asylum, they must also appear for the interview and bring their identity/travel documents if in their possession.

11. **INTERVIEW.** An Asylum Officer will interview you under oath, make an assessment of your claim and your eligibility for asylum. If you cannot speak English fluently, you are required to bring along an interpreter who is fluent in both English and your native language. Quality interpretation may be crucial to your claim; such assistance should be obtained at your expense prior to the interview. A list of agencies willing to assist you in finding qualified interpreters may be available from local INS District or Asylum Offices.

Until a final decision is made in your case, you will be permitted to remain in the United States. If your application to an Asylum Office is denied, you are entitled to renew your claim with an Immigration Judge.

12. **WITHHOLDING OF DEPORTATION.** Your asylum application is also considered to be an application for withholding of deportation to a specific country or countries under Section 243(h) of the Immigration and Nationality Act (8 U.S.C. 1253), as amended. If asylum is not granted, you may still be eligible for withholding of deportation.

In order to qualify for withholding of deportation, you must establish that your life or freedom would be threatened on account of race, religion, nationality, membership in a particular social group, or political opinion. Therefore, you must establish a clear probability of persecution if you return to your home country, (i.e., it must be more likely than not that you will be persecuted on account of one of the five factors.)

13. **WORK AUTHORIZATION.** You may request permission to work while your asylum application is pending. Generally, work authorization, if granted, will be valid, if renewed as required, at least until a final decision is made on your application. Submit a **Form I-765, Application for Employment Authorization**, with this form for each person seeking permission to work.

14. **PENALTY.** Title 18, United States Code, Section 1546, provides, "... Whoever knowingly makes under oath, or as permitted under penalty of perjury under Section 1746 of Title 28, United States Code, knowingly subscribes as true, any false statement with respect to a material fact in any application, affidavit, or other document required by the immigration laws or regulations prescribed thereunder, or knowingly presents any such application, affidavit, or other document containing any such false statement - shall be fined in accordance with this title or imprisoned not more than five years, or both.

15. **REPORTING BURDEN.** We try to create forms and instructions that are accurate, can be easily understood, and which impose the least possible burden on you to provide us with information. Often this is difficult because some immigration laws are very complex. Accordingly, the reporting burden for this collection of information is computed as follows: (1) learning about the form, 30 minutes; (2) completing the form, 60 minutes; and (3) assembling and filing the form, (includes the required interview and travel time, after filing of application), 2 hours, for an estimated average of 3 hours and 30 minutes per response. If you have comments regarding the accuracy of this burden estimate, you can write to both the U.S. Department of Justice, Immigration and Naturalization Service, Room 5304, Washington, DC 20536; and to the Office of Management and Budget, Paperwork Reduction Project: OMB No. 1115-0086, Washington, DC 20503.

U.S. Department of Justice
Immigration and Naturalization Service

OMB NO. 1115-0086
Request for Asylum in the United States

DO NOT WRITE IN THIS BLOCK - FOR INS USE ONLY

Asylum Office:	Basis of Asylum Claim:	Action:	
	1. ☐ Race	Asylum:	Withholding of deportation:
INS-FCO:	2. ☐ Religion	☐ Granted ☐ Denied	☐ Granted ☐ Denied
Received date:	3. ☐ Nationality	Date: _____	Date: _____
	4. ☐ Membership in a Particular Social Group		
G-28 or VOLAG #	5. ☐ Political Opinion	Adjudicating Officer	

PART A - INFORMATION ABOUT YOU

1. Alien Registration Number: *(if applicable)*

2. Name: *(Family name in CAPS)* *(First)* *(Middle)*

   Other names used: *(include maiden name or aliases)*

3. Address in the U.S.: *(Number and Street, Apt. #)*

   (City or Town) *(State)* *(Zip Code)*

4. Address *prior to coming to U.S.*: *(Number and Street, Apt. #)*

   (City or Town) *(Province or State)* *(Country)*

5. Sex: ☐ Male ☐ Female

6. Marital Status: ☐ Single ☐ Married ☐ Divorced ☐ Widowed

7. Date of Birth: *(Mo./Day/Yr.)*

8. Place of Birth: *(City or Town)*

   (Province) *(Country)*

9. Nationality: at Birth: _____
   at Present: _____
   Other: _____
   If stateless, how did you become stateless?

10. Race/Ethnic or Tribal Group:

11. Religion:

12. Arrival in the U.S.:
    Date: *(Mo./Day/Yr.)* _____
    Place: *(City/State)* _____
    ☐ Not in the U.S.

13. Current Immigration Status: *(Crewman, Stowaway, Student, Visitor or Other)*
    Date authorized stay expires: *(Mo./Day/Yr.)*

14. Social Security Number: *(if applicable)*

15. Telephone Number:
    Home *(Area Code)* ( ) - ( )
    Work *(Area Code)* ( ) - ( )

PART B - INFORMATION ABOUT YOUR FAMILY

16. List your spouse and all your unmarried children under the age of 21:

Name:	A-Number: *(If Applicable)*	Sex	Date of birth:	Place of birth:	If in U.S. Date/Place of Arrival
(Spouse)					

If in the U.S., are your spouse/children included in your request for asylum:

Children ☐ No ☐ Yes   Spouse ☐ No ☐ Yes   If not, is your spouse making a separate application for asylum? ☐ No ☐ Yes   *(INS office _____ Results - Granted/Denied)*

Form I-589 (Rev. 08-01-91)N

17. My Spouse/Children Reside: ☐ with me ☐ apart from me *(if apart, give address)*

_____
(Number and street and Apt. #.)   *(City)*   *(Province)*   *(Country)*

PART C - INFORMATION ABOUT YOUR CLAIM FOR ASYLUM

18. Why are you seeking asylum? *(Explain fully what is the basis - attach additional sheets as needed.)*

19. What do you think would happen to you if you returned to your home country? *(Explain.)*

20. Have you or any member of your family ever belonged to or been associated with any organizations or groups in your home country (*i.e., a political party, student group, union, religious organization, military or para-military group, civil patrol, guerrilla organization, ethnic group, human rights group, or the press*)?

☐ No ☐ Yes *(If yes, provide the following information relating to each organization or group: Name of organization or group, dates of membership or affiliation, purpose of the organization, what, if any, you or your relative's duties or responsibilities were, and whether you are still an active member.)*

21. Have you or any member of your family, ever been mistreated/threatened by the authorities of your home country or by a group(s) controlled by the government, or by a group(s) which the government of your home country is unable or unwilling to control?

☐ No ☐ Yes. If yes, was it mistreatment or threat because of:

☐ Race ☐ Religion ☐ Nationality ☐ Membership in a particular social group ☐ Political opinion ☐ Other

(Specify for each instance: your relationship, what occurred and the circumstances, date, exact location, who took such action against you, what was his/her position in the government or group, reason why the incident occurred, names and addresses of a few of the people who may have witnessed these actions and who could verify these statements. Attach documents referring to these incidents, if available; attach additional sheets as needed.)

22. Have you or any member of your family, ever been: ☐ Arrested ☐ Detained ☐ Interrogated

☐ Convicted and sentenced ☐ Imprisoned in your country, any other country, or in the U.S.?

☐ No ☐ Yes *(If yes, specify for each instance: What occurred and the circumstances, dates, location, duration of the detention or imprisonment, reason for the detention or conviction, treatment during detention or imprisonment, what formal charges were placed against you, reason for the release, treatment after release, names and addresses of a few of the people who could verify these statements. Attach documents referring to these incidents, if any.)*

23. Have you applied for asylum in the U.S. before?

☐ No ☐ Yes (Date_____INS office_____Results - Granted/Denied)

PART D - OTHER INFORMATION

24. Have you traveled to the United States before? How many times?_____

☐ No ☐ Yes (If so, give date, purpose and duration of trip.)

25. List all current travel or identity documents in your possession such as national passport, refugee convention travel document, safe conduct, or national identity card:

Document type	Document number	Issuing country or authority	Date of issue	Date of expiration

26. Date of departure from your country of nationality (Mo./Day/Yr.)

27. Was exit permission required to leave your country?

☐ No ☐ Yes (If yes, obtained by whom)

28. After leaving your home country, did you travel through or reside in any other country before entering the U.S.?

☐ No ☐ Yes (If yes, identify each country, length of stay, purpose of stay, address, reason for leaving, and whether you are entitled and willing to return to that country for residence purposes.)

29. Have you returned to your country of claimed persecution since your departure? How many times?_____

☐ No ☐ Yes (If so, give date, purpose and duration of trip.)

30. Have you applied for asylum or refugee status in any other country?

☐ No ☐ Yes (Date_____Country_____Results - Granted/Denied)

31. Have you been recognized as a refugee by another country or by the United Nations High Commissioner for Refugees?

☐ No ☐ Yes (If yes, Date_____Country_____)

32. Have you ever caused harm or suffering to any person because of his/her race, religion, nationality, membership in a particular social group, or political opinion or ordered or assisted in such acts?

☐ No ☐ Yes *(If yes, describe nature of the incidents and your own involvement.)*

33. Please provide any additional statement relevant to your case.

PART E - SIGNATURE

Under penalty of perjury, I declare that the above and all accompanying documents are true and correct to the best of my knowledge and belief.

_____   _____
Signature of applicant   *Date*

Signature of person preparing form if other than above:
I declare that this document was prepared by me at the request of the applicant and is based on information provided by the applicant.

Print Name _____   *Address* _____

Signature _____   *Date* _____ *G-28 or VOLAG #* _____

Applicant is not to sign the application below until he or she appears before an Asylum Officer of the Immigration and Naturalization Service for examination. I_____ swear (affirm) that I know the contents of this application that I am signing including the attached documents; that they are true to the best of my knowledge; and that corrections numbered ( ) to ( ) were made by me or at my request and that I signed this application with my full, true name:

_____
(Complete and true signature of applicant)

Signed and sworn to before me by the above-named applicant at_____ on _____
                                                                                                    (Month) (Day)   (Year)

_____
(Signature and title of interviewing officer)

U.S. Department of Justice
Immigration and Naturalization Service

OMB No 1115-0053
Application to Register Permanent Residence or Adjust Status

Purpose of this Form.
This form is for a person who is in the United States to apply to adjust to permanent resident status or register for permanent residence while in the U S It may also be used by certain Cuban nationals to request a change in the date their permanent residence began

Who May File.
Based on an immigrant petition. You may apply to adjust your status if
- an immigrant visa number is immediately available to you based on an approved immigrant petition, or
- you are filing this application with a complete relative, special immigrant juvenile, or special immigrant military petition which if approved, would make an immigrant visa number immediately available to you

Based on being the spouse or child of another adjustment applicant or of a person granted permanent residence . You may apply to adjust status if you are the spouse or child of another adjustment applicant, or of a lawful permanent resident, if the relationship existed when that person was admitted as a permanent resident in an immigrant category which allows derivative status for spouses and children

Based on admission as the fiance(e) of a U.S. citizen and subsequent marriage to that citizen You may apply to adjust status if you were admitted to the U S as the K-1 fiance(e) of a U S citizen and married that citizen within 90 days of your entry If you were admitted as the K-2 child of such a fiance(e), you may apply based on your parent's adjustment application.

Based on asylum status You may apply to adjust status if you have been granted asylum in the U S and are eligible for asylum adjustment [Note In most cases you become eligible after being physically present in the U S for one year after the grant of asylum if you still qualify as a refugee or as the spouse or child of refugee]

Based on Cuban citizenship or nationality You may apply to adjust status if
- you are a native or citizen of Cuba, were admitted or paroled into the U S after January 1, 1959, and thereafter have been physically present in the U S for at least one year, or
- you are the spouse or unmarried child of a Cuban described above, and you were admitted or paroled after January 1, 1959, and thereafter have been physically present in the U S for at least one year

Based on continuous residence since before January 1, 1972 You may apply for permanent residence if you have continuously resided in the U S since before January 1, 1972

Other basis of eligibility If you are not included in the above categories, but believe you may be eligible for adjustment or creation of record of permanent residence, contact your local INS office

Applying to change the date your permanent residence began If you were granted permanent residence in the U S prior to November 6, 1966, and are a native or citizen of Cuba, his or her spouse or unmarried minor child, you may ask to change the date your lawful permanent residence began to your date of arrival in the U S or May 2, 1964, whichever is later

Persons Who Are Ineligible
Unless you are applying for creation of record based on continuous residence since before 1/1/72, or adjustment of status under a category in which special rules apply (such as asylum adjustment, Cuban adjustment, special immigrant juvenile adjustment, or special immigrant military personnel adjustment), **you are not eligible for adjustment of status if any of the following apply to you**
- you entered the U S in transit without a visa,
- you entered the U S as a nonimmigrant crewman,
- you were not admitted or paroled following inspection by an immigration officer;
- your authorized stay expired before you filed this application, you were employed in the U S , prior to filing this application, without INS authorization, or you otherwise failed to maintain your nonimmigrant status, other than through no fault of your own or for technical reasons, unless you are applying because you are an immediate relative of a U S citizen (parent, spouse, widow, widower, or unmarried child under 21 years old), a K-1 fiance(e) or K-2 fiance(e) dependent who married the U S petitioner within 90

days of admission, or an "H" or "I" special immigrant (foreign medical graduates, international organization employees or their derivative family members),
- you are or were a J-1 or J-2 exchange visitor, are subject to the two-year foreign residence requirement, and have not complied with or been granted a waiver of the requirement,
- you have A, E or G nonimmigrant status, or have an occupation which would allow you to have this status, unless you complete Form I-508 (I-508F for French nationals) to waive diplomatic rights, privileges and immunities, and if you are an A or G nonimmigrant, unless you submit a completed Form I-566,
- you were admitted to Guam as a visitor under the Guam visa waiver program,
- you were admitted to the U S as a visitor under the Visa Waiver Pilot Program, unless you are applying because you are an immediate relative of a U S citizen (parent, spouse, widow, widower, or unmarried child under 21 years old),
- you are already a conditional permanent resident,
- you were admitted as a K-1 fiance(e) but did not marry the U S citizen who filed the petition for you, or were admitted as the K-2 child of a fiance(e) and your parent did not marry the U S citizen who filed the petition

General Filing Instructions.
Please answer all questions by typing or clearly printing in black ink Indicate that an item is not applicable with **"N/A"**. If the answer is **"none"**, write **"none"** If you need extra space to answer any item, attach a sheet of paper with your name and your alien registration number (A#), if any, and indicate the number of the item to which the answer refers You must file your application with the required **Initial Evidence**. Your application must be properly signed and filed with the correct fee If you are under 14 years of age, your parent or guardian may sign your application

Translations. Any foreign language document must be accompanied by a full English translation which the translator has certified as complete and correct, and by the translator's certification that he or she is competent to translate from the foreign language into English

Copies. If these instructions state that a copy of a document may be filed with this application, and you choose to send us the original, we may keep the original for our records

Initial Evidence.
You must file your application with following evidence

- **Birth certificate** Submit a copy of your birth certificate or other record of your birth
- **Photos.** Submit two (2) identical natural color photographs of yourself, taken within 30 days of this application [Photos must have a white background, be unmounted, printed on thin paper, and be glossy and unretouched They must show a three-quarter frontal profile showing the right side of your face, with your right ear visible and with your head bare You may wear a headdress if required by a religious order of which you are a member The photos must be no larger than 2 X 2 inches, with the distance from the top of the head to just below the chin about 1 and 1/4 inches Lightly print your A# (or your name if you have no A#) on the back of each photo, using a pencil]
- **Fingerprints.** Submit a complete set of fingerprints on Form FD-258 if you are between the ages of 14 and 75 [Do not bend, fold, or crease the fingerprint chart You should complete the information on the top of the chart and write your A# (if any) in the space marked "Your no OCA" or "Miscellaneous no MNU" You should not sign the chart until you have been fingerprinted, or are told to sign by the person who takes your fingerprints The person who takes your fingerprints must also sign the chart and write his/her title and the date you are fingerprinted in the space provided on the chart You may be fingerprinted by police, sheriff, or INS officials or other reputable person or organization You should call the police, sheriff, organization or INS office before you go there, since some offices do not take fingerprints or may take fingerprints only at certain times]

Form I-485 (Rev. 09-09-92)N

- **Medical Examination.** Submit a medical examination report on the form you have obtained from INS [Not required if you are applying for creation of record based on continuous residence since before 1/1/72, or if you are a K-1 fiance(e) or K-2 dependent of a fiance(e) who had a medical examination within the past year as required for the nonimmigrant fiance(e) visa.]
- **Form G-325A,** Biographic Information Sheet. You must submit a completed G-325A if you are between 14 and 79 years of age.
- **Evidence of status.** Submit a copy of your Form I-94, Nonimmigrant Arrival/Departure Record, showing your admission to the U.S. and current status, or other evidence of your status.
- **Employment letter/Affidavit of Support.** Submit a letter showing you are employed in a job that is not temporary, an affidavit of support from a responsible person in the U.S., or other evidence that shows that you are not likely to become a public charge [Not required if you are applying for creation of record based on continuous residence since before 1/1/72, asylum adjustment, or a Cuban or a spouse or unmarried child of a Cuban who was admitted after 1/1/59]
- **Evidence of eligibility.**
  - **Based on an immigrant petition.** Attach a copy of the approval notice for an immigrant petition which makes a visa number immediately available to you, or submit a complete relative, special immigrant juvenile, or special immigrant military petition which, if approved, will make a visa number immediately available to you.
  - **Based on admission as the K-1 fiance(e) of a U.S. citizen and subsequent marriage to that citizen.** Attach a copy of the fiance(e) petition approval notice and a copy of your marriage certificate.
  - **Based on asylum status.** Attach a copy of the letter or Form I-94 which shows the date you were granted asylum.
  - **Based on continuous residence in the U.S. since before 1/1/72.** Attach copies of evidence that shows continuous residence since before 1/1/72.
  - **Based on Cuban citizenship or nationality.** Attach evidence of your citizenship or nationality, such as a copy of your passport, birth certificate or travel document.
  - **Based on you being the spouse or child of another adjustment applicant or person granted permanent residence based on issuance of an immigrant visa.** File your application with the application of that other applicant, or with evidence it is pending with the Service or has been approved, or evidence your spouse or parent has been granted permanent residence based on an immigrant visa and
    - If you are applying as the spouse of that person, also attach a copy of your marriage certificate and copies of documents showing the legal termination of all other marriages by you and your spouse, or
    - If you are applying as the child of that person, also attach a copy of your birth certificate, and, if the other person is not your natural mother, copies of evidence, (such as a marriage certificate and documents showing the legal termination of all other marriages, and an adoption decree), to demonstrate that you qualify as his or her child
  - **Other basis for eligibility.** Attach copies of documents proving that you are eligible for the classification.

Where To File.
File this application at the local INS office having jurisdiction over your place of residence.

Fee. The fee for this application is $120, except that it is $95 if you are less than 14 years old. The fee must be submitted in the exact amount. It cannot be refunded. **DO NOT MAIL CASH.** All checks and money orders must be drawn on a bank or other institution located in the United States and must be payable in United States currency. The check or money order should be made payable to the Immigration and Naturalization Service, except that
- If you live in Guam, and are filing this application in Guam, make your check or money order payable to the "Treasurer, Guam."
- If you live in the Virgin Islands, and are filing this application in the Virgin Islands, make your check or money order payable to the "Commissioner of Finance of the Virgin Islands."

Checks are accepted subject to collection. An uncollected check will render the application and any document issued invalid. A charge of $5.00 will be imposed if a check in payment of a fee is not honored by the bank on which it is drawn.

Processing Information.

Acceptance. Any application that is not signed, or is not accompanied by the correct fee, will be rejected with a notice that the application is deficient. You may correct the deficiency and resubmit the application. An application is not considered properly filed until accepted by the Service.

Initial processing. Once an application has been accepted, it will be checked for completeness, including submission of the required initial evidence. If you do not completely fill out the form, or file it without required initial evidence, you will not establish a basis for eligibility, and we may deny your application.

Requests for more information. We may request more information or evidence. We may also request that you submit the originals of any copy. We will return these originals when they are no longer required.

Interview. After you file your application you will be notified to appear at an INS office to answer questions about the application. You will be required to answer these questions under oath or affirmation. You must bring your Arrival-Departure Record (Form I-94) and any passport to the interview.

Decision. You will be notified in writing of the decision on your application.

Travel Outside the U.S. If you plan to leave the U.S. to go to any other country, including Canada or Mexico, before a decision is made on your application, contact the INS office processing your application before you leave. In many cases, leaving the U.S. without advance written permission will result in automatic termination of your application. Also, you may experience difficulty upon returning to the U.S. if you do not have written permission to reenter.

Penalties.
If you knowingly and willfully falsify or conceal a material fact or submit a false document with this request, we will deny the benefit you are filing for, and may deny any other immigration benefit. In addition, you will face severe penalties provided by law, and may be subject to criminal prosecution.

Privacy Act Notice.
We ask for the information on this form, and associated evidence, to determine if you have established eligibility for the immigration benefit you are filing for. Our legal right to ask for this information is in 8 USC 1255 and 1259. We may provide this information to other government agencies. Failure to provide this information, and any requested evidence, may delay a final decision or result in denial of your request.

Paperwork Reduction Act Notice.
We try to create forms and instructions that are accurate, can be easily understood, and which impose the least possible burden on you to provide us with information. Often this is difficult because some immigration laws are very complex. The estimated average time to complete and file this application is computed as follows (1) **20** minutes to learn about the law and form, (2) **25** minutes to complete the form, and (3) **270** minutes to assemble and file the application, including the required interview and travel time, for a total estimated average of **5** hours and **15** minutes per application. If you have comments regarding the accuracy of this estimate, or suggestions for making this form simpler, you can write to both the Immigration and Naturalization Service, 425 I Street, N.W., Room 5304, Washington, D.C. 20536, and the Office of Management and Budget, Paperwork Reduction Project, OMB No. 1115-0053, Washington, D.C. 20503.

U.S. Department of Justice
Immigration and Naturalization Service

Application to Register Permanent Residence or Adjust Status

OMB No 1115-0053

START HERE - Please Type or Print

Part 1. Information about you.

Family Name	Given Name	Middle Initial

Address - C/O

Street Number and Name	Apt #

City

State	Zip Code

Date of Birth (month/day/year)	Country of Birth
Social Security #	A # (if any)
Date of Last Arrival (month/day/year)	I-94 #
Current INS Status	Expires on (month/day/year)

Part 2. Application Type. (check one)

I am applying for adjustment to permanent resident status because:

a. ☐ an immigrant petition giving me an immediately available immigrant visa number has been approved (attach a copy of the approval notice), or a relative, special immigrant juvenile, or special immigrant military visa petition filed with this application will give me an immediately available visa number if approved

b. ☐ My spouse or parent applied for adjustment of status or was granted lawful permanent residence in an immigrant visa category which allows derivative status for spouses and children

c. ☐ I entered as a K-1 fiance(e) of a U S citizen whom I married within 90 days of entry, or I am the K-2 child of such a fiance(e) (attach a copy of the fiance(e) petition approval notice and the marriage certificate)

d. ☐ I was granted asylum or derivative asylum status as the spouse or child of a person granted asylum and am eligible for adjustment.

e. ☐ I am a native or citizen of Cuba admitted or paroled into the U S after January 1, 1959, and thereafter have been physically present in the U S for at least 1 year

f. ☐ I am the husband, wife, or minor unmarried child of a Cuban described in (e) and am residing with that person, and was admitted or paroled into the U S. after January 1, 1959, and thereafter have been physically present in the U S for at least 1 year

g. ☐ I have continuously resided in the U S since before January 1, 1972

h. ☐ Other-explain _____

I am already a permanent resident and am applying to have the date I was granted permanent residence adjusted to the date I originally arrived in the U.S. as a nonimmigrant or parolee, or as of May 2, 1964, whichever is later, and (Check one)

i. ☐ I am a native or citizen of Cuba and meet the description in (e), above

j. ☐ I am the husband, wife or minor unmarried child of a Cuban, and meet the description in (f), above

Form I-485 (09-09-92)N

Continued on back.

FOR INS USE ONLY

Returned	Receipt
Resubmitted	
Reloc Sent	
Reloc Rec'd	

☐ Applicant Interviewed

Section of Law
☐ Sec 209(b), INA
☐ Sec 13, Act of 9/11/57
☐ Sec 245, INA
☐ Sec 249, INA
☐ Sec 1 Act of 11/2/66
☐ Sec 2 Act of 11/2/66
☐ Other_____

Country Chargeable

Eligibility Under Sec. 245
☐ Approved Visa Petition
☐ Dependent of Principal Alien
☐ Special Immigrant
☐ Other_____

Preference

Action Block

To Be Completed by Attorney or Representative, if any
☐ Fill in box if G-28 is attached to represent the applicant

VOLAG#

ATTY State License #

Part 3. Processing Information.

A

City/Town/Village of birth	Current occupation
Your mother's first name	Your father's first name

Give your name exactly how it appears on your Arrival /Departure Record (Form I-94)

Place of last entry into the U S (City/State)	In what status did you last enter? *(Visitor, Student, exchange alien, crewman, temporary worker, without inspection, etc)*
Were you inspected by a U.S Immigration Officer? ☐ Yes ☐ No	
Nonimmigrant Visa Number	Consulate where Visa was issued
Date Visa was Issued (month/day/year)	Sex ☐ Male ☐ Female	Marital Status ☐ Married ☐ Single ☐ Divorced ☐ Widowed

Have you ever before applied for permanent resident status in the U S? ☐ No ☐ Yes (give date and place of filing and final disposition)

B List your present husband/wife, all of your sons and daughters (if you have none, write "none" If additional space is needed, use separate paper)

Family Name	Given Name	Middle Initial	Date of Birth (month/day/year)
Country of birth	Relationship	A #	Applying with you? ☐ Yes ☐ No
Family Name	Given Name	Middle Initial	Date of Birth (month/day/year)
Country of birth	Relationship	A #	Applying with you? ☐ Yes ☐ No
Family Name	Given Name	Middle Initial	Date of Birth (month/day/year)
Country of birth	Relationship	A #	Applying with you? ☐ Yes ☐ No
Family Name	Given Name	Middle Initial	Date of Birth (month/day/year)
Country of birth	Relationship	A #	Applying with you? ☐ Yes ☐ No
Family Name	Given Name	Middle Initial	Date of Birth (month/day/year)
Country of birth	Relationship	A #	Applying with you? ☐ Yes ☐ No

C. List your present and past membership in or affiliation with every political organization, association, fund, foundation, party, club, society, or similar group in the United States or in any other place since your 16th birthday Include any foreign military service in this part If none, write "none" Include the name of organization, location, dates of membership from and to, and the nature of the organization If additional space is needed, use separate paper

Form I-485 (Rev 09-09-92) N   Continued On Next Page

Part 3. Processing Information. *(Continued)*

Please answer the following questions (If your answer is **"Yes"** on any one of these questions, explain on a separate piece of paper does not necessarily mean that you are not entitled to register for permanent residence or adjust status)   Answering **"Yes"**

1. Have you ever, in or outside the U.S.
    a. knowingly committed any crime of moral turpitude or a drug-related offense for which you have not been arrested?
    b. been arrested, cited, charged, indicted, fined, or imprisoned for breaking or violating any law or ordinance, excluding traffic violations?
    c. been the beneficiary of a pardon, amnesty, rehabilitation decree, other act of clemency or similar action?
    d. exercised diplomatic immunity to avoid prosecution for a criminal offense in the U.S.? ☐ Yes ☐ No

2. Have you received public assistance in the U.S. from any source, including the U.S. government or any state, county, city, or municipality (other than emergency medical treatment), or are you likely to receive public assistance in the future? ☐ Yes ☐ No

3. Have you ever
    a. within the past 10 years been a prostitute or procured anyone for prostitution, or intend to engage in such activities in the future?
    b. engaged in any unlawful commercialized vice, including, but not limited to, illegal gambling?
    c. knowingly encouraged, induced, assisted, abetted or aided any alien to try to enter the U.S. illegally?
    d. illicitly trafficked in any controlled substance, or knowingly assisted, abetted or colluded in the illicit trafficking of any controlled substance? ☐ Yes ☐ No

4. Have you ever engaged in, conspired to engage in, or do you intend to engage in, or have you ever solicited membership or funds for, or have you through any means ever assisted or provided any type of material support to, any person or organization that has ever engaged or conspired to engage, in sabotage, kidnapping, political assassination, hijacking, or any other form of terrorist activity? ☐ Yes ☐ No

5. Do you intend to engage in the U.S. in
    a. espionage?
    b. any activity a purpose of which is opposition to, or the control or overthrow of, the Government of the United States, by force, violence or other unlawful means?
    c. any activity to violate or evade any law prohibiting the export from the United States of goods, technology or sensitive information? ☐ Yes ☐ No

6. Have you ever been a member of, or in any way affiliated with, the Communist Party or any other totalitarian party? ☐ Yes ☐ No

7. Did you, during the period March 23, 1933 to May 8, 1945, in association with either the Nazi Government of Germany or any organization or government associated or allied with the Nazi Government of Germany, ever order, incite, assist or otherwise participate in the persecution of any person because of race, religion, national origin or political opinion? ☐ Yes ☐ No

8. Have you ever engaged in genocide, or otherwise ordered, incited, assisted or otherwise participated in the killing of any person because of race, religion, nationality, ethnic origin, or political opinion? ☐ Yes ☐ No

9. Have you ever been deported from the U.S., or removed from the U.S. at government expense, excluded within the past year, or are you now in exclusion or deportation proceedings? ☐ Yes ☐ No

10. Are you under a final order of civil penalty for violating section 274C of the Immigration Act for use of fraudulent documents, or have you, by fraud or willful misrepresentation of a material fact, ever sought to procure, or procured, a visa, other documentation, entry into the U.S., or any other immigration benefit? ☐ Yes ☐ No

11. Have you ever left the U.S. to avoid being drafted into the U.S. Armed Forces? ☐ Yes ☐ No

12. Have you ever been a J nonimmigrant exchange visitor who was subject to the 2 year foreign residence requirement and not yet complied with that requirement or obtained a waiver? ☐ Yes ☐ No

13. Are you now withholding custody of a U.S. Citizen child outside the U.S. from a person granted custody of the child? ☐ Yes ☐ No

14. Do you plan to practice polygamy in the U.S.? ☐ Yes ☐ No

Form I-485 (Rev. 09-09-92)N   **Continued on back**

Part 4. Signature. *(Read the information on penalties in the instructions before completing this section. You must file this application while in the United States.)*

I certify under penalty of perjury under the laws of the United States of America that this application, and the evidence submitted with it, is all true and correct. I authorize the release of any information from my records which the Immigration and Naturalization Service needs to determine eligibility for the benefit I am seeking.

| Signature | Print Your Name | Date | Daytime Phone Number |

Please Note: *If you do not completely fill out this form, or fail to submit required documents listed in the instructions, you may not be found eligible for the requested document and this application may be denied.*

Part 5. Signature of person preparing form if other than above. *(Sign Below)*

I declare that I prepared this application at the request of the above person and it is based on all information of which I have knowledge.

| Signature | Print Your Name | Date | Day time Phone Number |

Firm Name
and Address

Form I-485 (Rev 09-09-92) N

Form **9003** (January 1992)	Department of the Treasury—Internal Revenue Service **Additional Questions to be Completed by All Applicants for Permanent Residence in the United States**	OMB Clearance No. 1545-1065 Expires 8-31-94

This form must accompany your application for permanent residence in the United States

Privacy Act Notice: Your responses to the following questions will be provided to the Internal Revenue Service pursuant to Section 6039E of the Internal Revenue Code of 1986. Use of this information is limited to that needed for tax administration purposes. Failure to provide this information may result in a $500 penalty unless failure is due to reasonable cause.

On the date of issuance of the Alien Registration Receipt Card, the Immigration and Naturalization Service will send the following information to the Internal Revenue Service: your name, social security number, address, date of birth, alien identification number, occupation, class of admission, and answers to IRS Form 9003.

Name (Last—Surname—Family)   (First—Given)   (Middle Initial)

Taxpayer Identification Number . . . .

Enter your Social Security Number (SSN) if you have one. If you do not have an SSN but have used a Taxpayer Identification Number issued to you by the Internal Revenue Service, enter that number. Otherwise, write "NONE" in the space provided, i.e., "⌴⌴⌴⌴⌴NONE"

	Mark appropriate column	
	Yes	No
1. Are you self-employed? Mark "yes" if you own and actively operate a business in which you share in the profits other than as an investor		
2. Have you been in the United States for 183 days or more during any one of the three calendar years immediately preceding the current calendar year? Mark "yes" if you spent 183 days or more (not necessarily consecutive) in the United States during any **one of the three prior** calendar years **whether or not you worked** in the United States.		
3. During the last three years did you receive income from sources in the United States? Mark "yes" if you received income paid by individuals or institutions located in the United States. Income includes, but is not limited to, compensation for services provided by you, interest, dividends, rents, and royalties		
4. Did you file a United States Individual Income Tax Return (Forms 1040, 1040A, 1040EZ or 1040NR) in any of the last three years?		

If you answered yes to question 4, for which tax year was the last return filed? . . . . 19 ___ ___

Paperwork Reduction Act Notice—We ask for the information on this form to carry out the Internal Revenue laws of the United States. You are required to give us the information. We need it to ensure that you are complying with these laws and to allow us to figure and collect the right amount of tax.

The time needed to complete and file this form will vary depending on individual circumstances. The estimated average time is 5 minutes. If you have comments concerning the accuracy of this time estimate or suggestions for making this form more simple, we would be happy to hear from you. You can write to both the **Internal Revenue Service,** Washington, DC 20224 Attention: IRS Reports Clearance Officer, T:FP, and **Office of Management and Budget.** Paperwork Reduction Project (1545-1065) Washington, DC 20503. **DO NOT send this form to either of these offices. Instead, return it to the appropriate office of the Department of State or the Immigration and Naturalization Service.**

Remarks

Cat No 10126D

1. FILE COPY

Form **9003** (Rev. 1-92)

229

Form **9003**
(January 1992)

Department of the Treasury—Internal Revenue Service

Additional Questions to be Completed by All Applicants for Permanent Residence in the United States

OMB Clearance No 1545-1065
Expires 8-31-94

This form must accompany your application for permanent residence in the United States

Privacy Act Notice: Your responses to the following questions will be provided to the Internal Revenue Service pursuant to Section 6039E of the Internal Revenue Code of 1986 Use of this information is limited to that needed for tax administration purposes Failure to provide this information may result in a $500 penalty unless failure is due to reasonable cause

On the date of issuance of the Alien Registration Receipt Card, the Immigration and Naturalization Service will send the following information to the Internal Revenue Service your name, social security number, address, date of birth, alien identification number, occupation, class of admission, and answers to IRS Form 9003

Name *(Last—Surname—Family)* *(First—Given)* *(Middle Initial)*

Taxpayer Identification Number ....

Enter your Social Security Number (SSN) if you have one If you do not have an SSN but have used a Taxpayer Identification Number issued to you by the Internal Revenue Service, enter that number Otherwise, write "NONE" in the space provided, i e, "|_|_|_|_|N,O,N,E|"

	Mark appropriate column	
	Yes	No
1. Are you self-employed? Mark "yes" if you own and actively operate a business in which you share in the profits other than as an investor		
2 Have you been in the United States for 183 days or more during any one of the three calendar years immediately preceding the current calendar year? Mark "yes" if you spent 183 days or more (not necessarily consecutive) in the United States during any **one of the three prior** calendar years **whether or not you worked** in the United States		
3. During the last three years did you receive income from sources in the United States? Mark "yes" if you received income paid by individuals or institutions located in the United States Income includes, but is not limited to, compensation for services provided by you, interest, dividends, rents, and royalties		
4. Did you file a United States Individual Income Tax Return (Forms 1040, 1040A, 1040EZ or 1040NR) in any of the last three years?		

If you answered yes to question 4, for which tax year was the last return filed? . . . 19 __ __

Paperwork Reduction Act Notice—We ask for the information on this form to carry out the Internal Revenue laws of the United States You are required to give us the information We need it to ensure that you are complying with these laws and to allow us to figure and collect the right amount of tax

The time needed to complete and file this form will vary depending on individual circumstances The estimated average time is 5 minutes. If you have comments concerning the accuracy of this time estimate or suggestions for making this form more simple, we would be happy to hear from you You can write to both the **Internal Revenue Service,** Washington, DC 20224 Attention IRS Reports Clearance Officer, T.FP, and **Office of Management and Budget.** Paperwork Reduction Project (1545-1065) Washington, DC 20503 **DO NOT send this form to either of these offices. Instead, return it to the appropriate office of the Department of State or the Immigration and Naturalization Service.**

Remarks

Cat No 10126D

2. FOR ADIT AND STATISTICAL REPORTS

Form **9003** (Rev. 1-92)

U.S. Department of Justice
Immigration and Naturalization Service

OMB #1115-0009
Application for Naturalization

INSTRUCTIONS

Purpose of This Form.
This form is for use to apply to become a naturalized citizen of the United States

Who May File.
You may apply for naturalization if:
- you have been a lawful permanent resident for five years;
- you have been a lawful permanent resident for three years, have been married to a United States citizen for those three years, and continue to be married to that U.S. citizen;
- you are the lawful permanent resident child of United States citizen parents; or
- you have qualifying military service.

Children under 18 may automatically become citizens when their parents naturalize. You may inquire at your local Service office for further information. If you do not meet the qualifications listed above but believe that you are eligible for naturalization, you may inquire at your local Service office for additional information.

General Instructions.
Please answer all questions by typing or clearly printing in black ink. Indicate that an item is not applicable with "N/A" If an answer is "none," write "none" If you need extra space to answer any item, attach a sheet of paper with your name and your alien registration number (A#), if any, and indicate the number of the item.

Every application must be properly signed and filed with the correct fee If you are under 18 years of age, your parent or guardian must sign the application

If you wish to be called for your examination at the same time as another person who is also applying for naturalization, make your request on a separate cover sheet Be sure to give the name and alien registration number of that person

Initial Evidence Requirements.
You must file your application with the following evidence

A copy of your alien registration card

Photographs. You must submit two color photographs of yourself taken within 30 days of this application. These photos must be glossy, unretouched and unmounted, and have a white background. Dimension of the face should be about 1 inch from chin to top of hair. Face should be 3/4 frontal view of right side with right ear visible. Using pencil or felt pen, lightly print name and A#, if any, on the back of each photo. This requirement may be waived by the Service if you can establish that you are confined because of age or physical infirmity.

Fingerprints If you are between the ages of 14 and 75, you must sumit your fingerprints on Form FD-258. Fill out the form and write your Alien Registration Number in the space marked "Your No OCA" or "Miscellaneous No MNU" Take the chart and these instructions to a police station, sheriff's office or an office of this Service, or other reputable person or organization for fingerprinting (You should contact the police or sheriff's office before going there since some of these offices do not take fingerprints for other government agencies) You must sign the chart in the presence of the person taking your fingerprints and have that person sign his/her name, title, and the date in the space provided Do not bend, fold, or crease the fingerprint chart

U S Military Service If you have ever served in the Armed Forces of the United States at any time, you must submit a completed Form G-325B If your application is based on your military service you must also submit Form N-426, "Request for Certification of Military or Naval Service "

Application for Child If this application is for a permanent resident child of U S citizen parents, you must also submit copies of the child's birth certificate, the parents' marriage certificate, and evidence of the parents' U.S. citizenship If the parents are divorced, you must also submit the divorce decree and evidence that the citizen parent has legal custody of the child

Where to File.
File this application at the local Service office having jurisdiction over your place of residence.

Fee.
The fee for this application is $90 00. The fee must be submitted in the exact amount It cannot be refunded. DO NOT MAIL CASH

All checks and money orders must be drawn on a bank or other institution located in the United States and must be payable in United States currency The check or money order should be made payable to the Immigration and Naturalization Service, except that.
- If you live in Guam, and are filing this application in Guam, make your check or money order payable to the "Treasurer, Guam."
- If you live in the Virgin Islands, and are filing this application in the Virgin Islands, make your check or money order payable to the "Commissioner of Finance of the Virgin Islands "

Checks are accepted subject to collection. An uncollected check will render the application and any document issued invalid. A charge of $5 00 will be imposed if a check in payment of a fee is not honored by the bank on which it is drawn

Form N-400 (Rev 07/17/91) N

Processing Information.

Rejection. Any application that is not signed or is not accompanied by the proper fee will be rejected with a notice that the application is deficient. You may correct the deficiency and resubmit the application. However, an application is not considered properly filed until it is accepted by the Service.

Requests for more information. We may request more information or evidence. We may also request that you submit the originals of any copy. We will return these originals when they are no longer required.

Interview. After you file your application, you will be notified to appear at a Service office to be examined under oath or affirmation. This interview may not be waived. If you are an adult, you must show that you have a knowledge and understanding of the history, principles, and form of government of the United States. There is no exemption from this requirement.

You will also be examined on your ability to read, write, and speak English. If on the date of your examination you are more than 50 years of age and have been a lawful permanent resident for 20 years or more, or you are 55 years of age and have been a lawful permanent resident for at least 15 years, you will be exempt from the English language requirements of the law. If you are exempt, you may take the examination in any language you wish.

Oath of Allegiance. If your application is approved, you will be required to take the following oath of allegiance to the United States in order to become a citizen:

"I hereby declare, on oath, that I absolutely and entirely renounce and abjure all allegiance and fidelity to any foreign prince, potentate, state or sovereignty, of whom or which I have heretofore been a subject or citizen; that I will support and defend the Constitution and laws of the United States of America against all enemies, foreign and domestic; that I will bear true faith and allegiance to the same; that I will bear arms on behalf of the United States when required by the law; that I will perform noncombatant service in the armed forces of the United States when required by the law; that I will perform work of national importance under civilian direction when required by the law; and that I take this obligation freely without any mental reservation or purpose of evasion; so help me God."

If you cannot promise to bear arms or perform noncombatant service because of religious training and belief, you may omit those statements when taking the oath. "Religious training and belief" means a person's belief in relation to a Supreme Being involving duties superior to those arising from any human relation, but does not include essentially political, sociological, or philosophical views or merely a personal moral code.

Oath ceremony. You may choose to have the oath of allegiance administered in a ceremony conducted by the Service or request to be scheduled for an oath ceremony in a court that has jurisdiction over the applicant's place of residence. At the time of your examination you will be asked to elect either form of ceremony. You will become a citizen on the date of the oath ceremony and the Attorney General will issue a Certificate of Naturalization as evidence of United States citizenship.

If you wish to change your name as part of the naturalization process, you will have to take the oath in court.

Penalties.

If you knowingly and willfully falsify or conceal a material fact or submit a false document with this request, we will deny the benefit you are filing for, and may deny any other immigration benefit. In addition, you will face severe penalties provided by law, and may be subject to criminal prosecution.

Privacy Act Notice.

We ask for the information on this form, and associated evidence, to determine if you have established eligibility for the immigration benefit you are filing for. Our legal right to ask for this information is in 8 USC 1439, 1440, 1443, 1445, 1446, and 1452. We may provide this information to other government agencies. Failure to provide this information, and any requested evidence, may delay a final decision or result in denial of your request.

Paperwork Reduction Act Notice.

We try to create forms and instructions that are accurate, can be easily understood, and which impose the least possible burden on you to provide us with information. Often this is difficult because some immigration laws are very complex. Accordingly, the reporting burden for this collection of information is computed as follows: (1) learning about the law and form, 20 minutes; (2) completing the form, 25 minutes; and (3) assembling and filing the application (includes statutory required interview and travel time, after filing of application), 3 hours and 35 minutes, for an estimated average of 4 hours and 20 minutes per response. If you have comments regarding the accuracy of this estimate, or suggestions for making this form simpler, you can write to both the Immigration and Naturalization Service, 425 I Street, N.W., Room 5304, Washington, D.C. 20536; and the Office of Management and Budget, Paperwork Reduction Project, OMB No. 1115-0009, Washington, D.C. 20503.

U.S. Department of Justice
Immigration and Naturalization Service

OMB #1115-0009
Application for Naturalization

START HERE - Please Type or Print

Part 1. Information about you.

Family Name	Given Name	Middle Initial

U.S. Mailing Address - Care of

Street Number and Name		Apt #

City	County

State	ZIP Code

Date of Birth (month/day/year)	Country of Birth

Social Security #	A #

Part 2. Basis for Eligibility *(check one)*.

a ☐ I have been a permanent resident for at least five (5) years
b ☐ I have been a permanent resident for at least three (3) years and have been married to a United States Citizen for those three years
c ☐ I am a permanent resident child of United States citizen parent(s)
d ☐ I am applying on the basis of qualifying military service in the Armed Forces of the U.S. and have attached completed Forms N-426 and G-325B
e ☐ Other (Please specify section of law) _____

Part 3. Additional information about you.

Date you became a permanent resident (month/day/year)	Port admitted with an immigrant visa or INS Office where granted adjustment of status

Citizenship

Name on alien registration card (if different than in Part 1)

Other names used since you became a permanent resident (including maiden name)

Sex ☐ Male ☐ Female	Height	Marital Status ☐ Single ☐ Married	☐ Divorced ☐ Widowed

Can you speak, read and write English? ☐ No ☐ Yes

Absences from the U.S.:

Have you been absent from the U.S. since becoming a permanent resident? ☐ No ☐ Yes

If you answered **"Yes"**, complete the following, Begin with your most recent absence. If you need more room to explain the reason for an absence or to list more trips, continue on separate paper

Date left U.S.	Date returned	Did absence last 6 months or more?	Destination	Reason for trip
		☐ Yes ☐ No		
		☐ Yes ☐ No		
		☐ Yes ☐ No		
		☐ Yes ☐ No		
		☐ Yes ☐ No		
		☐ Yes ☐ No		

Form N-400 (Rev 07/17/91)N

Continued on back.

FOR INS USE ONLY

Returned	Receipt

Resubmitted

Reloc Sent

Reloc Rec'd

☐ Applicant Interviewed

At interview
☐ request naturalization ceremony at court

Remarks

Action

To Be Completed by *Attorney* or *Representative*, if any
☐ Fill in box if G-28 is attached to represent the applicant

VOLAG#

ATTY State License #

Part 4. Information about your residences and employment.

A. List your addresses during the last five (5) years or since you became a permanent resident, whichever is less. Begin with your current address. If you need more space, continue on separate paper

Street Number and Name, City, State, Country, and Zip Code	Dates (month/day/year)	
	From	To

B. List your employers during the last five (5) years. List your present or most recent employer first. If none, write "None". If you need more space, continue on separate paper

Employer's Name	Employer's Address Street Name and Number - City, State and ZIP Code	Dates Employed (month/day/year) From	To	Occupation/position

Part 5. Information about your marital history.

A. Total number of times you have been married _____ If you are now married, complete the following regarding your husband or wife

Family name	Given name	Middle initial

Address

Date of birth (month/day/year)	Country of birth	Citizenship
Social Security#	A# (if applicable)	Immigration status (If not a U.S. citizen)

Naturalization (If applicable)
(month/day/year) _____   Place   (City, State) _____

If you have ever previously been married or if your current spouse has been previously married, please provide the following on separate paper. Name of prior spouse, date of marriage, date marriage ended, how marriage ended and immigration status of prior spouse

Part 6. Information about your children.

B. Total Number of Children _____ Complete the following information for each of your children. If the child lives with you, state "with me" in the address column, otherwise give city/state/country of child's current residence. If deceased, write "deceased" in the address column. If you need more space, continue on separate paper

Full name of child	Date of birth	Country of birth	Citizenship	A - Number	Address

Form N-400 (Rev 07/17/91)N   **Continued on next page**

Continued on back

Part 7. Additional eligibility factors.

Please answer each of the following questions. If your answer is "**Yes**", explain on a separate paper.

1. Are you now, or have you ever been a member of, or in any way connected or associated with the Communist Party, or ever knowingly aided or supported the Communist Party directly, or indirectly through another organization, group or person, or ever advocated, taught, believed in, or knowingly supported or furthered the interests of communism? ☐ Yes ☐ No
2. During the period March 23, 1933 to May 8, 1945, did you serve in, or were you in any way affiliated with, either directly or indirectly, any military unit, paramilitary unit, police unit, self-defense unit, vigilante unit, citizen unit of the Nazi party or SS, government agency or office, extermination camp, concentration camp, prisoner of war camp, prison, labor camp, detention camp or transit camp, under the control or affiliated with
    - a. The Nazi Government of Germany? ☐ Yes ☐ No
    - b. Any government in any area occupied by, allied with, or established with the assistance or cooperation of, the Nazi Government of Germany? ☐ Yes ☐ No
3. Have you at any time, anywhere, ever ordered, incited, assisted, or otherwise participated in the persecution of any person because of race, religion, national origin, or political opinion? ☐ Yes ☐ No
4. Have you ever left the United States to avoid being drafted into the U.S. Armed Forces? ☐ Yes ☐ No
5. Have you ever failed to comply with Selective Service laws? ☐ Yes ☐ No
   If you have registered under the Selective Service laws, complete the following information
   Selective Service Number _____ Date Registered._____
   If you registered before 1978, also provide the following
   Local Board Number _____ Classification _____
6. Did you ever apply for exemption from military service because of alienage, conscientious objections or other reasons? ☐ Yes ☐ No
7. Have you ever deserted from the military, air or naval forces of the United States? ☐ Yes ☐ No
8. Since becoming a permanent resident, have you ever failed to file a federal income tax return? ☐ Yes ☐ No
9. Since becoming a permanent resident, have you filed a federal income tax return as a nonresident or failed to file a federal return because you considered yourself to be a nonresident? ☐ Yes ☐ No
10. Are deportation proceedings pending against you, or have you ever been deported, or ordered deported, or have you ever applied for suspension of deportation? ☐ Yes ☐ No
11. Have you ever claimed in writing, or in any way, to be a United States citizen? ☐ Yes ☐ No
12. Have you ever
    - a. been a habitual drunkard? ☐ Yes ☐ No
    - b. advocated or practiced polygamy? ☐ Yes ☐ No
    - c. been a prostitute or procured anyone for prostitution? ☐ Yes ☐ No
    - d. knowingly and for gain helped any alien to enter the U.S. illegally? ☐ Yes ☐ No
    - e. been an illicit trafficker in narcotic drugs or marijuana? ☐ Yes ☐ No
    - f. received income from illegal gambling? ☐ Yes ☐ No
    - g. given false testimony for the purpose of obtaining any immigration benefit? ☐ Yes ☐ No
13. Have you ever been declared legally incompetent or have you ever been confined as a patient in a mental institution? ☐ Yes ☐ No
14. Were you born with, or have you acquired in same way, any title or order of nobility in any foreign State? ☐ Yes ☐ No
15. Have you ever
    - a. knowingly committed any crime for which you have not been arrested? ☐ Yes ☐ No
    - b. been arrested, cited, charged, indicted, convicted, fined or imprisoned for breaking or violating any law or ordinance excluding traffic regulations? ☐ Yes ☐ No

(If you answer yes to 15, in your explanation give the following information for each incident or occurrence the **city**, **state**, and **country**, where the offense took place, the **date** and **nature** of the offense, and the **outcome** or **disposition** of the case)

Part 8. Allegiance to the U.S.

If your answer to any of the following questions is "**NO**", attach a full explanation
1. Do you believe in the Constitution and form of government of the U.S.? ☐ Yes ☐ No
2. Are you willing to take the full Oath of Allegiance to the U.S.? (see instructions) ☐ Yes ☐ No
3. If the law requires it, are you willing to bear arms on behalf of the U.S.? ☐ Yes ☐ No
4. If the law requires it, are you willing to perform noncombatant services in the Armed Forces of the U.S.? ☐ Yes ☐ No
5. If the law requires it, are you willing to perform work of national importance under civilian direction? ☐ Yes ☐ No

Form N-400 (Rev 07/17/91)N

Continued on back

Part 9. Memberships and organizations.

A. List your present and past membership in or affiliation with every organization, association, fund, foundation, party, club, society, or similar group in the United States or in any other place. Include any military service in this part. If none, write "none". Include the name of organization, location, dates of membership and the nature of the organization. If additional space is needed, use separate paper.

_____
_____
_____
_____

Part 10. Complete only if you checked block " C " in Part 2.

How many of your parents are U S citizens? ☐ One ☐ Both (Give the following about one U S citizen parent)

Family Name	Given Name	Middle Name

Address

Basis for citizenship
☐ Birth
☐ Naturalization Cert No

Relationship to you (check one) ☐ natural parent ☐ adoptive parent
☐ parent of child legitimated after birth

If adopted or legitimated after birth, give date of adoption or, legitimation (month/day/year) _____

Does this parent have legal custody of you? ☐ Yes ☐ No

(Attach a copy of relating evidence to establish that you are the child of this U.S. citizen and evidence of this parent's citizenship.)

Part 11. Signature. *(Read the information on penalties in the instructions before completing this section)*

I certify or, if outside the United States, I swear or affirm, under penalty of perjury under the laws of the United States of America that this application, and the evidence submitted with it, is all true and correct. I authorize the release of any information from my records which the Immigration and Naturalization Service needs to determine eligibility for the benefit I am seeking.

Signature   Date

Please Note: If you do not completely fill out this form, or fail to submit required documents listed in the instructions, you may not be found eligible for naturalization and this application may be denied.

Part 12. Signature of person preparing form if other than above. *(Sign below)*

I declare that I prepared this application at the request of the above person and it is based on all information of which I have knowledge.

Signature   Print Your Name   Date

Firm Name
and Address

DO NOT COMPLETE THE FOLLOWING UNTIL INSTRUCTED TO DO SO AT THE INTERVIEW

I swear that I know the contents of this application, and supplemental pages 1 through _____ , that the corrections , numbered 1 through _____ , were made at my request, and that this amended application, is true to the best of my knowledge and belief.

Subscribed and sworn to before me by the applicant

_____
(Complete and true signature of applicant)

_____
(Examiner's Signature)   Date

Form N 400 (Rev 07/17/91)N   FPI-LOM

U.S. DEPARTMENT OF JUSTICE
IMMIGRATION AND NATURALIZATION SERVICE

APPLICATION TO FILE PETITION FOR NATURALIZATION IN BEHALF OF CHILD

PLEASE TEAR OFF THIS SHEET BEFORE SUBMITTING PETITION

OMB No. 1115-0010

INSTRUCTIONS

This application may be completed by only one citizen parent or citizen adoptive parent of the child to be naturalized although if the other parent or the other adoptive parent is a citizen and desires to join in such action, he or she may do so. If only one parent or adoptive parent files this application, only that parent will be required to appear to file the petition for naturalization, and to be present at the hearing before the court.

Pages 1, 2 and 3 of this form must be filled out in ink or on the typewriter and signed with your full, true name(s), without abbreviations. UNLESS YOU ANSWER THE ITEMS IN FULL, IT MAY BE NECESSARY TO RETURN THE APPLICATION TO YOU. If you do not have enough space to answer a question completely, add the word "Continued" after the answer in the Application, then finish your answer on a separate sheet of paper this size, and show on that paper the number of the question(s) you are answering, the child's name, and his or her alien registration number.

YOU MUST SEND WITH THIS APPLICATION:

Photographs.—Three identical unglazed photographs of the child taken within 30 days of the date of this application. These photographs must be 2 by 2 inches in size. No other size should be submitted. The distance from the top of the head to the point of the chin should be approximately 1¼ inches. They must not be pasted on a card or mounted in any other way, must be on thin paper, must have a light background, and must clearly show a front view of the child's face without hat. They may be in natural color or in black and white, but black and white photographs which have been tinted or otherwise colored are not acceptable. Machine-made photographs are not acceptable. **Do not sign the photographs.** Using soft lead pencil to avoid mutilation of photographs, write the child's **Alien Registration number** lightly on the reverse of photographs, making sure that you place it in the center, away from the edges of the photograph.

IF THE CHILD IS 14 YEARS OF AGE OR OLDER, THE FOLLOWING MUST ALSO BE SUBMITTED:

Fingerprint Chart.—A record of the child's fingerprints, taken on the fingerprint chart furnished with the application. Write in the child's **Alien Registration number** on the chart in the space marked "Number," then take it with these instructions to any police station, sheriff's office, or office of the Immigration and Naturalization Service for fingerprinting. The child must then sign the chart in the presence of the officer taking the fingerprints, and the officer must sign his name and title and fill in the date in the space provided. Be sure the card bears the code of the office to which the application will be submitted. **Do not bend, fold, or crease the fingerprint chart.**

Biographic Information Form.—Every item in the biographic information form furnished with this application must be completed, and signed by the child on the line provided.

Alien Registration Receipt Card.—It is important that you show in the box on page 1 the name under which the child was registered under the Alien Registration Act of 1940 or a later act and the number exactly as it appears on the Alien Registration Receipt Card. **Do not send the child's card with this application.**

Authority for collection of the information requested on this form is contained in sections 322, 332, 334 and 335 of the Immigration and Nationality Act of 1952 (8 U.S.C. 1433, 1443, 1445 and 1446). Submission of the information is voluntary inasmuch as the immigration and nationality laws of the United States do not require an alien to apply for naturalization. If your Social Security Number is requested on a form, no right, benefit or privilege will be denied for your failure to provide such number. The principal purpose for which the information is solicited, is to enable designated officers of the Immigration and Naturalization Service to determine the eligibility of a natural or adopted child of a United States citizen parent, to be naturalized. All or part of the information solicited may, as a matter of routine use, be disclosed to courts, exercising naturalization jurisdiction and to other federal, state, local or foreign law enforcement and regulatory agencies, the Department of Defense, including any component thereof, the Department of State, the Department of the Treasury, Central Intelligence Agency, Interpol and individuals and organizations in the processing of the application or petition for naturalization, or during the course of investigation to elicit further information required by the Immigration and Naturalization Service to carry out its functions. Information solicited which indicates a violation or potential violation of law, whether civil, criminal or regulatory in nature, may be referred as a routine use, to the appropriate agency, whether federal, state, local or foreign, charged with the responsibility of investigating, enforcing or prosecuting such violations. Failure to provide any or all of the solicited information may result in an adverse recommendation to the court as to the child's eligibility for naturalization and denial by the court of the petition for naturalization.

Form N-402 (Rev. 4-15-82)Y   **(PLEASE TEAR OFF HERE BEFORE SUBMITTING PETITION)**

GPO . 1988 O - 213-254

U.S. DEPARTMENT OF JUSTICE
IMMIGRATION AND NATURALIZATION SERVICE

APPLICATION TO FILE PETITION FOR NATURALIZATION IN BEHALF OF CHILD
Under Section 322 of the Immigration and Nationality Act

OMB No. 1115-0010

Take or Mail to:
IMMIGRATION AND NATURALIZATION SERVICE,

CHILD's NAME AND ALIEN REGISTRATION NUMBER
Name ....
No ....

Date ...., 19........

I (We), the undersigned, desire that a petition for naturalization be filed in behalf of my (our) child.

(1) My full, true, and correct name is ....
        (Full, true name of citizen parent or citizen adoptive parent, without abbreviations)

(2) My present place of residence is ....
        (Apt No.) (Number and street) (City or town) (County) (State) (ZIP Code)

(3) I am a citizen of the United States of America and was born on .... in ....
        (Month) (Day) (Year)   (City, State, and Country)

(If not a native-born citizen) I was naturalized on .... at ....
        (Month) (Day) (Year)   (City and State)

certificate No ...., or I became a citizen of the United States through ....

(Is the child's other parent a citizen of the United States?   ☐ Yes   ☐ No)

(Complete (1a) to (3a) only if second parent wishes to join in application)

(1a) My full, true, and correct name is ....
        (Full, true name of second citizen parent or citizen adoptive parent, without abbreviations)

(2a) My present place of residence is ....
        (Apt No.) (Number and street) (City or town) (County) (State) (ZIP Code)

(3a) I am a citizen of the United States of America and was born on .... in ....
        (Month) (Day) (Year)   (City, State, and Country)

(If not a native-born citizen) I was naturalized on .... at ....
        (Month) (Day) (Year)   (City and State)

certificate No ...., or I became a citizen of the United States through ....

(4) I am (We are) the parent(s) of ....
in whose behalf this application for naturalization is filed
        (Full, true name of child, without abbreviations)

(5) The said child now resides with me (us) at ....
        (Apt No.) (Number and street) (City or town)

.... , is .... , and is a citizen, subject, or national of ....
(County) (State) (ZIP Code)   (Married) (Single)

(6) The said child was born on .... in ....
        (Month) (Day) (Year)   (City and Country)

(7) The said child was lawfully admitted to the United States for permanent residence on .... at ....
                                                                                         (Month) (Day) (Year)

.... under the name of ....
(City) (State)

.... and does .... intend to reside permanently in the United States

(8) I (We) desire the naturalization court to change the name of the child to ....
        (Give full name desired, without abbreviations)

(9) If application is in behalf of an adopted child
    I (We) adopted said child on .... in the ....
                              (Month) (Day) (Year)   (Name of court)

.... at ....
        (City or town) (State) (Country)

The said child has resided continuously in the United States with me (us) in my (our) legal custody since ....
                                                                                            (Month) (Day) (Year)

(1)

(10) Since such child's lawful admission to the United States for permanent residence, the child has not been absent from the United States at any time except as follows (if none, state "None"): _____
None

| DEPARTED FROM THE UNITED STATES || RETURNED TO THE UNITED STATES ||
PORT	DATE (MONTH, DAY, YEAR)	PORT	DATE (MONTH, DAY, YEAR)

(11) Has such child ever been a patient in a mental institution, or ever been treated for a mental illness? ☐ Yes ☐ No

(12) The law provides that a person may not be regarded as qualified for naturalization under certain conditions, if the person knowingly committed certain offenses or crimes, even though not arrested therefor. Has such child ever in or outside the United States:

(a) Knowingly committed any crime for which he/she has not been arrested? . . . . ☐ Yes ☐ No

(b) Been arrested, charged with violation of any law or ordinance, summoned into court as a defendant, convicted, fined, imprisoned, or placed on probation or parole, or forfeited collateral for any act involving a crime, misdemeanor, or breach of any law or ordinance? . . . . ☐ Yes ☐ No

If the answer to (a) or (b) is "Yes," on a separate sheet, give the following information as to each incident: when and where occurred, offense involved, and outcome of case if any.

(13) Are deportation proceedings pending against such child or has such child ever been deported or ordered deported, or has such child ever applied for suspension of deportation or for preexamination? . . . . . ☐ Yes ☐ No

(14) List the child's membership in every organization, association, fund, foundation, party, club, society, or similar group in the United States and in any other place, during the past ten years, and his foreign military service. (If none, write "None.")

(a) .... 19 ..... to 19 ....
(b) .... , 19 ..... to 19 ....
(c) .... , 19 ..... to 19 ....
(d) .... , 19 ..... to 19 ....

(15) Has such child ever served in the Armed Forces of the United States? . . . . ☐ Yes ☐ No

(16) (Answer only if the child is of an understanding age.) If the law requires it, is the child willing to bear arms or perform noncombatant service in the Armed Forces of the United States or perform work of national importance under civilian direction? If "No" explain fully on a separate sheet of paper . . . . ☐ Yes ☐ No

(17) Since the child's lawful admission to the United States for permanent residence, my wife (husband) and I have been absent from the United States as follows (if no absences, state "None"):

....

....

....

(18) My wife (husband) and I have been married as follows (give information as to each marriage):
(Use extra sheet of paper if necessary.)

DATE MARRIED	DATE MARRIAGE ENDED	NAME OF SPOUSE	HOW MARRIAGE ENDED (Death or divorce)

(2)

(19) A petition for naturalization has .... previously been filed on behalf of said child on ....
                                            (not)   (Month) (Day) (Year)

at ....in .... and denied
     (City)   (County)   (State)   (Name of court)

_____   _____
(Signature of 1st parent)   (Signature of 2d parent)

_____   _____
(Address of 1st parent)   (Address of 2d parent)

_____   _____
(Telephone No)   (Date)   (Telephone No)   (Date)

SIGNATURE OF PERSON PREPARING FORM, IF OTHER THAN APPLICANT(S)

I declare that this document was prepared by me at the request of the applicant(s) and is based on all information of which I have any knowledge.

_____   _____   _____
(Signature)   (Address)   (Date)

TO APPLICANTS: DO NOT WRITE BELOW THESE LINES

AFFIDAVIT

I do swear (affirm) that I know the contents of this application comprising pages 1 to 3, inclusive, subscribed by me, that the same are true to the best of my knowledge and belief; that corrections number ( ) to ( ) were made by me or at my request; and that this application was signed by me with my full, true name.

Subscribed and sworn (affirmed) to before me at the preliminary investigation (examination) at ....
this .... day of .... , 19........

I certify that before verification the parent(s) stated in my presence that he (she they) had .... read the
                                                              (heard)
foregoing application and corrections therein and understood the contents thereof

_____
(Complete and true signature of 1st parent)

_____   _____
(Complete and true signature of 2d parent)   (Naturalization Examiner)

Nonfiled ....

(Date, Reasons)

(3)

FEDERAL BUREAU OF INVESTIGATION
UNITED STATES DEPARTMENT OF JUSTICE
WASHINGTON, D.C. 20537

APPLICANT

TO OBTAIN CLASSIFIABLE FINGERPRINTS

1. USE BLACK PRINTER'S INK
2. DISTRIBUTE INK EVENLY ON INKING SLAB
3. WASH AND DRY FINGERS THOROUGHLY
4. ROLL FINGERS FROM NAIL TO NAIL AND AVOID ALLOWING FINGERS TO SLIP
5. BE SURE IMPRESSIONS ARE RECORDED IN CORRECT ORDER
6. IF AN AMPUTATION OR DEFORMITY MAKES IT IMPOSSIBLE TO PRINT A FINGER MAKE A NOTATION TO THAT EFFECT IN THE INDIVIDUAL FINGER BLOCK
7. IF SOME PHYSICAL CONDITION MAKES IT IMPOSSIBLE TO OBTAIN PERFECT IMPRESSIONS SUBMIT THE BEST THAT CAN OBTAINED WITH A MEMO STAPLED TO THE CARD EXPLAINING THE CIRCUMSTANCES
8. EXAMINE THE COMPLETED PRINTS TO SEE IF THEY CAN BE CLASSIFIED BEARING IN MIND THAT MOST FINGERPRINTS FALL INTO THE PATTERNS SHOWN ON THIS CARD (OTHER PATTERNS OCCUR INFREQUENTLY AND ARE NOT SHOWN HE

1. LOOP
CENTER OF LOOP
DELTA
THE LINES BETWEEN CENTER OF LOOP AND DELTA MUST SHOW

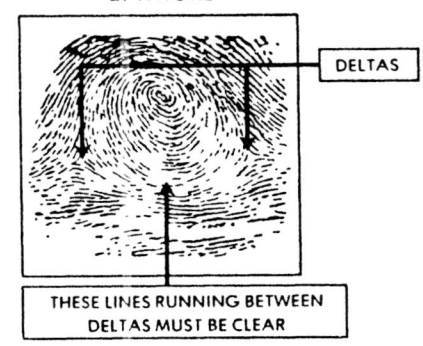

2. WHORL
DELTAS
THESE LINES RUNNING BETWEEN DELTAS MUST BE CLEAR

3. ARCH
ARCHES HAVE NO DELTAS

FD-258 (REV 12 29 82)

THIS CARD FOR USE BY:

1. LAW ENFORCEMENT AGENCIES IN FINGERPRINTING APPLICANTS FOR LAW ENFORCEMENT POSITIONS *

2. OFFICIALS OF STATE AND LOCAL GOVERNMENTS FOR PURPOSES OF EMPLOYMENT LICENSING AND PERMITS AS AUTHORIZED BY STATE STATUTES AND APPROVED BY THE ATTORNEY GENERAL OF THE UNITED STATES LOCAL AND COUNTY ORDINANCES UNLESS SPECIFICALLY BASED ON APPLICABLE STATE STATUTES DO NOT SATISFY THIS REQUIREMENT *

3. U S GOVERNMENT AGENCIES AND OTHER ENTITIES REQUIRED BY FEDERAL LAW **

4. OFFICIALS OF FEDERALLY CHARTERED OR INSURED BANKING INSTITUTIONS TO PROMOTE OR MAINTAIN THE SECURITY OF THOSE INSTITUTIONS

INSTRUCTIONS:

*1 PRINTS MUST FIRST BE CHECKED THROUGH THE APPROPRIATE STATE IDENTIFICATION BUREAU AND ONLY THOSE FINGERPRINTS FOR WHICH NO DISQUALIFYING RECORD HAS BEEN FOUND LOCALLY SHOULD BE SUBMITTED FOR FBI SEARCH

2 PRIVACY ACT OF 1974 (P L 93 579) REQUIRES THAT FEDERAL STATE OR LOCAL AGENCIES INFORM INDIVIDUALS WHOSE SOCIAL SECURITY NUMBER IS REQUESTED WHETHER SUCH DISCLOSURE IS MANDATORY OR VOLUNTARY BASIS OF AUTHORITY FOR SUCH SOLICITATION AND USES WHICH WILL BE MADE OF IT

**3 IDENTITY OF PRIVATE CONTRACTORS SHOULD BE SHOWN IN SPACE EMPLOYER AND ADDRESS THE CONTRIBUTOR IS THE NAME OF THE AGENCY SUBMITTING THE FINGERPRINT CARD TO THE FBI

4 FBI NUMBER IF KNOWN SHOULD ALWAYS BE FURNISHED IN THE APPROPRIATE SPACE

MISCELLANEOUS NO RECORD OTHER ARMED FORCES NO PASSPORT NO (PP) ALIEN REGISTRATION NO (AR) PORT SECURITY CARD NO (PS) SELECTIVE SERVICE NO (SS) VETERANS ADMINISTRATION CLAIM NO (VA)

☆ U.S.G.P.O. 1992 312-322/40014

LEAVE THIS SPACE BLANK

APPLICANT

LEAVE BLANK

TYPE OR PRINT ALL INFORMATION IN BLACK
LAST NAME **NAM**   FIRST NAME   MIDDLE NAME

FBI   **LEAVE BLANK**

SIGNATURE OF PERSON FINGERPRINTED

ALIASES **AKA**

ORI — USING BALTIMORE MD

RESIDENCE OF PERSON FINGERPRINTED

DATE OF BIRTH **DOB**   Month   Day   Year

DATE   SIGNATURE OF OFFICIAL TAKING FINGERPRINTS

CITIZENSHIP **CTZ**

SEX | RACE | HGT. | WGT | EYES | HAIR | PLACE OF BIRTH **POB**

YOUR NO **OCA**

EMPLOYER AND ADDRESS

LEAVE BLANK

FBI NO **FBI**

ARMED FORCES NO **MNU**

CLASS _____

REASON FINGERPRINTED

SOCIAL SECURITY NO **SOC**

REF _____

MISCELLANEOUS NO **MNU**

| 1 R THUMB | 2 R INDEX | 3 R MIDDLE | 4 R RING | 5 R LITTLE |
| 6 L THUMB | 7 L INDEX | 8 L MIDDLE | 9 L RING | 10 L LITTLE |

LEFT FOUR FINGERS TAKEN SIMULTANEOUSLY | L THUMB | R THUMB | RIGHT FOUR FINGERS TAKEN SIMULTANEOUSLY

U.S. IMMIGRATION & NATURALIZATION SERVICE

COLOR PHOTOGRAPH SPECIFICATIONS

◄ SAMPLE PHOTOGRAPH

HEAD SIZE (INCLUDING HAIR) MUST FIT INSIDE OVAL ►

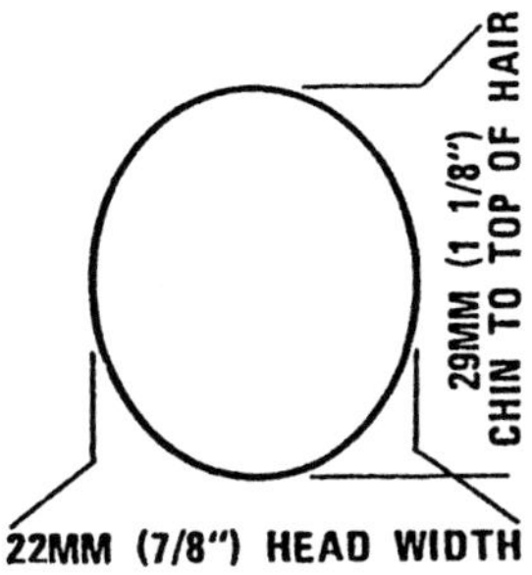

29MM (1 1/8") CHIN TO TOP OF HAIR
22MM (7/8") HEAD WIDTH

COLOR FILMS OF THE INTEGRAL TYPE, NON-PEEL-APART, ARE UNACCEPTABLE. THESE ARE EASILY RECOGNIZED AS THE BACK OF THE FILMS ARE BLACK. THE ACCEPTABLE INSTANT COLOR FILM HAS A WHITE BACKING.

- PHOTOGRAPH MUST SHOW THE SUBJECT IN A ¾ FRONTAL PORTRAIT AS SHOWN ABOVE
- RIGHT EAR MUST BE EXPOSED IN PHOTOGRAPH FOR ALL APPLICANTS, HATS MUST NOT BE WORN.
- PHOTOGRAPH OUTER DIMENSION MUST BE LARGER THAN 1¹/₄ W x 1³/₈ H, BUT HEAD SIZE, (INCLUDING HAIR) MUST FIT WITHIN THE ILLUSTRATED OVAL (OUTER DIMENSION DOES NOT INCLUDE BORDER IF ONE IS USED)
- PHOTOGRAPH MUST BE COLOR WITH A WHITE BACKGROUND EQUAL IN REFLECTANCE TO BOND TYPING PAPER
- SURFACE OF THE PHOTOGRAPH MUST BE GLOSSY
- PHOTOGRAPH MUST NOT BE STAINED, CRACKED, OR MUTILATED, AND MUST LIE FLAT
- PHOTOGRAPHIC IMAGE MUST BE SHARP AND CORRECTLY EXPOSED, PHOTOGRAPH MUST BE UN-RETOUCHED

- PHOTOGRAPHS MUST NOT BE PASTED ON CARDS OR MOUNTED IN ANY WAY
- 2 (TWO) PHOTOGRAPHS OF EVERY APPLICANT, REGARDLESS OF AGE, MUST BE SUBMITTED
- PHOTOGRAPHS MUST BE TAKEN WITHIN THIRTY (30) DAYS OF APPLICATION DATE
- SNAPSHOTS, GROUP PICTURES, OR FULL LENGTH PORTRAITS WILL NOT BE ACCEPTED
- USING CRAYON OR FELT PEN, TO AVOID MUTILATION OF THE PHOTOGRAPHS, LIGHTLY PRINT YOUR NAME (AND ALIEN REGISTRATION RECEIPT NUMBER IF KNOWN) ON THE BACK OF ALL PHOTOGRAPHS
- IMPORTANT NOTE - FAILURE TO SUBMIT PHOTOGRAPHS IN COMPLIANCE WITH THESE SPECIFICATIONS WILL DELAY THE PROCESSING OF YOUR APPLICATION

SAMPLES OF UNACCEPTABLE PHOTOGRAPHS

FACING WRONG WAY  | HEAD SIZE TOO LARGE  | HEAD SIZE TOO SMALL

DARK BACKGROUND | TOO DARK  | TOO LIGHT

ER-731
9/90 3230

Printed in the United States
50751LVS00009B/2